TERRORS OF UNCERTAINTY

From *Frankenstein* and *Dracula* to *Psycho* and *The Chainsaw Massacre*, horror fiction has provided our culture with some of its most enduring themes and narratives. Looking at horror fiction as a genre and as a social phenomenon, Joseph Grixti provides a theoretical and historical framework for reconsidering horror and the cultural apparatus that surrounds it. Examining classics from literature and film, hair-raisers like *Cannibal Holocaust* and *Zombie Flesh Eaters*, and bestsellers including James Herbert's *The Fog* and Stephen King's *The Shining*, he looks at shifts in the genre's meaning – its fascination with excess, its commentaries on the categories and boundaries of culture – and at interpretations of horror from psychology, psychoanalysis, sociology, cultural and media studies. Refusing any reductive position, Grixti examines the various arguments for and against horror fictions: assumptions that horror taps the 'beast within', notions of terror as catharsis, and debates on the effects of media violence. He reveals that both works of horror fiction and the texts which explain them have a similar ideological base; by cultivating fear within well-determined codes, with the help of an increasingly lucrative horror industry, they propagate a sense of personal helplessness and political impotence which is central to the maintenance of consumer culture.

Terrors of Uncertainty brings together a provocative range of perspectives from across the disciplines which combine to raise important questions about the relationship between fiction and society, and on the way we use fiction to resolve or evade our fears of uncertainty. It contextualizes a social phenomenon which is as topical and as urgent as it is controversial.

'Lucid, well-informed, and challenging, Grixti moves beyond historical or critical appraisal of horror fiction towards a complex theorization of the genre as discourse.'

Rosemary Jackson

Joseph Grixti is currently lecturing in Studies in Education at the Brisbane College of Advanced Education, Australia.

D1499874

TERRORS OF UNCERTAINTY

The Cultural Contexts of Horror Fiction

JOSEPH GRIXTI

ROUTLEDGE
London and New York

First published 1989 by Routledge
11 New Fetter Lane, London EC4P 4EE
29 West 35th Street, New York, NY 10001

©1989 J. Grixti

Photoset by Rowland Phototypesetting Ltd
Bury St Edmunds, Suffolk
Printed in Great Britain
by St Edmundsbury Press Ltd
Bury St Edmunds, Suffolk

British Library Cataloguing in Publication Data

Grixti, Joseph
Terrors of uncertainty: the cultural
contexts of horror fiction.
1. Horror stories, to 1980 –
Critical studies
I. Title
809.3'916

Library of Congress Cataloging in Publication Data

Grixti, Joseph, 1950–
Terrors of uncertainty: the cultural contexts of horror fiction
by Joseph Grixti.
p.   cm.
Bibliography: p.
Includes index.
1. Horror tales – History and criticism.   2. Literature and
society.   3. Literature – Psychological aspects.   I. Title.
PN3435.G75 1989
809.3'872 – dc 19

ISBN 0 – 415 – 02598 – 2 (PB)
0 – 415 – 02597 – 4 (HB)

CONTENTS

PREFACE

This book partly owes its origins to a group of teenaged schoolboys whom I overheard enthusing over horror books while I was browsing through the popular fiction section of a bookshop in Bristol a few years back. One boy was telling his mates about the wonders of James Herbert's *The Fog*, whose cover at the time displayed a clenched fist holding up a ghastly-looking human head prominently severed at the neck. Researching and writing the book has in large measure been an attempt to make sense of – contextualize and theorize – the issues which (on reflection) I have come to recognize as arising from their enthusiasm, and also from my (possibly symptomatic) reaction to it and to the types of texts which inspired it.

During the period since I started writing the book, the proportions of mass-marketed horror have continued to grow. New books and films, as well as countless imitations of successful antecedents and updated 'remakes' of products of earlier stages in the genre's history, continue to be made on a scale which suggests that the demand for horror fiction has anything but waned. The genre has also continued to expand in other ways – as evidenced in the growing number of children's books, cartoons, toys, games and films which have taken over the stock characters, images and themes of horror fiction and made them the focus of (frequently, but not always) lighthearted contemplation. A number of professional horror writers have also gone on to produce fantasy fiction specifically directed at children – often maintaining many of the stylistic techniques and ideological orientations which they developed while establishing themselves in the horror genre.

I make no claim to having kept up with all specific instances and nuances of these developments: this book is not intended as a directory of horror fiction and its offspring. But the fact that the contemplation of horrific eventualities has become an expanding industry with apparently vast investment potential raises important questions about the types of societies in which we live, and also about the manners in which our methods of developing fictions to help us make sense of experience have become inseparable from the demands and complex orientations of consumerism. In these terms, the contextualization and theorization of horror fiction as discourse assumes even more urgent dimensions.

It is difficult to decide which individuals to single out as indispensable contributors to the making of a project like this one. The book would probably not even have reached conception were it not for Fred Inglis: I am forever in his debt for his inspiration, friendship, challenging criticism and enthusiastic support throughout the period that I have had the pleasure of knowing him. A number of the ideas developed in the book have also benefited greatly from conversations I had with Marilyn Butler and Martin Barker at a time when I was still trying to identify the contours and boundaries of the subject of gothic and horror fiction. Philip Gammage's friendship and faith in the project kept me going during periods when the outlook seemed bleak. I am also indebted to friends, colleagues and students at the University of Bristol, the University Malta, the Geelong College and at the Brisbane C.A.E. for providing the intellectual and human contexts within which different parts of the book were researched and written.

The ideas which are developed in chapters 2, 5 and 6 have grown out of articles which originally appeared in *Use of English*, *Educational Studies* and *British Journal of Educational Studies* respectively.

My wife Roswitha has lived with the terrors, uncertainties, as well as the pleasures which have surrounded the writing of the pages which follow. In more than one sense this book would not exist were it not for her unflagging support and patient acceptance of the demands it has made on my time and pursuits. It is with love and gratitude that I now dedicate it to her and to our two daughters, Katja and Vanessa.

Brisbane
March 1989

INTRODUCTION:
Matter, method, and meaning

In the course of his systematic attempt at defining what he terms 'the regime of power–knowledge–pleasure that sustains the discourse on human sexuality in our part of the world', Foucault isolates a number of methodological issues which are as relevant to the subject of this book as they are to his analysis of 'the great process of transforming sex into discourse' (Foucault 1979: 22). According to Foucault, the central issue in this type of analysis (at least in the first instance) is not that of determining whether one formulates prohibitions or permissions, whether one asserts importances or denies effects, or whether one refines the words one uses to designate the phenomenon under consideration. The crucial point, rather, is

> to account for the fact that it is spoken about, to discover who does the speaking, the positions and viewpoints from which they speak, the institutions which prompt people to speak about it and which store and distribute the things that are said.
>
> (ibid: 11)

The point at issue, then, is the overall discursive fact: the way in which a human phenomenon has been put into discourse and made part of a specific cultural environment.

This book sets itself the first task of accounting for the fact that horrific possibilities of experience are spoken about in fictional terms. It is thus concerned with the exploration and evaluation of meaning. More specifically, the book directs itself to the task of identifying the values and meanings which inhere in some of the more popular forms of contemporary horror fiction, and of analysing these meanings against the background of a wider cultural debate. It is not my intention here to focus either on pointing to the merits of horror fiction as a literary (or cinematic) genre, or on endorsing the frequent attacks made on such fiction as an allegedly disturbing or depraving influence. I propose, rather, to consider some of the questions raised by horror fiction as a cultural phenomenon, and to try to understand what the fields of discourse surrounding such fiction imply about the ways in which contemporary society sees itself. The book is thus divided into two major parts. The first part (which could have been subtitled 'Forms of the customary life') examines representative samples of works of horror fiction. The second part ('Forms of the educated life') analyses a series of academic (mainly psychological) perspectives on horror fiction and 'mass-media violence'.

Literary critics frequently point to a distinction between horror fiction and a reportedly more respectable 'literature of terror'. Prawer, for instance, insists that there is a clear point of demarcation between 'fantasy terror' – which is ' "weird", "eerie", "ghostly", or "uncanny" rather than horrifying' – and 'horror' – which involves 'a *painful* emotion composed of repugnance and fear, a shudder of *loathing*, as well as terror' (Prawer 1980: 108; Prawer's italics). This distinction is frequently made to carry moral as well as aesthetic overtones. Thus, a work of 'fantasy terror' is designated as involving a stylized approach to horrible situations and as avoiding traffic 'with sadistic and erotic fantasies, with unhealthy nervous excitements that nourish no values, with the confirmation of social prejudice through the stereotypes that are made to carry the necessary menace' (ibid.: 110). It bears stressing at this stage that in this book I propose to cut across these distinctions and to take horror fiction to constitute a genre which is as vast as it is complex. Though I want to stress that there are very important differences and implications raised by tone, method, and connotations (moral, aesthetic, or otherwise) in stories dealing with horrific eventualities of experience, I wish to approach such stories generically as redescriptions of reality which are proposed to their readers as reflecting or suggesting adequate modes of viewing and evaluating ourselves and our environment. According to this definition, the genre of horror fiction includes a legion of works which vary greatly in artistry, merit, and value. It includes various influential or seminal classics like Mary Shelley's *Frankenstein*, Robert Louis Stevenson's *Strange Case of Dr Jekyll and Mr Hyde*, Bram Stoker's *Dracula*, Henry James's *Turn of the Screw*, the tales of Edgar Allan Poe, and a series of undoubtedly superior films like (to name two of the most influential) Robert Wiene's *Cabinet of Dr Caligari* and Alfred

Hitchcock's *Psycho*. But the genre also incorporates a very large and growing number of more suspect and controversial products like *I Spit on Your Grave, Cannibal Holocaust, Zombie Flesh Eaters*, and (the 1973 Mexican) *Santo and the Blue Demon vs. Dracula and the Wolfman*. In other words, horrific eventualities of experience can be and have been considered and evaluated in very different terms and tones within the genre of horror fiction. A number of representatives of the genre reflect considerable artistic, imaginative, and intellectual merit in their application of the conventions of the genre to a searching analysis of human concerns, and in their employment of standard images of horror to convey insights which can form the basis of constructive action. At the same time, the genre of horror fiction can also be said to harbour an increasing amount of popular material which thrives on cliché and which projects images and interpretations of experience which are as hollow and self-enclosed as they are pretentious. There is a tendency for this latter type of product to be either dismissed or denounced out of hand, or else popularized, defended, and even adulated in a 'camp' sort of way because of its unorthodox qualities – or because of its undeniable ability to arouse strong emotions, revulsion, and nausea. The decision to categorize and examine these very different exponents of the horror genre more broadly than is usually the case is based on the assertion that they are all social products which transform possibilities of experience into discourse, and which thus influence, reflect, and reinforce popular attitudes, assumptions, and prejudice. On these terms, popular horror fiction calls for a sharp and systematic exposition of what it is doing and how it works.

Further, the understanding of horror fiction which I adopt here includes all forms of narrative, irrespective of their medium of transmission. Here again, I wish to stress that this generalization is not meant as a negation of the importance and implications of the medium through which fictions are transmitted. Indeed, much of what follows underlines the critical roles played by the nature of different media in relation to the methods in which we understand, experience, and react to this type of fiction. Though most of the examples discussed in this book are taken from books and films, it is important to remember that horrific fictions are transmitted through a variety of other channels – including everyday conversation, periodical publications ('comics', popular magazines, etc.), radio, theatre, television, video recordings, songs, and recorded lyrics, and even computer video games. It should be clear that each of these media brings its own set of connotations and cognitive requirements which will have very important implications for the variety of methods in which the stories which are told through them will be presented, interpreted, and evaluated. But, though the media of transmission vary in critical ways, they can be said to have in common the fact that they transmit to a potentially large and diffuse audience redescriptions of reality and projected eventualities of a specific (horrific) nature. Partly because of the nature of specific media, and largely because of the orientations of the authors, these redescriptions and fictional projections also come loaded with evaluations which variously invite us to consider their subjects as disturbing, entertaining, nauseating, adventurous, threatening, humorous, etc. To take a fairly self-evident example, the playing of computer video games which involve us in galactic violations, or in helping Mr Pacman to evade or devour his would-be annihilators, can be seen as a form of traffic in fictional horrors. But it is a very specific form of traffic, and one which is very different from the types of cognitive, perceptual, and emotional activities which are involved when we sit at the cinema to watch a horror movie, or when we switch over a television channel to watch a late-night horror show, rent a video-recorded horror film, or curl up in bed to read a tale of terror on a cold winter night. And it is not just the media of transmission which become operative here: the conditions in each of those cases and the expectations which we bring to each of those exercises are of critical importance to our methods of decoding and responding to the narratives.

I am therefore approaching fictional horrors as social and cultural products which are of significance because they form part of the symbolic structures which we use to make sense of and ascribe meaning to our existence. Horror fiction, whatever its merits or faults and irrespective of its medium of transmission, is here taken to be a type of narrative which deals in messages about fear and experiences associated with fear. It is presented in these pages as a genre which proposes the contemplation and evaluation of areas of shared uncertainty. This is an approach which is intended as a corrective to the common supposition that exponents of this genre (and even tales and thrillers which involve the depiction of violent situations) are directly or exclusively geared towards the arousal and encouragement of sadistic or masochistic reactions. The type of fiction I am concerned with, therefore, is one which touches on large and diverse areas of experience which are frequently found disturbing because they fit no easy categories. It invites us to consider situations which elaborate and conjecture about the fact that human beings at times act in horrifically destructive manners. It projects images which have our vulnerability and superstitions as their points of focus – the discomfort we occasionally feel about our own psyche and about what may lurk in its dark depths; our worries and qualms about our own creations and about the technological advances which might be turning us into helpless robots in a ruthless world; our anxieties about the ways in which our bodies can let us down, about pain, death, and the dead, and about all forms of hostile forces which may at any moment (or so we are told) intrude into our uncertainly patched-up social and personal worlds. A focal contention of this book is that the roots and ramifications of such fears – both as they are revealed, explored, or exploited in the social products themselves, and in the reception such products are accorded by those who decode them – constitute an important component of contemporary reality, and of the tools we have developed for reading and dealing with it.

Popular horror fictions, then, form part of a complex discursive process which is an integral component of the models deployed by contemporary society (often tacitly and uncritically) to understand itself. In examining and trying to explain the phenomenon of contemporary horror fiction, this book is concerned with seeing it as an important signifying component of the contemporary mind which, as Harré et al. phrase it, 'is a shaping of the activities of the whole person . . . by socio-linguistic influences' (Harré et al. 1985: viii). Working from this premise, the book opens with an analysis of representative samples of contemporary horror fiction in order to identify the pictures of personal and social reality, the modes of perceiving, discussing, and evaluating experience, which these products project for their audience's contemplation and possible endorsement. Chapter 1 presents a broadly historical account of some of the major landmarks in the development of horror fiction as a genre and cultural phenomenon, indicating some of the more striking social concerns with which this type of fiction has been associated. Chapters 2 and 3 focus on the works of two contemporary bestselling writers of horror fiction, and discuss the pictures of personal and social reality which underscore the content and style of their writing. The dystopias and imagined realms of horror, as well as the world-saving devices which these bestsellers portray, are analysed in these chapters with the aim of identifying what kind of symbolic universe and overarching reality definitions are represented and implicitly endorsed in these social products and in the fact of their wide readership.

These models of reality are next located within academic research traditions and perspectives. The premise here is that horror fictions and the arguments which have grown around them need to be examined within the context of the various interactions which take place between a culture's customary and educated modes of discourse. I want to suggest that a number of the definitions, assumptions, fears, and uncertainties which underscore the content and uses of horror fiction also underlie some of the more prominent attempts at explaining their alleged potential value and functions, as well as the reactions and condemnations which are frequently aroused by marketed representations of horror. In these terms, I wish to question the viability of the meanings which have been ascribed to human motivation and behaviour by the popular and academic discursive conventions which are most commonly applied to the consideration of fearful fantasies.

Narratives of terror have held a peculiar fascination from time immemorial, and there is nothing unprecedented about the fact that horror books, films, and videos currently appear to be enjoying a peak of popularity. Given the fact that there is a tradition of horror fiction, however, there are a number of significant changes in just what is today taken to constitute the horrific and shocking, and in the manners in which the subject is handled. There is also nothing unprecedented about the claims which frequently appear in the press about, say, the 'video nasties' being the plague of society and the soul-soilers of the young. Very similar claims were made about horror comics before these were banned by Act of Parliament in Britain in the 1950s – often, as Barker (1984a) points out, with little justification or proof beyond impassioned references to 'common sense'. Popular concern about the possible bad effects which the cinema and (later) television might be having on the young were also given great prominence and paralleled by all types of experimental and field investigations when these particular media started to reach a wide audience. Recent concern about the consequences of 'mass media violence' and marketed horrors, however, is insistent that there are disturbing developments within the industry, and that the types of horrors to which the young are being exposed today have reached a level of nauseatingly graphic detail and putrefying corruption which is unprecedented. The proponents of this view appear convinced that the influence which such fare might have on impressionable children and corruptible adolescents is of a kind which calls for and justifies very grave, passionate, and (to be effective) legislating and punitive concern. At the same time, the arguments and claims made in defence of the horror genre (by its exponents and producers, by 'horror buffs', and also by a number of social theorists) have kept pace with the moral crusaders and have attained a level of relative complexity which also manages to combine the assumptions of 'common sense' with scientific-sounding and often subtly worded claims about (most frequently) the 'vicarious satisfaction' and the 'cathartic release' provided by the experience of violence and horror in synthetic forms. Such claims (whether in favour or against the representation of horrific subjects on different media) and the fact that all manner of exercises in horrific fantasy continue to enjoy great popularity (though not, it should be stressed, exclusively among the young) need to be placed in a coherent perspective. This is not only because these phenomena raise very pertinent questions about the way we live now, about the ways in which we see ourselves, and about the type of future in which we would like to live, but also because the tones and thrust of the arguments surrounding contemporary horror fiction form part of a much broader cultural debate and are based on assumptions of wider resonance and implications.

In chapter 4 of this book I analyse the logic and provenance of the explanations which are most frequently offered to account for the popularity and appeal of horror fiction. Foremost among such explanations is the claim that fictional horrors and 'mass-media violence' perform the social ('cathartic') function of appealing to, exercising, and hence 'discharging' a set of sadistic or cowardly dispositions which allegedly form an essential component of our genetic make-up. This claim is here argued to be based on historically complex but essentially compromised conceptions of human nature. Its underlying assumptions can be said to form part of a long discursive tradition which accounts for disturbing phenomena and unpalatable manifestations of human destructiveness by ascribing them to 'inherited', 'inevitable', or 'natural' characteristics which are allegedly located 'inside' the individual but which are also con-ceptualized as being alien and opposed to the rational mind or spirit. During the past century, one explanation of this type which has received great prominence as well as frequent adaptive modification as a result of constant interaction between academic and popular discourse has been that epitomized in the image of the 'beast within' – i.e. the assertion that human beings and human societies act and are interested in what is destructive and nasty because they are innately beastly, and as such inevitably and 'naturally' inclined to bestiality. Though I am very critical of the more popular uses made of this image by a number of (psychodynamically oriented) writers, I also wish to stress its interpretative and dramatic uses and applications as these have been developed in some of the more sophisticated psychoanalytic accounts of catharsis.

Chapter 5 looks critically at a number of widely publicized assertions about the effects of horror fiction and 'mass-media violence'. I want to suggest that there are important points of contact between the assumptions and intentions informing claims about depraving and/or desensitizing influences, and those inspiring assertions about the release of unpleasant urges through the 'safety-valve' of synthetic horrors. A recurring tendency informing the models of humanity which underlie both approaches (and, indeed, much of horror fiction itself) is that of conceptualizing behaviour and motivation in terms of the requirements of classical mechanics. This reveals itself in the regularity with which the effects of fictional horrors are assumed to take place in an unmediated fashion, as though their carriers and those affected by them were no more than surfaces which come in direct contact and produce a reaction – much in the manner of a stone hitting somebody's head. This assumption is at the base of what has been variously referred to as the 'magic bullet', the 'hypodermic needle', or the 'stimulus–response' theory of mass communcations. I am particularly concerned with showing some of the major inadequacies of the research methods employed in the bulk of experimental and field studies intended to prove that 'mass-media violence' can be shown to influence behaviour directly. Questions of intentions and the socio-linguistic conventions which give them shape and direction are generally and deliberately evaded in such studies, and this is an omission which puts their findings in serious doubt. Such questions have, however, been considered by a number of researchers interested in the social cognitive aspects of mass communications – particularly in relation to the impact which fearful or fear-reinforcing fictions might have on social perceptions and attitudes.

Chapter 6 considers the contours of this impact by examining how social and cultural realities might be affected by the fact that individuals and institutions produce, endorse, and are entertained by the types of fantasies, redescriptions, and evaluations which continue to be encoded in mass-marketed horror fictions. The chapter thus examines how our perceptions of the environment are influenced by the myths of our times, and hence how these processes are linked to fear and anxiety. By considering how playful activities frequently allow us to explore threatening possibilities of experience from safe and reassuring positions, chapter 6 also discusses the appeal and implications of horror in terms of the ways in which we use fiction to define reality and resolve or evade the worries and discomforts of uncertainty.

The exercise of deconstructing customary models of reality and of showing them to be based on questionable assumptions does not make such models or their influence disappear. An analysis of the type undertaken here can make for an awareness of the nature of the speculative instruments which are at our disposal and which continue to form the basis of our attempts to make sense of existence and behaviour, but it does not by itself alter or replace them. To state this differently, understanding why personal and social uncertainties are expressed, evaluated, or resolved in a particular fashion, or why horror fiction should have become the focus of so much popular as well as educated attention and controversy, does not by itself change the facts that the horror industry is very lucrative, and that the models and concepts encoded in its redescriptions have helped to shape reality as we customarily understand it today. The importance of understanding influences and intentions lies in its role as a necessary preliminary to deliberate and progressively purposeful action. Given the centrality which meaning and explanations have in our lives, this importance cannot be overstressed.

The method of analysis adopted in the chapters which follow is therefore interdisciplinary, exploratory, and selective. In order to familiarize myself with the conventions of horror fiction I started my exploration by reading a large number of popular horror stories and viewing as many as possible of the horror movies screened regularly on television and at the cinema. Inevitably, of course, I have become aware of the existence of an endless list of horror books and films which I could not possibly explore, even if I were inclined to do so or felt that I should. I have therefore taken evidence of current bestselling popularity as my criterion for the selection of a relatively small number of representative samples. I have also been inevitably influenced by the experience of reading and viewing these books and films, in that my reactions have ranged from fascination to mild interest to boredom, and have included feelings of excitement, shock, nausea, depression, anger, confusion, and (importantly if somewhat grudgingly at times) fear. This is not to suggest that I believe the experience to have made me a better or worse person, or that it has 'released', 'cleansed', 'sullied', 'desensitized', or 'depraved' me. But the pages which follow are inescapably and necessarily partly motivated by the desire to understand and place these reactions and feelings (as well as their implications) within a coherent and viable perspective. I am very much aware of the fact that these reactions and my consequent ruminations on the horror genre have been heavily influenced by the shape of my own biography and by my position within a specific and complex cultural reality. These conditions constitute an indispensable frame marking the boundaries of this enquiry. Within those boundaries, the following chapters set out to explain cultural phenomena through redescription, and by looking at their historical origins in a complex ground of ideas and social formation.

Part I

HORROR AND HELPLESSNESS IN CONTEMPORARY BESTSELLERS

There is something peculiarly horrible and paralyzing in the terror of sleep. It lays the energies of the soul prostrate before it, crushes them to the earth as beneath the weight of an enormous vampyre, and equalizes for a time the courage of the hero and the child. . . . Courage and philosophy are frequently opposed in vain to these appalling terrors. The latter dreads what it disbelieves; the spectral forms, spectral voices, and all the other horrid superstitions of sleep arise to vindicate their power over that mind, which, under the fancied protection of reason and science, conceived itself shielded from all such attacks, but which, in the hour of trial, often sinks beneath their influence as completely as the ignorant and unreflecting hind, who never employed a thought as to the real nature of these fantastic and illusive sources of terror.

(R. Macnish, *The Philosophy of Sleep*, 1834: 68)

Chapter 1

HORROR FICTION AND SOCIAL UNEASE – AN OVERVIEW

'The horror of that moment,' the King went on, 'I shall never, *never* forget!' 'You will though,' the Queen said, 'if you don't make a memorandum of it.'
(Lewis Carroll, *Through the Looking Glass*)

PRELUDE: GENRE AND CULTURE

The next three chapters aim to place the phenomenon of contemporary horror fiction within the context of a wider cultural debate. This will involve the alignment of the more prominent of this fiction's underlying assumptions and concerns with some of the theories, beliefs, and anxieties which have dominated our century's attempts to understand itself, and with some of the images which contemporary society has found fit to express its conception of itself and of its habitat. The arguments developed here build on the understanding that our perceptions of the environment both determine and are expressed in the myths of our times. These chapters therefore analyse representative samples of contemporary horror fiction in order to identify the pictures of personal and social reality, the modes of perceiving, discussing, and evaluating experience, which these products project for their audience's contemplation and possible endorsement. The present chapter proposes to clarify the implications of all this by presenting an introductory and broadly historical account of some of the landmarks in the development of horror fiction as a genre, indicating some of the social and cultural concerns with which this fiction has been associated.

That statement of intent and the method of examination adopted here make a number of assumptions which need to be spelled out by way of introduction. The reading and writing of fiction are here understood to constitute what Inglis calls 'a social, sociable, heavily conventional means of exploring and defining our private fantasies and their relation to our realities' (Inglis 1975: 122). Such explorations, of course, can be conducted in more than one medium, and in the pages which follow I shall be referring to works of popular horror fiction which function through different media (films, books, comics, etc.). This is not to imply that the media employed make little or no difference. Such an assertion would not only be untenable, it would also run counter to some of the main arguments developed in this book as a whole. The eclectic approach adopted here is, rather, intended to underline an aspect of these social products which forms the focus of this enquiry – i.e. their function and uses as institutionalized methods of contemplating experience and projected eventualities. Fiction (in whatever medium) is here understood to constitute

> a social convention, an institutionalised technique of discussion, by means of which an author invites us to join him in discussing a possibility of experience that he regards as interesting and to share with him attitudes towards it, evaluations of it, that he claims to be appropriate.
>
> (Harding 1967: 13)

The satisfaction which millions of readers (or viewers) appear to derive from horror fiction is here therefore taken to indicate no more and no less than the nuances implied by the fact of this social convention. It is in terms of a constantly qualifying awareness that such satisfaction is experienced within an institutionalized convention that its implications are here contended to be of significance. As Harding notes of the relation between spectator and author:

> Implicitly we think of a work as being offered to us by someone, as having had significance for another person and not being an impersonal accident like the flickering of flames. Part of our own satisfaction is the sense that some other human being found it satisfying to contemplate such and such possibilities of experience and evaluate them in such and such a way, that when we share his satisfaction some mutual sanctioning of values is occurring, and that we have this quasi-social relation with him even if he is dead or totally inaccessible.
>
> (ibid. 1971: 311)

In this sense, there is much which an examination of fictional horrors can tell us about the workings of popular culture and about the types of significance ascribed to reality and fantasy in the habitual modes of discourse and consciousness which the popularity of such fictions implies. This does not mean that the texts of horror fiction (or any fiction, for that matter) can be taken as straight blueprints of such elusive and impossibly generalized notions as those described in terms like 'the collective unconscious', or the conglomerate (and often hazily and condescendingly discussed) 'mass culture' or 'mass consciousness'. For one thing, wide as are the appeal and following which this type of fiction appears to command, they cannot be claimed to cover anything like the majority, even of the so-called masses. Further, the reading and viewing of horror fictions, even among the most avid of fans, is but one of a large variety of cultural activities and influences which operate on a concurrent basis and which form a broad and complex context of awareness within the perspectives of which horror fiction usually plays a limited and constantly qualified role. This is one of the reasons why (as later chapters will illustrate) arguments and claims about a direct series of effects (corrupting or cathartic) ascribed to this type of product cannot but be inconclusive and of limited applicability. But, even though simple equations between cultural products and generalized consciousness can only stand their ground if they are willing to concede a host of qualifications, the reading of works of popular fiction as reflectors and affirmations of social and cultural realities remains valid and profitable. A work of horror fiction is (of its very nature) an exponent of genre – it works within a set of conventionalized parameters which constrain it towards a norm. As Tudor puts it, 'A genre is a relatively fixed culture pattern. It defines a moral and social world, as well as a physical and historical environment. By its nature, its very familiarity, it inclines toward reassurance' (Tudor 1974: 180). What this inclination towards reassurance implies in the culture pattern encoded in contemporary works of horror fiction will need to be examined sharply in the pages which follow. It bears noting at this stage that among the claims made for horror fiction by one of its foremost contemporary exponents (a writer whose work is examined in chapter 3) is the assertion that 'its main purpose is to reaffirm the virtues of the norm by showing us what awful things happen to people who venture into taboo lands' (King 1982a: 442–3), and that the finest representatives of the genre 'tell us truths about ourselves by telling us lies about people who never existed' (ibid.: 282). Such claims embrace an assumed set of shared values and ideas about what constitutes the norm and about which 'truths' will apply within the conventions of that norm. It is to the identification of those presumed norms and truths that this part of the book (i.e. chapters 1, 2, and 3) directs itself.

If the fearful fantasies encoded in works of horror fiction are to be seen as forming part of a larger cultural reality, then an account of the modes of functioning associated with such fiction will need to take on a number of weighty considerations. According to Ricoeur, 'we understand ourselves only by the long detour of the signs of humanity deposited in cultural works' (Ricoeur 1981: 143). Horror fiction is one of these signs – its texts are social products packed with messages within which are encoded meanings related to human experience. The task of unravelling the countless configurations assumed by the signs of humanity – whether one chooses to call this exercise one of deconstruction, analysis, practical criticism, or interpretation – is (again in Ricoeur's terms) 'the reply to the fundamental distanciation constituted by the objectification of man in works of discourse, an objectification comparable to that expressed in the products of his labour and his art' (ibid.: 138). It is through following this hermeneutical detour that we can begin to form a clear understanding of some of the systems of meaning with which human thought and action are imbued. To adapt a phrase from Silverstone, these products both speak to and speak of 'the modes of thought and feeling that orient our actions in the daily round' (Silverstone 1981: 6). In this important sense they are (like television, which is Silverstone's subject) 'not so much a guide to action, or a guide for the perplexed, but rather a commentary on the categories and boundaries of culture and an exploration of the ambiguities and uncertainties that are endemic to it' (ibid.).

The texts of horror fiction (as of other fiction), therefore, are commentaries – representations which explore and evaluate (and in this sense influence) a set of cultural and cognitive experiences. The texts themselves are made up of messages – coded meanings which constitute what Hall calls a 'differentiated moment, in which the formal rules of discourse and language are in dominance':

> Before this message can have an 'effect' (however defined), satisfy a 'need' or be put to a 'use', it must first be appropriated as a meaningful discourse and be meaningfully decoded. It is this set of decoded meanings which 'have an effect', influence, entertain,

instruct or persuade, with very complex perceptual, cognitive, emotional, ideological or behavioural consequences.

(Hall 1980: 130)

The methods in which the meanings encoded in such messages are appropriated and decoded are in their turn dependent on our culture's ways of seeing and on what Fiske and Hartley call 'our common experience, our culturally determined intersubjectivity' (Fiske and Hartley 1978: 38). Among the many complexities of contemporary common experience which influence our methods of decoding (and hence responding to) messages about violence and horror are the traditions of 'mass-media violence' and horror fiction themselves, as well as the controversies which have surrounded them. The cognitive implications of horror fiction – i.e. what this type of fiction reflects about our modes of knowing and seeing, as well as the influence it can be claimed to exert – are therefore importantly conditioned by the fact that such fiction forms part of a distinct tradition which constitutes a genre. It is as a genre that horror fiction can be argued to form a signifying (and significant) component of our culturally determined intersubjectivity. Like other genres, it works within a set of conventionalized parameters (and hence within the form of a specific set of formal rules of discourse and language) which are determined and maintained by a complex series of forces and attitudes which are conservative (possibly circular) but not static. Precisely because of the processes of interaction endemic to the encoding–decoding exercise, genre involves development. We can therefore speak of innovators within a genre – writers or film-makers who explore, stretch, and extend the boundaries and signifying properties of the tradition within which they work. Critics also speak, for instance, of 'explosive periods . . . in the cycle of shudder art' (Twitchell 1983: 41), of 'the principal phases of the international history of the horror film' (Punter 1980: 346), and even of 'a more linear, temporally more straightforward development conditioned by the film-makers' desire to test out various degrees of explicitness and thresholds of acceptability' (Prawer 1980: 42). Some of these developments and their implications are explored in the rest of this chapter. At this point it is worth stressing that the processes in operation here are manifestly more complex than is allowed for by the assumption that works of horror fiction exist exclusively to satisfy or encourage a sadistic or masochistic delight in bathing in gore.

It is time to consider some specific examples.

A FEARFUL FLIGHT BETWEEN SCIENCE
AND SUPERSTITION

I take my first example from a relatively mild, technically accomplished, and respectable representative of the genre of fantasy horror: the film *The Twilight Zone*, issued in 1983 by Warner Brothers, and produced by two of the most successful and popular of the new generation of film-makers currently working in Hollywood – Steven Spielberg and John Landis. The film was co-directed by Spielberg and Landis together with Joe Dante and George Miller, each of whom was responsible for one of the four separate tales which make up the piece. All of these directors had already made a name for themselves with works belonging to (or else containing elements and techniques deriving from) the genre of fantasy horror. Spielberg had had his first success with *Jaws* in 1975, and had by now become a household name after further successes like *ET* and *Raiders of the Lost Ark*. Landis's *An American Werewolf in London* (1981) had combined traditional horror motifs and calculated clichés with humour and impressive special effects to produce an unusually entertaining version of the werewolf story – a version, incidentally, which is full of respectful references to earlier renderings. Dante's earlier films included *Piranha* (made in the wake of the success of *Jaws*) and *The Howling*, while Miller had already directed the first two *Mad Max* films about the struggle for survival in a post-nuclear landscape. As its title suggests, the 1983 *Twilight Zone* is a conscious act of homage to Rod Serling's long-running American television series of the same name, made and first transmitted between 1959 and 1965, and the centre of a large and long-lived cult following. The television series presented a mixture of science fiction and whimsical tales whose point of focus was frequently provided by terror – a note generally underlined by Serling's demeanour as a uniformly grim and earnest host and master of ceremonies inviting viewers into what he called 'a fifth dimension beyond that which is known to man'. The 1983 film, in fact, follows the format and general style of the television series and even opens with a pre-credits sequence (written and directed by Landis) in which episodes from the Rod Serling series are enthusiastically recalled by two characters who are driving towards their own version of the 'middle ground . . . between science and superstition, between the pit of man's fears and the summit of his knowledge' (as Serling's invocation at the start of each instalment had it).

The story I wish to consider here constitutes the final segment of this film, directed by George Miller, with a screenplay and original story by Richard Matheson (who had also been responsible for some of the screenplays of the original television series). Matheson also provides an interesting indication of some of the general trends and directions taken by the fantasy-horror industry over the past thirty years or so. He has written extensively both as a novelist and as a screen-writer, and, as Daniels puts it, he 'is a leader of that group of fantasy writers who, perhaps partly inspired by the indefatigable Robert Bloch, have fattened their traditionally feeble finances by finding work in films' (Daniels 1977: 216). His early work dates from the 1950s, and the popular concerns which underscore his stories (the modes of thought and feeling to which and of which they speak) can readily be identified as characteristic of their period. Matheson's stories have also been highly successful. His 1954 novel *I Am Legend* was filmed twice within a decade – first as *The Last Man on Earth*, with Vincent Price in the lead role, and later (in 1971) as *The Omega Man*, with Charlton Heston. This was a tale which dealt with the vicissitudes of the last mortal on earth, an anachronistic freak, hunter by day, quarry by night, struggling for survival in a world peopled by the monstrous victims of a technologically precipitated plague of vampirism. The theme of horrific isolation in a once familiar world turned threateningly alien is also at the centre of *The Shrinking Man*, a novel which Matheson published in 1956 and which he turned into the screenplay of the film *The Incredible Shrinking Man* (directed by Jack Arnold) in 1957. The background to this story was a growing public anxiety about the dangers of radiation and other possible consequences of A-bomb testing, and the tale dwelt on the horror of helplessly becoming an alien in one's home and world as the protagonist literally shrinks into infinity (at the rate of one-seventh of an inch per day) after being exposed to a vagrant and sparkling cloud of radioactivity.

The final segment of the 1983 *Twilight Zone* is also concerned with isolation. In an age when air disasters and hijacks are frequently in the news, it invites us to consider the fear of flying from the perspective of a hyper-anxious air traveller. The situation is basically that of the boy who cried wolf. Having jeopardized his credibility by overreacting in a storm, the protagonist finds himself in the unenviable position of being the only person on the plane to realize that the flight's safety is threatened by a supernatural (and grotesquely

9

improbable) force. The opening shot is of a plane flying through a thunderstorm at night. 'This could be the end of a particularly frightful experience,' the narrator's voice informs us; 'it is only the beginning.' Inside the plane the stewardesses are concerned about one of the passengers, a Mr Valentine (played by John Lithgow), who has locked himself in the lavatory and is only with difficulty persuaded to return to his seat. Valentine knows all the statistics about flying being the safest means of transport, but these figures clearly give him little reassurance. He is also a scientist, and has written a highly technical book on computing – a copy of which is seen by one of the stewardesses and mistaken for science fiction. Left alone and wishing to distract himself, Valentine looks out of the window. Through the darkness he thinks he sees something unusual moving about on one of the wings. He peers more closely and a flash of lightning illuminates his view. The shots in this sequence have alternated between close-ups of Valentine's face as he squints through the rain-spattered window, and ill-defined shots of his angle of vision as the viewer too is invited to try to make out exactly what is on the wing. We next see Valentine from a grotesque angle (a hand-held camera looks up at his face) as he jumps from his seat and dementedly shouts that there is a man out on the wing. The initial reaction of his fellow-travellers is one of panic and confusion. They then become patronizing and reproachful: 'You used to be a normal person!' a rather unpleasant little girl tells him reprovingly.

Let us pause here and consider what this introduction to the tale is up to. The segment comes at the end of the film, so that we are viewing and responding to it after we have seen three other tales dealing with fantastic situations. We are, therefore, waiting for something unusual to happen. In this type of film, the unexpected is expected, and the thrill we experience when it arrives partly derives from the satisfaction of having our expectations confirmed in a reassuring and entertaining fashion. Since this story is emphatically presented as belonging to a genre and tradition of fantasy horror, the denouement will have to be out of the ordinary, magical. The audience is in a sense expecting to make again the reassuring discovery that everything is still in its culturally accustomed place: magic and the supernatural belong to fantasy fiction and to films and TV programmes like *The Twilight Zone* – and, within the well-ordered world of popular genres, good fences make good neighbours. Audience expectations and genre conventions are therefore determining (and restricting) factors in the story's development.

At the opening of the segment Valentine is presented as a somewhat ludicrous figure – the wide-angle close-ups of his terrified face in the lavatory mirror, the patronizing attitude of the stewardesses, and the disapproving looks of the other passengers, all suggest that here is a man who needs to get a good hold of himself and stop acting in this absurdly irrational fashion. But the film does not allow us to maintain this patronizing attitude for long. Valentine, we soon discover, is a scientist, well versed in statistics and technicalities, and in all probability more knowledgeable than either the stewardesses or his rather bizarre-looking fellow passengers. He also knows that he is making a fool of himself and understands the need to calm down. But he is still terrified. Logic and scientific knowledge are apparently as ineffective against his fearful gut reactions as are the mild sedatives which the senior stewardess encourages him to swallow.

In its relatively light-handed fashion, the segment can be argued to be inviting us to consider a very disturbing epistemological possibility. Underlying our fascinated consideration of the sequence of events narrated in this story is a vaguely formulated dread that our neatly schematized conceptions of reality and normality might be ill founded, that there might be vision and truth in the most absurd-sounding claims made by people whose behaviour we 'naturally' take to indicate instability and derangement. The narrative method adopted here only gradually courts us into seeing the situation from Valentine's perspective, and hence to the realization that this ostensibly unbalanced and irrationally terrified individual is in fact the one sensible person in the group. Valentine's most absurd-sounding discovery is thus also witnessed by the film's viewers: there is a gremlin tearing apart one of the engines on the wing outside his window. I shall be considering some further examples of this type of play on perspectives and its implications in chapter 3. What I wish to stress here is the manner in which this particular commentary on the ambiguities and uncertainties of our ways of seeing and knowing falls short of being really disturbing because of the context in which it is presented. Our sense of a well-ordered cognitive reality is in fact paradoxically confirmed here, and this reassurance is made possible by our continued awareness of the frame within which the tale is functioning. The story explores a potentially very disturbing consideration – i.e. that the world view of the condescendingly appraised madman, or absurd-looking doomsday prophet, might not be so ridiculous after all, that it is his version of reality which is the most practical, and that our survival might actually depend on our taking his warnings seriously. But all this is undercut by the frame within which this episode and its underlying ideas are set – the expectations and connotations which we (like the film's makers) have brought to it from our previous experiences of other representatives of this genre, of the TV series, and of the package provided by the film as a whole. It is this frame which provides the undercurrent of reassurance to the effect that our set of reality (our cognitive schemes or mental models) is ultimately still well founded and functional.

Throughout the film, we follow the narrative and consider the ideas and emotions to which it draws our attention as an exercise in fantasy, and 'fantasy' is a term which has popularly come to be associated with the unreal. The events and ideas which we are invited to consider are therefore perceived as having little contact with the world of the functional because they belong to a never-never land, a 'twilight zone' which Serling's TV series had made synonymous with what he called 'the dimension of imagination'. According to this conception, this is a dimension which we only explore when we have nothing better or more practical to do, and which we should not take too seriously anyway. It is a realm, in other words, which has already been clearly classified within our schematized set of reality as possibly providing entertainment and excitement, but as being basically inconsequential – much like the fleeting thrill of sitting on a big dipper in amusement parks, where the entire setting acts as a reassurance that all the 'dangers' we have chosen to endure are actually as controlled and safe as they are short-winded. And so, in this tale at least, what touched on a potentially disturbing concept turns out to be an exercise in reassurance, and by implication that reassurance can also be recognized as incorporating a reinforcement of some of our most cherished prejudices, stereotypical images, and unformulated assumptions.

The example I have been considering, then, skirts round the really frightening: it uses its own tradition as a buffer against the implications of the functional issues which it also makes the basis of the thrills it generates. There are, of course, many other representatives of the genre of fantasy horror which are not so reassuring and which deliberately set out to undermine our (common-sense) understanding of what constitutes the real by blurring the distinctions between what we normally take to belong to the world of everyday practical reality and that which we had categorized as belonging to a hermetically sealed world of 'fantasy' and 'imagination'. This is a point which I shall be considering in greater detail in chapter 3, but it bears stressing here that the assumptions and genre conventions underlying 'reassuring' works like *The Twilight Zone* are identical to those which inform more disturbing and frightening works of horror fiction. To state this differently, distinctions between 'fantasy' and 'reality' can be blurred in horror fiction because such distinctions are themselves frequently ill-founded and reductionist, in that the products of the imagination are inseparable from our interpretations of what constitute the practical and real. As Sartre put it, 'to experience any object as horrible, is to see it against the background of a world which reveals itself as *already* horrible':

> For the horrible is *not possible* in the deterministic world of the usable. The horrible can only appear in a world which is such that all the things existing in it are magical by nature, and the only defences against them are magical. This is what we experience often enough in the universe of dreams, where doors, locks and walls are no protection against the threats of robbers or wild animals for they are all grasped in one and the same act of horror. And since the act which is to disarm them is the same as that which is creating them, we see the assassins passing through doors and walls; we press the trigger of our revolver in vain, no shot goes off.
>
> (Sartre 1971: 89; italics in the original)

Sartre illustrates his account of fear as arising 'when the world of the utilisable vanishes abruptly and the world of magic appears in its place' (ibid.: 90–1) by considering how we perceive the sudden appearance of a face looking in at us from outside a window. The sequence from *The Twilight Zone* considered above includes just such a situation: the protagonist at one point suddenly lifts the blind on his port window and finds the grotesque features of the gremlin staring in at him. The scene refers to a long tradition, in that the image of a face at the window is one which has been used consistently, and often very strikingly, as a means of generating or suggesting fear in narratives of terror. As is made clear by one of the more memorable sequences in Henry James's *Turn of the Screw*, the tenor of such scenes is very often to project associations of supernatural powers and threatening malice on to the face and its owner. The magical qualities ascribed to such figures are mainly, as Sartre suggests, a product of the superstitious doubts and uncertainties of the person perceiving the image. The face, according to Sartre, is not appraised 'as that of a man, who might push the door open and take twenty paces to where we are standing':

> On the contrary, it presents itself, motionless though it is, as acting at a distance. The face outside the window is in immediate relationship with our body; we are living and undergoing its signification; it is with our own flesh that we constitute it, but at the same time it imposes itself, annihilates the distance and enters into us. Consciousness plunged into this magic world drags the body with it inasmuch as the body is belief and the consciousness believes in it.
>
> (ibid.: 86–7)

The fact that the image has become one of the standard clichés of horror fiction, of course, is a further influence on the manner in which we read scenes involving such figures. It is also not surprising to find that one of the figures of horror fiction most frequently portrayed in this position is that of the vampire – in works ranging from the Victorian penny dreadful *Varney the Vampire* (which opens with just this type of scene), to Stoker's *Dracula* and the various film versions made of it (including, most hauntingly perhaps, Murnau's silent *Nosferatu: a Symphony of Terror* in 1922), and Stephen King's' *Salem's Lot* (which has a child vampire peering in).

UNCANNY VAMPIRE FORMS AND THE GROWTH OF GOTHIC FICTIONS

We can get an idea of the ways in which a particular image can become the vehicle for very different meanings, and still retain an underlying thread of associations, by looking at some of the uses which have been made of the figure of the vampire in fiction. As is the case with other popular images associated with fearful fictions, the figure of the vampire is one whose history is interestingly intertwined with the public and private concerns of the epochs which popularized and endorsed it as an objectification of uncertainly understood and disturbing phenomena. Many interpretations have been given of the significance of this figure, which in the course of the past two centuries has become variously associated with the horrors of death and corruption as well as those of earthbound immortality; with the inexplicable spread of deadly diseases as well as with psychopathological disturbances like necrophilia and obsessions with blood;

14

with the lure of sexually perverse domination as well as suicidal submission and oblivion; with the dreadful quest for omnipotence outside the sanctioned aspirations of legalized religion, as well as with the anachronistic survival of an ambivalently perceived aristocracy whose 'noble blood' is nourished with the blood of lower classes (and even animals) in rituals involving degrading ('bestial') acts of violation.

The popular origins of the vampire myth are difficult to pin-point. According to Summers, there is evidence (though no direct reference) to suggest that 'vampirism was not unknown in Italy and in Greece of ancient times' (Summers 1929: 1). Marred as it is by its eccentric author's belief in vampires as physical realities, and by his straight-faced use of unorthodox sources (like *Varney the Vampire or, the Feast of Blood*[1]) as conclusive evidence of the ubiquity of vampires, Summers's work offers an extraordinary compendium of accounts (mostly of folk origin) about the dead returning to disturb or molest the living. There is a recurring pattern of functional meanings underlying these tales which suggests that, though popular images of horror take on different associations according to the period of their propagation, their trends and uses are fairly standard.

Writing about sixteenth- and seventeenth-century popular beliefs in spirits and ghosts as physical realities, Thomas has argued that these figures often served the function of personifying 'men's hopes and fears, making explicit a great deal which could not be said directly'(Thomas 1973: 717). According to Thomas, since the shapes assumed by these personifications and the interpretations ascribed to them were inevitably influenced by the manners in which 'mental and perceptual processes can be extensively conditioned by the cultural content of the society in which men live' (ibid.: 711), ghosts and other supernatural beings were also a useful sanction for social norms. To take an example cited by Summers (1929: 133–43), in 1653 Henry More published a treatise entitled *An Antidote to Atheism* which included two accounts of events allegedly occurring in Silesia and involving dead corpses walking from their graves and disturbing or attacking the living. Both were cases in which a Christian burial had been given to men who, according to the creed of the time, did not deserve it – one was a suicide, the other a hypocritical sinner, but these facts were kept secret from the rightful authorities by the dead men's relatives. It was only when these bodies (showing no signs of decomposition) were finally exhumed, cut to pieces, and burned that the disturbance to the living (including the dead men's relatives) came to an end. 'I cannot so much as imagine', commented More at the end of his account, 'what the *Atheist* will excogitate for a subterfuge or hiding place, from so plain and evident Convictions' (ibid.: 143).

Yet, according to Jones's account at least, excogitations about the significance of delayed decomposition in cases like these were very much an ecclesiastical concern:

> Unfortunately the Greek Orthodox Church – it is said in a spirit of opposition to the Roman Catholic pronouncement that the bodies of saints do not decompose – supported the dogma that it is the bodies of the wicked, unholy, and especially excommunicated, persons which do not decompose. Just as the Roman Catholic Church taught that heretics could be turned into Werewolves, the Greek Orthodox Church taught that heretics became Vampires after death.
>
> (Jones 1931: 103)

While the thrust of Jones's (psychoanalytic) account is to stress a sexual origin to beliefs in vampires and nightmares connected with them, he is also careful to note how 'in the Middle Ages there was a close correlation between visitations of the Black Death and outbreaks of Vampirism', and this because plagues 'have always been associated in the popular – and to some extent in the medical – mind with the notion of stench, particularly from decomposing sewage' (ibid.: 123). In this connection, Jones cites William of Newburgh's account of the Vampire of Alnwick Castle, who 'was actually believed to have caused an extensive plague through the evil odors he spread, and it ceased when his corpse was adequately dealt with' (ibid.).

Fearful fantasies of this nature, then, frequently performed important social functions by providing graspable (and in this sense reassuring) explanations to account for phenomena and misfortunes which were otherwise incomprehensible. I shall be considering some of the psychological implications of this point more closely in part II, but it is worth noting at this stage how this idea also has important implications in relation to the historical development of the genre of horror fiction. The Gothic fictions of the eighteenth century have generally been taken to represent the point of origin of the horror genre as we know it today. Tales of supernatural horrors have of course been told from antiquity, and monsters and their terrors figure prominently in works ranging from the *Odyssey* and the Book of

Revelation to *Beowulf* and *La Divina Commedia*. Horrific scenes of violence and violation also form part of many works of literature written before the eighteenth century. To cite some famous examples from a period when these type of horrors appear to have enjoyed great popularity, one can mention the violence and gore in Shakespeare's *Titus Andronicus*, the blinding of Gloucester in *King Lear*, the torture and murder of Marlowe's Edward II, and the proliferation of murders depicted in Jacobean tragedies. But there is an important difference to be underlined between the presentation and connotations of these horrors and those which first reveal themselves in the early Gothic fictions of the eighteenth century, and this was a difference which had important cultural implications. According to Punter, what happened in the eighteenth century was that 'the medieval, the primitive, the wild, became invested with positive value in and for itself' (Punter 1980: 6), and this was reflected in a growing taste for a type of art which endorsed and encouraged a fascination with excess and exaggeration. It is to this point in the history of literary and cultural developments that we can ascribe the origins of the frame of reassurance which I have argued surrounds contemporary works of horror fantasy like *The Twilight Zone*. According to Daniels, 'modern audiences are so accustomed to tales which are obvious inventions that they fail to realize the extent to which their ancestors expected and believed their stories to be gospel truth' (Daniels 1977: 8). Daniels notes that the year of England's last witchcraft trial (1717) also saw the birth of Horace Walpole, the author of 'the first modern horror story' (*The Castle of Otranto*), and he argues that 'stories of the sinister supernatural really began to come into their own after belief in the uncanny had been almost extinguished', so that the horror story as a distinct entity 'developed almost simultaneously with the idea of fiction' (ibid.: 19–20, 7–8). As Barker elaborates,

> Whilst religion held sway, the supernatural world would seem as natural as, if not more so than, the scientific. This meant that surprise and amazement at the odd and the inexplicable could not be separated out, and treated as exceptional and as a possible subject for bravura and delicious daring. The fears were too central and close to home to be the subject for fantastic reconstruction; but in another sense they were also taken as too normal, however terrifying.
>
> (Barker 1984a: 125–7)

On this issue, Butler also notes how the growth of the taste for Gothic fictions in the eighteenth century coincided with a taste for new, very emotional or millenarian religious cults, both in England and on the continent. She draws attention to Thomas's (1973) suggestion that the religious reforms of the Restoration deprived populations in western Europe of certain magical comforts by making a stricter distinction between orthodox Christianity and magic, and thus led to vulgar and educated recourse to witchcraft and astrology in the sixteenth and seventeenth centuries:

> Even in the 'rational' eighteenth century, a population which was not offered scientific explanation for its ills, and had no scientific protection (for medicine offered little until the twentieth century), had the same need of reassurance which earlier generations sought from a more naive Christianity or from witchcraft. And in this connection it is striking how Gothic fiction, with its strangely recurring motifs, has an almost ritual aspect.
>
> (Butler 1981: 28)

A fascination with excess and a need for reassurance thus found their point of fusion in a growing type of fiction which explored the macabre, the unorthodox, the supernatural, and other areas of human experience which defied logical explanation.[2] Part of the reassurance such fictions could provide grew out of their implicit distinction from everyday reality – their exotic settings, stereotypical or larger-than-life characters, unusual or anachronistic situations. The frame of reassurance which such fictions came to assume was also inseparable from their predictability – the 'almost ritual aspect' of their recurring motifs. Given the popularity of such titillating exercises in reassurance, it is not surprising that horror fictions and their protagonists were soon also recognized to be highly marketable as commodities. And, in this connection, the uses which have been made of the vampire motif over the past hundred years or so present a very revealing picture.

According to Johnson, the audience and resonance which have been achieved by the vampire myth in the twentieth century are both unparalleled and paradoxically apposite in a period which has been 'the great age of de-bunking, of secularisation and de-mythologisation' (Johnson 1982: 432). Similarly, in his eulogic account of what he terms 'the English Gothic cinema 1946–1972', Pirie notes how, among the many 'Gothic prototypes' which have 'commanded an astonishing success since their original composition', it is the popularity of *Dracula* and its various offshoots which 'goes beyond everything else – including *Frankenstein* – by a very long way' (Pirie 1973: 82). Pirie notes that Bram Stoker's novel has scarcely ever been out of print since it was first published in May 1879, and how as a play it turned out to be one of the most successful theatrical productions of the 1920s and 1930s, breaking record after record in England and France:[3]

> Most profitable of all, the film series has proved quite unstoppable and Michael Carreras, Hammer's managing director, recently confirmed that of all the monsters Hammer has introduced into its repertoire – including Frankenstein, the Werewolf, the Gorgon, Zombie, the Mummy, and many others – Dracula remains by far the most acceptable in terms of box-office receipts and continued audience response.
>
> (ibid.)

The 'acceptability' of Dracula is also reflected in the ways in which this figure has found its way into comics and cartoons (sometimes in unlikely guises like that of Quackula the vampire duck) as well as its selling value in such forms as 'vampire-shaped' ice-lollies and (in America at least) a 'vitamin-enriched vampire cereal' called Count Chocula. The 'acceptability' of Dracula and the vampire motif 'in terms of box-office receipts' was also largely responsible for the spate of Universal Pictures horror movies of the 1930s and early 1940s (as well as their many imitators). According to Clarens, Tod Browning's 1931 film version of *Dracula* (which had Bela Lugosi in the lead role that was to make him famous and, according to his own account, the recipient of a vast fan mail in the 1930s) became Universal's biggest money-maker of the year and 'dispelled the last doubt about the marketability of horror films' (Clarens 1968: 79–80).

The vampire's market value at the cinema is also underlined by Silver and Ursini's (1975) catalogue of sixty-six feature films made before the mid-1970s and dealing explicitly with fictional vampires. The list includes classics like Carl Dreyer's 1932 *Vampyr*; routine productions like Hammer's *Taste the Blood of Dracula* (1969), *Lust for a Vampire* (1971), and *The Vampire Circus* (1972); spoofs like Roman Polanski's 1967 *Dance of the Vampires* (which also went by the title *The Fearless Vampire Killers or Pardon Me but Your Teeth Are in My Neck*); as well as more suspect efforts like (the Mexican) *Santo and the Blue Demon vs. Dracula and the Wolfman* (1973), (the Italian) *Goliath and the Vampires* (1961) and (the American) *Plan 9 from Outer Space* (an incredibly cheap and incompetent 1955 production which included Bela Lugosi's last and most unfortunate screen appearance as a vampire). The list has of course continued to grow steadily, and vampire films continue to be made in fairly large quantities, frequently by unimaginative film hacks keen on exploiting a motif which has been proved to pull the crowds, but often also by directors and actors of considerable talent offering reinterpretations of an ancient theme of undisputed fascination. Thus, George Romero's *Martin* (1977) was intended to call into question or, as Romero put it, to 're-vamp' the traditional vampire myths and their anachronistic associations by exploring the character and sexual problems of a young man whose family has led him to believe that it has a history of vampirism and that he is himself an 84-year-old vampire. John Badham's 1978 version of *Dracula* (which had Laurence Olivier and Donald Pleasance in the roles of Dr Van Helsing and Dr Seward) underlined the seductive and virile appeal of the vampiric count (played by a Byronic-looking Frank Langella), in a manner which seemed to be touching on the ambiguities associated with the peculiarly Fascist lure of violent young men – a phenomenon to which public attention has been drawn at regular intervals by cases like those of Charles Manson's followers, the 'conversion' of Patty Hearst, and the frequently photographed girlfriends of terrorists facing trial. In Badham's version, Lucy is courted to become the vampire's favourite bride because of her vitality and spirit, and the changes which take place in her character are emphasized as constituting a release of passion and energy from the restricting conventionalities of a regional Edwardian existence. The conventionally respectable characters in this film (Dracula's antagonists as well as his victims) live in the upstairs quarters of Dr Seward's sanatorium, leading an apparently normal bourgeois existence and holding polite conversations during cordial dinner parties, while downstairs the patients at the sanatorium rage, roar, or whimper away their sordid existence in grated passageways and bolted cells. It is on this underground of sordid madness in the edifice of bourgeois civilization that Dracula is shown to thrive in this film. The brittle inadequacies of middle-class values also form the point of focus in Werner Herzog's sombre remake of F. W. Murnau's 1922 *Nosferatu* in 1979. Far from being romanticized, the vampire here is presented as a sick and sickening disease spreading its influence over a world which is portrayed (in line with Herzog's earlier films) as a desert into which the vampire rides to the ironic but ominous sound of Gounod's *Sanctus* in the film's final scene. In this version, the letting loose of the vampire is initiated by one of the more obviously demented representatives of the business class: the vampire disciple Renfield, who is here an incongruously giggling estate agent who knowingly sends his assistant to sell town property to Count Dracula at his castle. In one of the film's more memorable sequences, the vampire's field of action is depicted as a rat-infested and plague-ridden city, its squares littered with coffins and dreary bonfires, while at one end a group of primly dressed people invite the viewer to join them at their morbidly lavish last supper. In Herzog's version, the vampire–count looks hideously and uncompromisingly grotesque (as was the case with Max Schreck's portrayal in the 1922 version), but Klaus Kinsky's rendering of the part, and particularly the softly modulated, world-weary tones of his voice, succeeded in adding pathos and grim dignity to the cadaverous figure with its skull-like head, red-rimmed eyes, rodent fangs, and mandarin-clawed hands. The theme of disease and decadence dominates, so that there is no traditional confrontation here between good and evil, light and darkness, or science and superstition: the town's council are shown to be ineffectual, while Dr Van Helsing is presented as a feeble and senile scientist without real insight, arrested at the end by a feeble old man representing what is left of authority for the 'murder' of the staked (but not destroyed) vampire.

The conscious processes of reinterpretation exemplified in these films involve a realignment of the anachronistic images of the vampire motif with those concerns and experiences which the films' directors consider to be symptomatic of contemporary society. Such realignments (less consciously conducted, perhaps) can also be shown to underlie many of the more box-office oriented renderings of the Dracula story. Significantly, Silver and Ursini note the regularity with which vampire films underline the degenerative and bestial aspects of the vampire. In Universal Pictures' 1936 *Dracula's Daughter*, they point out, the protagonist is 'painfully aware of her uncontrollable bestiality but . . . naive as to its necessary consequences' (Silver and Ursini 1975: 113). In the first Hammer version of *Dracula* (directed by Terence Fisher in 1958), 'the emphasis on the bestial – low angle shots of the Count framed against the rapacious gargoyles which crown the battlements of his castle, Lee's hissing and growling

– also hinted at the deteriorative or atavistic cause underlying vampirism' (ibid.: 83). Similarly, in the 1960 *Brides of Dracula* (also directed by Fisher for Hammer Studios), 'the young male vampire is a spoiled son of the aristocracy whose profligacy and licentiousness eventually degenerate into what Van Helsing terms the 'disease' of vampirism (ibid.). In the mid-1980s, while AIDS both dominated and radically transformed the tenor and trend of discussions about sexual behaviour and relations, adaptations of the vampire motif more onerously associated promiscuity with bestiality, disease, and death. The protagonists of films like *Once Bitten*, *Fright Night*, and *Vamp* are teenagers who are shown to be attracted by the apparently opulent and loose life-style of the creatures of the night, but who learn to appreciate and endorse the values of safe sex, clean living, and the satisfactions of their mundane (middle-class) existence.

PSYCHOPATHIC VIOLATORS AND INVADING DEMONS

The shapes assumed by the fictions of the imagination, then, are importantly influenced and structured by the context in which we live, by our perception and understanding of experienced reality, and by the modes of discourse (social norms, political and moral/religious structures, the various systems of signs, symbols, language, and gestures) which mediate and also give shape and meaning to our attempts at understanding and explanation. Viewed from this perspective, broadly phrased assertions about the 'intrinsic value' or 'instinctive need' of the pleasures, thrills, and 'escape' provided by fantasy in themselves amount to little more than expressions of a complex set of presuppositions and ideological influences. Fantasy is known and experienced in terms of the shapes which it assumes. It is not an ethereal, mystical, or magical quality which serves as a balm for the rigours of science and rationalism, or which belongs to an exclusive and isolable realm of emotion – and this because, as I shall be arguing more fully in part II, such a realm does not exist. We are more likely to make adequate and constructive sense of the ways in which human fantasies manifest themselves if we recognize their interconnections with common-sense understanding as well as with political and scientific speculation. We need, in other words, to recognize human fantasies (fearful or otherwise) as an important index of the concerns, purposes, and understanding of reality which predominate in a particular context and time.[4] As Geertz puts it, 'ideation, subtle or otherwise, is a cultural artefact': like class or power it is something to be characterized by 'construing its expressions in terms of the activities that sustain them' (Geertz 1983: 152).

Viewed from this perspective, the various themes which seem to predominate in the horror fiction of different periods, or the various cycles which have often been argued to mark the history of horror films, reflect further complex levels of connotation. To take a recent development, it is worth noting how in the late 1970s and early 1980s there has been a growth in the number of films which explore situations and project images involving liberated women being sexually violated by pathologically violent men. Hitchcock's *Frenzy* (1972) in many respects set the tone, and the tide has grown with films like *Looking for Mr Goodbar* (in which a confidently and aggressively promiscuous Diane Keaton is horrifically stabbed to death by a young man with sexual problems), *Halloween, Dressed to Kill, Lipstick, Friday the Thirteenth, He Knows You're Alone*, and *I Spit on Your Grave*. According to Twitchell, this trend suggests a fear of women which 'may tell us more than we want to know about the sadistic misogyny engendered by the Women's Movement' (Twitchell 1983: 41–2). At times of gradual cultural shifts, Twitchell argues, 'people need some "object" toward which they can direct their anxieties'. The implications of this phenomenon when it expresses itself in works of horror fiction like the ones just mentioned are complex and potentially regressive – particularly when they endorse and compound stereotypical and ideologically motivated images like those of non-domesticated women being punished for transgressing traditionally established sexual boundaries (which is a recurring motif in many of these films). The theme of pathological violence as it is explored and evaluated in films like these also raises a number of questions about the manners in which contemporary society explains to itself the origins and nature of destructiveness and violation among humans. Violence (as chapters 2 and 3 will illustrate more fully) is frequently equated with a streak of madness, an allegedly uncontrollable component of our inherited nature which in extreme cases is said to break down all culturally transmitted restraints and to give full vent to bloodlust and chaotic plunder.

The most noted images to which this notion has given rise are the werewolf and Mr Hyde, and it is no accident that the horror film industry has also produced countless renderings and variations of tales involving these figures. Such renderings include the first American film production of *Dr Jekyll and Mr Hyde* in 1908 (a photographic record of a stage-play); the differing portrayals of the Jekyll–Hyde figure presented by John Barrymore, Fredric March, and Spencer Tracy (in 1920, 1932, and 1941 respectively); Lon Chaney Jr's many appearances as the Wolf Man in the 1940s; and so on to more recent variations like the Hammer versions of the 1960s (which included an early appearance by Oliver Reed as the lycanthropic protagonist in 1961), as well as little remembered efforts of the 1950s like Herman Cohen's *I Was a Teenage Werewolf* (1957)[5] and Jack Arnold's *Monster of the Campus* (1958). Arnold's film rather clumsily elaborated on an aspect of the Jekyll–Hyde story which had been made explicit in Fredric March's 1932 portrayal of Hyde as prehistoric savage – a note which has underscored most of the versions made of this tale since then at least. In the opening scenes of *Monster of the Campus* the protagonist, a university professor interested in evolution, explains to his rather dim but pretty assistant that humans have inherited their violent nature from their ape antecedents. In the course of his experiments he is contaminated by one of his prize possessions – a prehistoric fish which has bypassed evolution and retained a grotesque appearance and adjuncts like clawed feet which allow it to walk on the sea-bed. The rest of the film is taken up with the professor's transformations from civilized scientist to primate savage – until he is shot dead by the representatives of (civilized) law and order.[6] There are a number of culturally based assumptions underlying this as well as more subtle explorations of an allegedly primitive origin to violence and destructiveness which I shall be examining in some detail in the chapters which follow. What I wish to underline at this stage is the frequency with which contemporary works of horror fiction project and reinforce a set of assumptions about the degenerative, diseased, and compulsive characteristics of this 'primitive tendency'. Fearful fantasies about the psychopathological destructiveness which is assumed to derive from this tendency are also frequently juxtaposed against a set of stereotypical images of the reassuringly controlling (though equally ruthless) representatives of civilized law and order.

DeFleur and Dennis note that a study of popular American TV dramas of the crime-adventure variety (*Starsky and Hutch*, *Kojack*, *Charlie's Angels*, etc.) suggests that the most dangerous offenders depicted in these stories tend to be presented as being 'criminally insane' (DeFleur and Dennis 1985: 396–400). According to this study,[7] scenes portraying acts of horrific violation frequently showed murderers, rapists, slashers, snipers, or bombers as having glassy eyes, grimacing strangely, or giggling incongruously as they committed their crimes:

> Some laughed strangely and sobbed or cried. Others mumbled incoherently and screamed irrationally. Another bared his teeth and snarled as he jumped on his victims to suck blood from their jugular veins. Still another squeezed raw meat through his fingers and rubbed it on his gun as he prepared to kill his next victim.
>
> (ibid.: 398)

According to DeFleur and Dennis, the trend of such presentations, and of the popular vocabulary of madness which goes with them, is to use the mentally ill to represent evil. Against this evil the forces for law and order fight and win to protect society. In other words, a culturally based fear of a stigmatized sector of the population is invoked and reinforced, while reassurance is provided about the efficiency and (sane) toughness of the guardians of the status quo. I shall be considering some of the issues raised by this juxtaposition more fully in chapter 2, but it is worth noting here how (in this type of popular fiction as in the early Gothic fictions of the eighteenth century) a fascination with the wild and threateningly unorthodox has been transformed into an exercise in ideological reassurance.

Titillation and ideological reassurance can also be argued to have been motivating forces in the making and viewing of the series of films about invasions from outer space which were made in the America of the 1950s – i.e. during the height of the Cold War. This trend was perhaps most effectively and memorably caught in Don Siegel's 1956 *Invasion of the Body Snatchers*, but there were other (less accomplished) products like *Invasion of the Saucer-Men* (1957), *Earth vs. the Flying Saucers* (1957), *I Married a Monster from Outer Space* (1958), and *The Blob* (a 1958 production in which a young Steve McQueen led a band of quick-witted teenagers in destroying the eponymous alien which had grown from a handful of glutinous substance by absorbing the citizens of an all-American town). As a number of critics have pointed out, such films reflected a growing concern about potential invasion or infiltration by dark forces coming from behind what had come to be known as 'the Iron Curtain'.[8] It is also worth recalling that films like these were being produced and popularly patronized at a period when interest in space exploration was growing fast, and when the race for space (highlighted by the successful launching of the first Russian satellite in 1957) was on. Similarly, the spate of films about demonic pregnancies and child monsters produced in the late 1960s and early 1970s (*Rosemary's Baby*, *The Omen*, *It's Alive*, to name the most famous) reflected a complex set of popular anxieties (superstitious as well as political) about possible invasion by malevolent alien forces and about the vulnerability of helpless innocence in the face of evil. The successful marketing of these films also coincided with mounting awareness and concern over diminishing global resources and a growing public debate about the widespread availability of effective methods of birth-control, the legalization of abortion, and the long- and short-term effects of pregnancy-related drugs like thalidomide and fertilization pills. As Prawer puts it, 'the gusto with which films like *The Omen* make the audience wish for the child's destruction has something deeply suspect about it' (Prawer 1980: 71). Yet this film grossed over four million dollars during its first three days' showing, and eventually made over a hundred million dollars at the box-office.

The contemplation of horrifically 'possessed' or pathologically violent youngsters was perhaps most influentially conducted in William Friedkin's *The Exorcist* (1973) and Stanley Kubrick's *A Clockwork Orange* (1971). It is worth recalling in this connection that most of the complaints and indignation directed against Kubrick's film at the period of its release involved claims about the horrifying and depraving effects it was alleged to be having on the young. The violating protagonists of *A Clockwork Orange* – in contrast to the staid, withdrawn, and opulently self-regarding victims – were emphatically young and they moved about in a psychedelic world which at times had the appearance of a global disco. It was this aspect of the film which projected a highly disturbing but also clearly cognizable vision of futuristic youth gone badly sour, callously alienated, and rhythmically antisocial. The young men in this film were as worrying in their violation of traditional social and ethical norms as was the blaspheming and horrifically transformed teenage girl in *The Exorcist*. Both films appeared at a period of much publicized student unrest, the flower movement, an allegedly growing drug generation intent on hedonistic pursuits, and frequent youthful protest against traditional (largely middle-class) values – popularly caught in Bob Dylan's song 'The times they are a-changing', which exhorted mothers and fathers to admit that their sons and daughters were beyond their command.

In this general context, films like *A Clockwork Orange* and *The Exorcist* can be argued to have touched chords of alarm among audiences imbued with ambivalent conceptions of adolescence and the related vigilante anxieties, uncertainties, and often beleaguered dreams which in the course of the present century have been increasingly and at times frantically projected on to the young.[9] In this connection Fraser notes what he terms the paradox that it was Kubrick's *A Clockwork Orange* rather than Francis Ford Coppola's *The Godfather* which did the most to set off complaints in the early 1970s about excessive violence in movies (Fraser 1976: 14). Fraser lists the profusion of vividly realistic scenes of violence in *The Godfather* and contrasts them to the stylized and relatively restrained depiction of fewer such scenes in *A Clockwork Orange*. In Fraser's view, it was precisely the 'alienated and alienating style' of Kubrick's approach which was so disquieting, particularly in the much-commented-on rape scene in a secluded country house, in which the violation of the helpless couple was accompanied by the protagonists' chanting of 'Singin' in the rain', while the hand-held camera appeared to provide stylistic support to the aggressiveness of the young invaders dressed in masquerade costume. Unlike the thoroughly familiar and 'almost *respectable*' moral ambiguousness of *The Godfather*'s depiction of gangsters and mafiosi (of long acquaintance in their Hollywood garbs), the ambiguities of *A Clockwork Orange* were far from respectable. Fraser notes that, while film gangsters have often been ambivalently viewed as 'types of individualistic resistance fighters against society' (ibid.: 16), the stylized presentation of violation in *A Clockwork Orange* appeared to 'reinforce and in a sense confirm the psycho-pathological vision of the violators' while the victims 'virtually disappeared as suffering consciousness' (ibid.: 24–5). Kubrick's cinematic style, Fraser continues, converted life into artifice and the whole of the rape scene into 'cinema'. It thus later became difficult to believe that one of the victims had been killed and the other crippled after 'the burlesque-elegant snipping away of the wife's jumpsuit' (which 'began by making it seem as if she too were in fancy dress, a partner in a curious ritual, and ended by leaving her looking like a large denuded doll'), and after the punctuation of the kicking inflicted on the husband with distancing soft-shoe dancing and singing allusions to the Donen–Kelly musical classic (ibid.: 25). In Fraser's view, it was this 'aesthetising and distancing of violence' (which finds its cinematic sources in the earlier movies of Jean-Luc Godard and in *Bonnie and*

Clyde) which made the film so emotionally ambiguous and aroused uneasiness about the psychopathic in 'what may be called the collective intellectual psyche of our time' (ibid.: 25–6).

Thus, to return to the implications of an argument which has threaded most of this chapter, while the violence and horrific violations graphically depicted in films like *The Godfather* are well padded in their (genre-generated and maintained) frame of reassurance, the aestheticizing and distancing of violence in exercises like *A Clockwork Orange* paradoxically draws attention to the contours and implications of that frame by taking its licence to its logical ('artistic') conclusions. In both cases, to labour a point, the story's message and meaning, as well as the audience's response, have their roots firmly in the social and cultural concerns of the period of their making. This is not to suggest that all exercises in horror fiction can be neatly classified as having been directly inspired or instigated by transparent sets of moral controversies, political concerns, or public debates. What I have emphasized in this chapter are some of the functions such fictions perform as institutionalized methods of contemplating experience and projected eventualities, and as commentaries on the categories and boundaries of culture. In the next two chapters I propose to examine more closely some of the values and ideologies which are endorsed and encoded in such commentaries by focusing on the tales and techniques of two of the most successful writers of popular horror fiction currently working in Britain and America.

Chapter 2

HEROICS
AND HELPLESSNESS –
THE CASE
OF JAMES HERBERT

A gust of wind sterte up behind
  And whistled through his bones;
Through the holes of his eyes and the hole of his mouth
  Half-whistles and half-groans.
                    (S. T. Coleridge, *The Ancient Mariner*)

PRELIMINARIES

In the next two chapters I propose to examine some of the values
encoded in a specific set of contemporary images of fear by focusing on
the work of two bestselling writers of horror fiction. My concern here
is to identify the psychological assumptions and the pictures of
personal and social reality which underscore the content and style of
these authors' tales – the dystopias and imagined realms of terror as
well as the world-saving devices which they portray. The violence and
vomit, the threats, haunting images, and nagging doubts which these
writers place at the centre of the narratives they offer for their readers'
contemplation, are here considered in juxtaposition to the extent to
which they reflect any evidence of a wider viable reality, of 'a larger
sense, embracing and surrounding [them] all the time, of an order
without' (Hoggart 1958: 268).

The authors selected for discussion in these chapters are initially
chosen because of their current wide popularity, particularly as
reflected in the frequent claims which are made about the millions of
copies of their works sold, the impressive number of reprints into
which their novels have run in a comparatively short period (both had
their first success in 1974), and the relative speed with which the
movie industry has been translating their books into films. But there
are also other reasons behind these chapters' choice of the often

29

disturbing, sometimes engrossing, and frequently nauseating material which constitutes the phenomenon of contemporary horror fiction as exemplified in the novels and short stories of these two writers. As I argued in chapter 1, these social products can be read as commentaries on some of the categories and boundaries of culture. The continued popularity of these authors' work suggests that the subjects they repeatedly consider and the values they ascribe to them are (at the very least) also repeatedly contemplated and found congenial by their many readers. In this sense, the distinctive tones and poses with which James Herbert and Stephen King approach their material not only shed a revealing light on the popular concepts and values which go into making a convention riddled with clichés look up to date and trendy, but also raise important questions about the seriousness and viability of those concepts, and about what their values reveal about our culture's methods of dealing with unpleasant or threatening phenomena.

JAMES HERBERT: CONTEXT AND TRADITION

In a promotional article which appeared in the *Telegraph Sunday Magazine* on 27 December 1981, Daniel Farson (great-nephew of Bram Stoker and sometime writer of macabre tales and illustrated children's guides to mythical monsters and occult ogres) asserted that 'To millions of young British readers who do not normally buy books, James Herbert is a favourite writer. His reputation advances by word of mouth.' The world sales of Herbert's first nine bestsellers were (late in 1983) claimed to be fifteen million.[1] The British paperback edition of his novel *The Fog* (first published in December 1975) was in its twentieth reprint before 1985. Its predecessor, *The Rats*, had fourteen reprints between 1974 and 1984, and (in 1981, 1984, and 1985 respectively) *The Jonah, Shrine*, and *Domain* followed a series of popular successes by rocketing (as the media would have it) into the lists of bestselling paperbacks and spending a number of weeks there. Among the 'millions of young British readers' of Herbert's works, it would seem, is also no less a celebrity than the Princess of Wales, who on 25 February 1983 was reported in the *Guardian* as having purchased a copy of Herbert's *Lair* ('a book about lots of people being eaten alive by giant rats').

Herbert lives and writes in the south of England. The horrors and catastrophes which litter his stories usually take place in London and the southern regions, a setting which he can expect the majority of his readers to find familiar: 'This was their own doorstep,' he points out in one of his novels, 'the British people could relate to it' (Herbert 1975: 20). But it is not just on a geographical level that the novels court their readers' empathy. Herbert's readers are also expected to understand that the macabre events described are natural extensions of a shared world view – a view, incidentally, which is also implicit in the texture of his writing. In the course of a BBC radio interview (*Midweek*, Radio 4, 26 January 1983) he asserted that his reason for writing about 'such horrible things' is that 'life is far more horrible' and that events in each of his books have 'been paralleled by an event afterwards'. When one of his characters comments that the unpredictability of the weather 'goes with the times' (Herbert 1975: 43), the assumed community of values Herbert is appealing to is taken as much for granted as are his affirmations about 'the most crazy things [happening] in a crazy world' (ibid.: 17). Like many of his colleagues in the horror industry, Herbert insists that he is 'a lovely person really . . . very pragmatic, if you like, very down to earth' (*Midweek*, Radio 4, 26 January 1983). Writing horror stories, 'instead of going to a psychiatrist's couch', he insists, enables him to get rid of 'so many phobias': 'I'm getting all these nasty ideas out on to paper, whereas most people just keep it inside them' (ibid.). This self-styled 'pragmatism' and the attendant 'down-to-earth' daub of a human nature plagued with bottled-up nasty ideas and phobias not only fit unequivocally into a generalized popular conception of humanity which we shall have occasion to examine in detail in later chapters of this enquiry – in Herbert's writing it comes dressed in an urbanity of tone and a brand of cynicism which bear close consideration.

Herbert's plots and characters fit quite readily within a tradition of horror entertainment which the media (ranging from the cinema to comics) have kept in the popular imagination for most of this century. The irresponsible professors (in *The Rats* and *The Fog*) experimenting with mutant rats and 'mutated mycoplasma' – which proceed to destroy their creators along with a sizeable proportion of the British population – are direct descendants of Baron Frankenstein (particularly as he was portrayed by Peter Cushing in the Hammer Film variations on Mary Shelley's story made in the 1960s and early 1970s). The vampire legends and the many Dracula stories derived from Bram Stoker's novel can be traced below the contemporary pseudo-scientific surface of a novel like *The Dark* (Herbert 1980), while the Jekyll–Hyde syndrome, as well as the many related popular varieties of the werewolf legend, can be recognized in the emphasis on evil and irrational tendencies and their horrific release catalogued in *The Fog*, *The Dark*, and *The Jonah*. Tales of ghosts, demonic possession, and reincarnation are also hazily dressed up in ersatz technological jargon in *The Survivor* (ibid.: 1976), *Fluke* (ibid.: 1977), and *Shrine* (ibid.: 1983). Herbert's novels also reflect many of the characteristics of the tradition of popular horror fiction which proliferated in American pulp-magazines in the first half of this century. That tradition often concentrated on violent death, bloody confrontation, overtones of sadistic and often kinky sex, and frequently virile young heroes and busty damsels in distress.[2] It included such dubious hack-work products of the 1930s as *Spicy Mystery* and *Dime Mystery*, but also boasted relatively respectable pulp-magazines like *Unknown Worlds* (1939–43) and *Weird Tales* (1923–54), whose contributors included H. P. Lovecraft, Robert E. Howard (creator of Conan the Barbarian), and Robert Bloch (author of *Psycho*).[3] That tradition also included the much-maligned and feverishly attacked EC comics of the 1950s (most notably campaigned against in Frederic Wertham's 1954 *Seduction of the Innocent*),[4] and it had its British counterpart in the Americanized products incisively reviewed in Orwell's essay on 'Raffles and Miss Blandish' and in Hoggart's *Uses of Literacy* (among which products were also the early instalments of the long-running Hank Janson novels).[5]

In his defiantly favourable estimate of Herbert's work, King regrets that 'he is held in remarkably low esteem by writers in the genre on both sides of the Atlantic', and insists on proclaiming his worth by placing him squarely in the pulp tradition, asserting that 'James Herbert is probably the best writer of pulp horror to come along since the death of Robert E. Howard' (King 1982a: 404):

> James Herbert comes at us with both hands, not willing to simply engage our attention; he seizes us by the lapels and begins to shout in our faces. It is not a tremendously artistic method of attack, and no-one is ever going to compare him to Doris Lessing or V. S. Naipaul . . . but it works.

(ibid.: 407)

Implicit in this type of dubiously trendy praise is the tautological assumption that the popularity of pulp fiction can be condescendingly explained in terms of an ability to provide its readers with a no-nonsense, virile-cum-viraginous read which their limited abilities make them relish. But, still, to point to the circuitous unhelpfulness of such an account is not to negate that in their own symptomatic way these novels do 'work'. Littered as they are with clichés and monotonous repetitions, their gruesome descriptions evince a compulsive quality which defies easy dismissal. It is to a closer examination of that quality that the next section directs itself.

MATTERS OF LIFE AND DEATH

Herbert's writing is at its most heady when the horrors come in quick succession, so that the reader is left breathless and as confused as the victim into whose terrified consciousness the author has chosen to lure and lock him. In the following extract from *The Fog*, the maid in a huge country house has just staggered to the room where she expects to find her employers having breakfast. She is looking for help, having moments before discovered the hideously mutilated body of her friend the cook ('its skull cleaved open to the bridge of the nose'). There is an almost perversely clinical attention to minute gory details, carefully juxtaposed against the recognizably ordinary and homely – the maid, for instance, suggests having 'a nice cuppa' just before she sees the cook's body. The narrative manages to recreate the feeling of being caught in a nightmare world in which one's helplessness is mercilessly exposed and threatened since the security normally offered by the people and objects which one had previously assumed to know intimately has been horrifically transformed, though they also remain mockingly recognizable:

She stumbled through the open door and stopped short at the sight confronting her.

Her mistress lay sprawled on the floor in a pool of blood, only a few tendons in her neck holding her head to her body. It lay parallel to her left shoulder, grinning up at her. The Colonel lay spreadeagled on the huge dining table, long nails through the palms of his hands and the flesh of his ankles to pin him there. A man stood over him, an axe dripping with blood in his hands.

As the maid watched, dumb-struck, unable to move with the horror of it, the man raised the axe above his head and brought it down with all his strength. It severed a hand and splintered the wood beneath. The man struggled to free the weapon from the table and raised it again. By the time he'd cut off the other hand, the Colonel was unconscious. By the time he'd hacked off both feet, the Colonel was dead.

The maid finally began to scream when the man with the axe turned his head and looked at her.

(Herbert 1975: 29)

The clichés with which such writing is riddled ('pool of blood', 'the horror of it') enable the writer, in Q. D. Leavis's phrase, 'by a few clumsy strokes to evoke a composite picture that is already stowed away in the readers' minds' (Leavis 1932: 194). They are also of a piece with the uncomplicated and unchallenging pattern of the sentences, and it is this fluidity and unexceptionable quality of style which causes us both to read fast and also to flinch uncomfortably as we are made to focus on the macabre minutiae ('only a few tendons', 'the flesh of his ankles'). The horrors in effect seem to be lodged exclusively in the language which is too entangled in the figurative possibilities of its own restricted and mannered rhetoric to maintain any real hold on the 'down-to-earth' realities it claims to emulate. The almost mathematical details ('It lay parallel to her left shoulder', 'lay spreadeagled') give only an apparent and linguistically theatrical solidity to this nightmare world, and serve to reflect a refusal or inability on the author's part to give full imaginative consideration to the horrific situation he is inviting us to contemplate. One gets the feeling that, like the mistress's disssevered head in the extract, the author is grinning at us as he dispassionately lists the horrors which he expects to make us gasp for breath. 'By the time he'd cut off the other hand, the Colonel was unconscious. By the time he'd hacked off both feet, the Colonel was dead.' The slick externality and self-conscious cleverness of style, the neat juxtaposition of patterned clauses, are the only means of escape which we are allowed from the house of horrors through which the author has promised to guide us. This constitutes, in effect, a further (value-laden) deployment of what in chapter 1 I termed the frame of reassurance surrounding this type of horror fiction. The use of convention here becomes an exercise in mocking the flesh it feeds on, of teasing our emotional need of reassurance about our individual and communal vulnerability after it has placed itself at an artificially safe distance from the issues which underscore that vulnerability. The style, which King eulogizes as 'that clear, lucid, grammatical prose', used by Herbert like 'combat boots' as he 'goes out to assault the reader with horror' (King 1982a: 404–5), is an open invitation for the reader to join the author on his tenuous perch.

Here is another instance of Herbert's way of talking about death. The girl in this passage has had a last-minute change of mind about committing suicide over the loss of her lesbian lover, only to find herself trampled into the sea by thousands of people who join in what the blurb at the back of the book calls 'a monstrous act of self-destruction':

> Her eyes were open as the last bubbles of air escaped from her lips. The terror had gone. There was no pain. There was no recollection of her life, no memories to taunt her in her dying. Just a misty blankness. No thoughts of God. No question why. Just a descending white veil. Not a veil of peace, nor one of horror. Not even one of emptiness. Free of emotion and free of coldness. She was dead.
>
> (Herbert 1975: 119–20)

'Free of emotion and free of coldness': it is in clichés of this kind that one finds the one bleak offer which the novels hold out. And again, even in a pseudo-philosophical passage such as this, one catches the unmistakable tones of the disc jockey and the market salesman (Herbert's early career, appropriately enough perhaps, started in rock-and-roll singing and advertising art direction): 'Not a veil of peace, nor one of horror. Not even one of emptiness' ('I'll let you have it not for ten pounds, nor for eight. I won't even ask for five pounds.'). To speak of matters of life and death in these tones is not only to reflect a conception of human nature which deprives it of all vestiges of dignity – it also casts a disturbing light on our post-industrial way of seeing ourselves. Life and death become analogous here to cut-price and shoddily manufactured artefacts. I shall return to the implications of this attitude in chapter 3. At this stage it bears stressing that reading these novels one is frequently reminded of the pat and often inane manner in which many TV compères conduct their variety or quiz programmes, or of the self-sufficiency which runs through the style of the popular daily tabloids. In this respect, Herbert makes his allegiances very clear: the hero of *The Rats* is a young teacher who reads the *Mirror* 'on the bus on the way to school – he loved to leave it around the staff-room, to the disapproval of his colleagues who thought any newspaper other than *The Times* or The *Guardian* were comic-books' (Herbert 1974: 46). Nor does Herbert seem to have any doubts about the universal goodness and light cast by the mass media: 'And the public weren't that stupid any more. The media had broadened their minds, given them an insight, however vague, into things that years ago would have been unheard of, let alone believed' (ibid. 1975: 137). That parenthetical 'however vague' can be read as much as a qualification as a reminder of the author's (and presumably his patronized and patronizing reader's) own superior and broad mind. The attitude is also inseparable from the cynicism of the protagonists who can see through the corruption and self-seeking inefficiency of institutionalized authority but put it all down to a natural meanness in mankind.

There are many examples one can cite from Herbert's novels of the way in which people in positions of authority and those under that authority almost invariably despise each other. Among these are characters like the police officer 'enjoying the fact that the man he had to be servile to had to be servile to others' (ibid. 1980: 321); the young teachers who 'hide smiles of pleasure behind their hands' when their deputy head is snapped at (ibid. 1974: 107); the young soldiers who delight in the fact that the older Corporal in charge of them 'couldn't even piss in front of them' because 'their mocking faces caused a mental block – or a block somewhere else' (ibid. 1975: 185); and the officer from the GLC who thanks God that 'someone was stupid enough' to work in the London sewers (ibid. 1980: 184). The examples and the manner in which Herbert writes about them have overtones of overgrown schoolboyishness. Their very method of surreptitious giggling at the expense of members of different social positions does little more than reaffirm and endorse the status quo of social formations and injustices. When Herbert's writing assumes the 'down-to-earth' pose of 'pragmatic' philosophizing, the effect is even more hollow:

> No, it was no good becoming over-wrought with authority, for he knew too well that apathy existed on all levels. The gasman who neglected to fix a leaky pipe. The mechanic who failed to tighten a screw. The driver who drove at fifty miles an hour in the fog. The milkman who left one pint instead of two. It was a matter of degree. Wasn't that what Original Sin was supposed to be all about? We're all to blame. He fell asleep. (ibid. 1974: 64)

The list deliberately ranges from the potentially lethal to the banal. It is very much a home-baked philosophy of life whose recipe and ingredients come wholesale from popularized litanies of human depravity and helplessness: society is ultimately irredeemable, injustice and inefficiency are an unchangeable part of human nature, the present social structures stink because of apathy, the fault is in ourselves not in our technological cultures – 'Wasn't that what Original Sin was supposed to be all about?' It is also of significance that these considerations are presented as little more than a thought for bedtime. The final sentence of the passage (like the cameo appearance of the mischievous milkman) underlines the mindless smugness with which unnerving threats are fitted into a top-of-the-pops picture of manageable reality. The attitude is one which hunts for scapegoats to soothe its discomfort and sets up as its hero the type of man who 'reached a certain point, and knowing there was nothing he could do about the situation, his mind walked away from it' (ibid.: 64). And, again, Herbert's position in this respect is unequivocal. Asked in an interview where he stands in relation to the victims and violators in his stories, he answered:

> I'm the hero that eventually wins. I mean, every author I think puts himself, a bit of himself, into the hero, and the point of all my books – and this is not to say I'm pompous – but the point is that it is always the one individual against the system.
>
> (*Midweek*, Radio 4, 26 January 1983)

Repeatedly in Herbert's novels the hero is a young, disillusioned suburban individualist in sneakers, whose instincts are his sword and whose armour is the vast edifice of institutionalized authority against which he directs his bitterest invectives. 'You're a loner,' one of these heroes is told, 'you don't conform to organisation' (Herbert 1981: 23). Similarly, the doting girlfriend of another of the heroes made in Herbert's projected image and likeness reflects how, 'Despite all the technological advances of science, it seemed survival still depended on the action of a man. One man' (ibid. 1975: 177). The contradictions endemic to these visions are worth underlining. 'Individualist' as they are claimed to be, these heroes are repeatedly shown as effecting their world-saving gestures with the aid of a technology or spuriously updated white magic strong enough to balance the powers which created the scientific monsters or malevolent forces in the first place. The hopeless circularity of this vision is further reflected in the fact that the contrasts which the novels offer to the many horrors and unpleasant characters packing Herbert's world are the peep-hole to the protagonists' sex life and a caricatured post-Romantic country innocence peopled by nice old ladies who give sweets to cute little children just before they disappear through the jaws of disaster (which is precisely what happens at the start of *The Fog*).

'NAKED ANIMAL BEHAVIOUR', 'RAW EMOTIONS', AND 'INSTINCT'

'Christ, Kelso,' alliterates the hero's girlfriend in *The Jonah*, 'you're in the Force, you know just how thin that barrier between civilisation and naked animal behaviour is' (ibid. 1981: 68). If one takes the trouble to unpack this, one finds that by 'civilisation' one is meant to understand the playing of the grudgingly well-domesticated but ultimately unhoodwinked citizen. 'Naked animal behaviour' is taken to be synonymous with the perpetration of the most gruesome and obscene violences on self and others which can be imagined. The concept that man's mind is cohabited by a technological ape and a primeval roaring beast consistently informs Herbert's plots and colours most of his style. The fog and the dark (in the novels of those names) let loose the 'animal' in man – or, rather, the 'animal' as he is popularly misconstrued. 'Animal, sometimes known as The Beast to his friends,' is also a football hooligan who makes what ends up as a predictably explosive appearance in *The Dark*:

> Personally, he didn't care much about the game either. It was the excitement he liked, not the excitement of the competition but, although he couldn't have expressed it himself, the raw emotion the game produced, feelings that could be demonstrated without embarrassment.
>
> (ibid. 1980: 133)

It is this understanding of 'raw emotion' and 'feelings' which Herbert presents as lying at the root of destructive violence. It is also the suggestion that people cease being human when this 'raw emotion' controls their actions without restraint that makes it possible for Herbert's heroes to physically attack and hurt their mentally de-ranged lovers, or kill other human beings. The refusal or inability to consider the implications of all this is brought out in the way

Herbert's heroes blot out moral considerations in the interests of immediate action:

> Holman felt the car bump as it passed over their bodies, but he kept his foot down hard on the pedal, gathering speed, sending the men on the roof flying off. It ploughed through the thronging mass and Holman closed his mind from thoughts of his unfortunate victims. Perhaps it was because he regarded them as a threat rather than human beings. Perhaps he thought they were less human because of their madness. Or perhaps it was because he didn't have time to think at all that enabled him to carry on.
>
> (ibid. 1975: 224)

Such listing of possibilities and inconclusive catalogues of 'perhaps' clauses occur repeatedly in Herbert's novels at moments when thorny issues are briefly sniffed at before the author's mind, 'knowing there was nothing he could do about the situation', walks away from them. The last sentence in the passage just quoted also touches a chord which recurs very often in Herbert's work. 'Instincts', 'spontaneous', and their synonyms are among the most frequently used words in the novels, and they seem to form an essential part of the heroes' survival kit. The rational, on the other hand, is assumed to be antithetical to instinct and hence mistrusted since it is believed to be ineffective in the face of danger. Thus, the victims in the novels are usually 'too stunned to react quickly' (ibid. 1980: 263) because their attempts to fit the macabre into a familiar world can only lead to confusion and paralysing terror (which, Herbert almost invariably informs us, is usually accompanied by involuntary urination).

Evil and threatening figures in Herbert's work are generally associated with madness, or with the pent-up dynamos of violent irrationality which he believes to constitute 'naked animal behaviour'. Many of his horrific effects depend on the magnification to grotesque proportions of vaguely understood notions of the unconscious self and the unnerving doubts about what may lurk in its dark alleyways. Within this context, the release of evil is presented as deriving from 'the cold logic of a fanatic' (ibid.: 163) on the one hand, and a mist of bogus technicalities on the other:

> The Church had always insisted that Satan was a reality: for them it helped to prove the existence of God. Freud had confounded the Church and demonologists alike by explaining that each of us had

been through a phase of individual development corresponding to that animistic stage in primitive man, that none of us has traversed it without preserving certain traces of it which can be re-activated. Everything which now strikes us as 'uncanny', fulfils those vestiges of animistic mental activity within us.

(ibid.)

In the sequence where this passage occurs, its function is principally that of giving a spurious air of updated scientific credibility to the supernatural happenings in the story. The explanation is ascribed to the good and wise professor who, in good Van Helsing tradition, is and sounds foreign, and supplies the impressive-sounding erudition which no one is really expected to bother trying to understand but which is presumably essential for combating the novel's powers of evil. The potted rendering of Freud in the passage is in fact taken almost verbatim from Freud's essay on 'The uncanny',[6] with the important difference that where Freud's account (or rather the standard translation) speaks of 'residues and traces' of the 'animistic stage in primitive man' being 'still capable of manifesting themselves', in Herbert we have 'traces . . . which can be re-activated'. Such an account projects human nature as basically (rather than analogically) no different from an electrical contraption whose different components can be 're-activated' at any stage by external forces. The manner in which the dynamic and hydraulic imagery in Freud's account of the unconscious and motivation has here been taken to its literal extreme in a quasi-electronic account of motivation and behaviour is patent. The novels as a whole, in fact, assume a sense of universal helplessness, within the arbitrariness of which men can only hope that in moments of crisis activity will be taken over by their 'instincts' (sharp, irrational, and mechanical enough to help towards survival) but that their 'raw emotions' will not take over so completely as to turn them into possessed engines of mad destruction.

POPULAR HEROICS AND SOCIAL UNEASE

Below the slick tone of self-satisfied knowingness and the pose of the worldly-wise man about town, Herbert's writing betrays an unease about the human condition which is only superficially evaded in the onanistic portrayals of the sceptical 'individual against the system'. The awed emotions of confused dread and displaced admiration for inane heroics which give these novels a lot of their peculiar impetus are impossibly locked within a magical mode of thinking which has but spurious contact with practical reality. Herbert insists frequently on the necessity of action in the face of crises, but the 'practical' activities his heroes invariably indulge in are of the hard-punching and tough-talking variety which prevail in the fast-moving and slick world of mass-media thrillers. Like the hard-jawed, casually dressed-for-action and fast-paced macho protagonists of television series like *The Professionals*, Herbert's heroes invariably have a world-saving mission to perform, and this is taken to mean that they must not allow themselves any time to reflect or feel pity for their victims.[7] In spite of their (ultimately proto-Fascist) individualism, and their criticism of worthless figures in positions of power or authority, they usually get their marching orders from, and perform their heroics to sustain, a hierarchical structure which is as inefficient as it is corrupt. This is of course an inevitably symptomatic contradiction, since the values underscoring the admiration for tough heroics are inspired by an awe for power which almost compulsively venerates authority. I am not suggesting that Herbert is a Fascist writer. What I am saying is that the values endorsed in his and similar popular fictions are of the kind which could form a congenial breeding-ground for Fascist ideologies. There is also something truncated in the veneration for the type of heroics projected in these stories. Jungian psychologists argue that the hero figure in myths and legends symbolizes a developing consciousness of the self, struggling through the hurdles of growing up. But there is very little which suggests growth or development of any kind in the individualism associated with Herbert's heroes. The process here is more circular. Thus, the hero of *The Fog* assumes his James Bond role, complete with licence to kill, on instructions from the Prime Minister, who 'talked long and hard at him, telling him the choice was not his, that one life meant little compared to the millions that were in danger' (ibid. 1975: 221). The heroes promise themselves to expose the 'crass stupidity' of the authorities responsible for the catastrophes once 'the time for constructive action was over' (ibid.: 161), but this amounts to little more than a muzzled growl and what is believed to be a necessary pose within an ultimately compromised system of values. Herbert himself epitomizes the incorporeality of this confused ideal in the protagonist of *The Survivor* (ibid. 1976) – a jumbo-jet co-pilot who seems to have miraculously survived an air disaster, only to discover at the end (with the equally baffled reader)

41

that he has really been a ghost all along, left behind, in good medieval tradition, to exact vengeance on the lunatic who planted a bomb on the plane.

The areas of social unease at the back of the horrors described in Herbert's novels are both symptomatic of our age and needful of rational exploration and realistic confrontation. It is on the grounds that these novels are essentially vacuous in their approach to crucial issues that one can express concern about the versions of reality and the 'pragmatic' values which they propose as appropriate to their predominantly young readers. This applies especially to the caricatured sense of helplessness conveyed by Herbert's writing in the face of what he symptomatically calls 'the subconscious will for self-destruction every mind possesses, hidden deep down in the darkest recesses of the brain, but always ready to be brought to the surface' (ibid. 1975: 273). It is also significant that the images of death and destruction conveyed in Herbert's novels are usually presented on a very large scale and linked to what Winston Churchill called 'the dark powers of destruction unleashed by science'. Again, the underlying attitude behind this portrayal of death has its roots in the contemporary popular consciousness, and its symptoms can also be traced in the spate of disaster movies on which millions of dollars were spent in the 1970s. As Cannadine puts it, 'death in the second half of the twentieth century has taken on a global aspect' under the shadow of possible nuclear annihilation: 'For the threat of mass, accidental death and the desire to avoid it, has permeated all our lives and experiences and expectations, to some extent' (Cannadine 1981: 236). Invariably in Herbert's novels it is the fate of millions which hangs in the balance and the horrors of agonizing and undignified death are as arbitrary as they are omnipresent. To write appropriately and responsibly about such a subject is difficult enough: its vocabulary is patently not part of the repertory of the slick showman. The bloodlessly smug tone which permeates Herbert's writing and the setting up of puerilely conceived strapping fellows to save the world betray an evasion of the momentousness of the issues underlying a communal unease. Writing about 'the apparently simple grammar of desire', Williams argues that an emphasis on the possibility of a better world can go in one of two directions:

> into revolutionary effort, when history is moving; into a resigned settlement when it goes wrong or gets stuck. The utopian mode has

to be read, always, within that changing context, which itself determines whether its defining subjunctive mood is part of a grammar which includes a true indicative and a true future, or whether it has seized every paradigm and become exclusive, in assent and dissent alike.

(Williams 1980: 208)

The pose of hard-punching bravado assumed in Herbert's novels is in reality an endorsement of resigned settlement: it domesticates the shadows of dystopia by fitting them into a callow conception of reality dominated by spectacular gestures and idealized heroics which have more in common with the antics of Popeye the Sailorman than with the type of 'magical activity' which, according to Collingwood, can act as 'a kind of dynamo, supplying the mechanism of practical life with the emotion that drives it' (Collingwood 1938: 69).

On these grounds, Herbert's novels can be argued to reflect a tendency to evade the threats of uncertainty by resorting to grotesque and hollow illusions of control and accommodation. This tendency, along with the related characteristics the novels share with an endless host of popular and 'pulp' thrillers, can be said to partially account for their appeal in a context where insecurity and unease about the threats of destruction are often nervously swept under a magical carpet of technological wonders and industrial efficiency. 'We have looked for so long at foggy landscapes reflected in misty mirrors', as Booth puts it, 'that we have come to *like* fog' (Booth 1961: 372). The popularity of a horror-story writer like James Herbert is one of the manifestations of that sense of moral insecurity and evasive indecision which our age has made its birthright. In extension of a term I developed in chapter 1, one can say that the frame of reassurance which these fictions hold out to their readers (young or otherwise) constitutes an irresponsible betrayal of trust. The map (to alter the metaphor) offering a reliable path through and out of our epoch's maze of horrors is not to be found here.

In the next chapter I propose to examine the work of an American writer of horror fiction whose approach is ostensibly more thoughtful and challengingly consistent than that of Herbert, and whose writing is more consciously evocative of the traditions of popular fantasy and horror fiction which form its progeny. Since Stephen King conveys a more knowledgeable air to the business which he compares with that of 'paralyzing an opponent with the martial arts . . . or finding vulnerable spots and applying pressure there' (King 1982a: 86), an analysis of his modes of attack and psychological assumptions can prove quite revealing. My concern in chapter 3, therefore, is with the further identification and appraisal of a set of widespread world views and popular conceptions about human nature and the human psyche. My point of focus will be the evaluations and commentaries on contemporary cultural experiences which are encoded in the fearful fantasies exchanged between King and the millions of readers of his tales.

Chapter 3

LANGUAGE, MODES OF SEEING, AND MAGIC – THE COVENANT OF STEPHEN KING

The heart of man is the place the Devil dwells in; I feel sometimes a hell within myself.

(Sir Thomas Browne, *Religio Medici*)

TRADITIONS OF TERROR AND INVITATIONS TO MADNESS

The blurbs to the paperback editions of Stephen King's horror stories have frequently introduced him as living in America with his wife and their three children and as having a 'remarkable talent for writing bestsellers' which has made him 'one of the most successful young writers in the United States' (e.g. King 1980, 1982b). King's first novel was published in 1974 and by 1983 his books were claimed to have sold over forty million copies (Herbert, H., 1983). A total of six film versions of his stories were made and issued between 1983 and 1985 (*The Dead Zone, Firestarter, Cujo, Christine, Children of the Corn*, and *Cat's Eyes*), with *Christine* (directed by John Carpenter) reputedly starting production before the book's publication in May 1983. Three of his earlier novels were also made into successful film versions involving big names in the industry: *Carrie*, by United Artists in 1976, directed by Brian De Palma and with Sissy Spacek and John Travolta in the leading roles; *'Salem's Lot* by Warner Brothers for television in 1979, directed by Tobe Hooper (at the time noted mostly for *The Texas Chainsaw Massacre*) and featuring James Mason and David Soul; and *The Shining* by Warner Brothers in 1980, with Stanley Kubrick as director and Jack Nicholson and Shelley Duvall as main actors. In 1982 King also collaborated with George Romero (whose 1968 low-budget *Night of the Living Dead* had by then long become established as a cult classic among horror movies). in the making of *Creepshow* – a film made up of a collection of macabre tales written by King himself, mainly inspired by and paying tribute to the horror comics of the 1950s, and with King and his young son Joe among the cast. A cartoon-book version of the film, again following the format of the EC comics of the 1950s, also appeared about the same time. Besides short introductory essays and numerous interviews published in various periodicals and popular magazines,[1] King has also written a long and chatty discussion on the horror genre (King, *Danse macabre*, 1982a) which offers a thoughtful and entertaining account of fictional horrors in various media (books, films, comics, radio programmes, TV shows), concentrating mainly on American products between 1950 and 1980.

His wide reading in, viewing of, and reflections about popular horror fiction are patent: his novels contain frequent direct and indirect references to important precursors in his field, his discursive analyses of classics as well as shoddy products within the genre reflect acumen as well as dedicated research, and, in spite of his old-fashioned pose of impatience with academics ('those lepidopterists of literature' – ibid.: 300), he has also taught courses in 'Themes in supernatural literature', creative writing, and other literature at the University of Maine.[2] His works in fact fit quite consciously and clearly within the main lines of the tradition of popular horror fiction which he has studied with loving attention. They almost unfailingly have a contemporary setting (usually with his native Maine as the backdrop), and consistently attempt to read the traditional themes and images of horror in terms of the anxieties, concerns, and vicissitudes – or, as he terms them, the 'phobic pressure points' (ibid.: 18) – of the contemporary western psyche as he sees it. Within the limitations of his chosen genre, he writes in a gripping and calculatedly popular manner. But what he calls the 'sub-texts' of his tales are also clearly and often challengingly considered and thought-provoking. That much needs to be acknowledged ungrudgingly, since a reading of his works underlines the inadequacy of belligerent predispositions to label all horror fiction as uniformly mindless, suspect, or unhealthy. 'There are levels and levels,' he asserts in one of his interviews, 'and I am doing the best I can' (Duncan 1983). He is often harsh on those he considers to be hacks in his business, and suggests that 'the biggest reason why the movies so often seem afflicted with a case of arrested development' may be related to something he had learnt from a Warner Brothers executive, i.e. 'that movie surveys show the average filmgoer to be fifteen years of age' (King 1982a: 197). And yet he is also insistent on his love even for what he terms the 'slice and dice' type of horror film since 'once you've seen enough horror films, you begin to get a taste for really shitty movies' (ibid.: 230). The mixture of 'camp' taste and concern about the genre maintaining or achieving some sort of intellectual or 'cultured' respectability is symptomatic of the ambiguous standing of contemporary horror fiction in general and of King's approach and attitudes in particular.

Like James Herbert, King is insistent that 'terrible things happen in the world, and they're things no-one can explain' (ibid. 1977: 446). The antidote, which is basically a latter-day version of the American Dream, is prescribed by one of his characters to the child protagonist of *The Shining* in the following terms: '"But see that you get on. That's your job in this hard world, to keep your love alive and see that you get on, no matter what. Pull your act together and just go on"' (ibid.). King's version of human nature too can be said to fit quite readily into the picture of attitudes to human destructiveness and psychopathology which I outlined in chapters 1 and 2 and which will be examined in some detail in the second part of this book. 'If we share a Brotherhood of Man,' he argues in *Danse macabre*, 'then we also share an Insanity of Man' (ibid. 1982a: 204). At the core of his writing is the conviction that we all carry a 'potential lyncher' within us and that there are 'anti-civilization emotions' or 'hungry alligators swimming around in that subterranean river beneath' our 'civilized forebrains' which need to be fed or let loose every now and then and allowed 'to scream and roll around on the grass' if mental and social equilibrium is to be maintained (ibid.: 204–5). This, he suggests, accounts for both the appeal and the function of horror fiction:

> Horror appeals to us because it says, in a symbolic way, things we would be afraid to say right out straight, with the bark still on; it offers us a chance to exercise (that's right; not *exorcise* but *exercise*) emotions which society demands we keep closely in hand. The horror film is an invitation to indulge in deviant, antisocial behavior by proxy – to commit gratuitous acts of violence, indulge our puerile dreams of power, to give in to our most craven fears. Perhaps more than anything else, the horror story or horror movie

says it's okay to join the mob, to become the total tribal being, to destroy the outsider.

(ibid.: 47)

He suggests that 'the very basis of the horror story' is made up of 'secrets best left untold and things best left unsaid' (ibid.: 66), and that, since the 'perfect reaction' which every horror writer and film-maker hopes for is a childlike 'total emotional involvement, pretty much undiluted by any real thinking process' (ibid.: 120), the horror story 'urges us to put away our more civilized and adult penchant for analysis and to become children again, seeing things in pure blacks and pure whites' (ibid.: 203):

> It may be that horror movies provide psychic relief on this level because this invitation to lapse into simplicity, and even outright madness is extended so rarely. We are told we may allow our emotions free rein . . . or no rein at all.

(ibid.)

Here too, then, the emotions are assumed to be antithetical to 'civilized behaviour', and thus 'the dream of horror is in itself an out-letting and a lancing . . . and it may well be that the mass-media dream of horror can sometimes become a nationwide analyst's couch' (ibid.: 27). The qualifiers in these passages ('it may be', 'on this level', 'it may well be', 'can sometimes') are worth noting. King is in fact aware that 'the term *catharsis* . . . has been used too glibly by some practitioners in [his] field to justify what they do' (ibid.), but he is unwilling or unable to forego the term's force of associations and also uncomfortable about using it – compromising with: 'but it still has its limited uses here' (ibid.). It is partly this awareness of the need to tread softly where others have been clumsy that both adds to King's congeniality as a writer and tends to give an, at times, illusory impression of complexity to his approach, even though his standpoint in this respect is basically not far from that of his glib colleagues.

Borrowing a phrase from Burton Hatlen ('an English professor at the University of Maine' – ibid.: 12) – who presumably borrowed it from Philip Larkin – King speaks at great length about the 'myth pool' which comprises the 'fictive literature in which all of us, even the non-readers and those who do not go to films, have communally bathed' (ibid.: 66). His own account of human motivation and behaviour can in fact be said to have its origins somewhere in the depths of that same 'myth pool', but this is a point he fails to note. He asserts that 'one of the things that make art a force to be reckoned with even by those who don't care for it is the regularity with which myth swallows truth . . . and without so much as a blurp of indigestion' (ibid.: 67). That much has been said before, and it is in fact not clear where King's version of 'truth' ends and where 'myth' begins, since his world picture is so heavily determined by the media's vast and uneven array of dreams of horror.

In the rest of this chapter I propose to examine some of the functional implications of this blurring of distinctions. One of the points I developed in the chapters preceding this was that genre associations and expectations can engender (with a variety of value-laden implications) a frame of reassurance around many examples of popular horror fiction. What I wish to illustrate more fully now is the manner in which the cultural and cognitive implications of an established genre (its traditional associations as well as its more technical aspects) can also be used as a force in the (artificial) creation of fearful and frightened reactions. To state this differently, I now propose to consider more closely how and why genre associations can be made into a self-sufficient, self-enclosed, and self-referring realm of childlike uncertainty and superstitious terror – a world (in Sartre's terms) 'which is such that all the things existing in it are magical by nature, and the only defences against them are magical' (Sartre 1971: 89).

'MYTHIC FIGURES' AND 'LUSHER CONCEPTS OF EVIL'

According to King, 'our lusher concepts of evil' are represented in contemporary western culture by 'an almost perfect Tarot hand' which has 'the Vampire, the Werewolf, and the Thing Without a Name' as its major components (King 1982a: 66), and which includes the Ghost ('the best-known mythic figure of the supernatural') and 'the Bad Place' (i.e. haunted houses) as further examples of what he terms (in another metaphor) 'those springs that feed the myth-pool' (ibid.: 296). It will be worth looking at King's handling of these 'supernatural mythic figures' and 'lusher concepts of evil', and also at his methods of updating them, in order to identify what is taken to constitute reality (and its absence) in this particular brand of popular horror fiction.

The central 'mythic figure' which ostensibly dominates King's novel *Cujo* (ibid. 1982b) is the monster, the 'Thing Without a Name' which in this instance takes the shape of an initially lovable 200-lb St Bernard dog which chases a rabbit into a bolthole, gets bitten by germ-carrying bats, and turns rabid to be transformed into an embodiment of mad destructiveness. The echoes of *Alice in Wonderland* are deliberate: the 'rabbit-hole' and the looking-glass are also used as gateways to dreams of horror and the 'sick wonders' of the imagination in *The Shining* (ibid. 1977: 419). King associates the physical monster in *Cujo* with a number of other unnerving threats facing his characters, so that it is meant both to symbolize and to prod 'phobic pressure points' of social and psychological dimensions. Thus the novel contains frequent references to the 'monsters' of advancing age and loneliness, to the 'monsters' of the mammoth of the advertising industry which threaten two advertising agents in the novel with career and financial ruin, and to the 'monster' which the 4-year-old boy in the novel senses to be lurking in his closet (another recurring motif in King's work). The monster-dog's name, it is pointed out, is the same as that taken by William Wolfe of the Symbionese Liberation Army ('a radical robber of banks and kidnapper of rich young heiresses' – ibid. 1982b: 152), and there are also insistent linking allusions to another 'monster' (one in fact which had figured in King's earlier novel *The Dead Zone*, 1980) which 'was not werewolf, vampire, ghoul or unnameable creature from the enchanted forest or from the snowy wastes' but 'a cop named Frank Dodd with mental and sexual problems' (ibid. 1982b: 7). The source of the generic monster's existence and threat is partly external and inexplicably arbitrary, and partly deriving from, or possibly feeding upon, the disease of madness which King (again like James Herbert) believes to lodge in men's souls. At the start of the novel, a 4-year-old child is terrified by 'a thing that might have been half man, half wolf' (ibid.: 8) lurking in his closet. The child's parents go to great lengths to explain that 'there were no monsters', that 'shadows could sometimes look like the bad things they sometimes showed on TV or in the comic books' (ibid.: 9), and proceed to demonstrate how the 'monster' their son had 'seen' was really nothing more than a pile of blankets, a teddy bear, and the reflections produced by the bathroom light. But such rational explanations hold no ground in a context where 'the sick wonders' of the imagination are projected as physical realities and where dreams, as Sheridan Le Fanu put it, 'come through stone walls, light up dark rooms, or darken light ones, and their persons make their exits and their entrances as they please, and laugh at locksmiths'.[3] The 'monster' in the child's closet does not go away, and when the parents return to bed it proceeds to whisper to the child in the darkness, 'I'll eat you', it promises, 'and you'll be in me':

> Tad stared at the creature in his closet with drugged, horrified fascination. There was something that . . . was almost familiar. Something he almost knew. And that was the worst, that almost knowing. Because –
>
> *Because I'm crazy, Tad. I'm here. I've been here all along.*
>
> (King 1982b: 12; italics in the original)

The 'half man, half wolf' which the child 'almost knew' is of course the werewolf, old Edward Hyde waiting to reverse his position from that of being locked away in the closet of men's hearts to that of 'eating' them and having their rational or 'civilized' selves subdued ('inside') for a change. This process is shown later in the novel as the 'possessed' dog's good nature gradually succumbs to the 'something, possibly destiny, or fate, or only a degenerative nerve disease called rabies' (ibid.: 344). 'Free will', King insists, 'was not a factor' (ibid.): 'The last of the dog that had been before the bat scratched its nose turned away, and the sick and dangerous dog, subverted for the last time, was forced to turn with it' (ibid.: 115).

As in James Herbert's stories, evil in King's work is repeatedly associated with a disease of madness, perennially lurking and festering in hiding. The concept is of course an ancient one. As Cavendish points out, 'The need for order and the fear of disorder have profoundly affected concepts of evil. Anything which threatens order and sanity is evil and may be caused by a great variety of supernatural beings' (Cavendish 1975: 7). The theological overtones raised here are worth pausing over, not least because King is clearly aware of them. In a culture where 'sizeable numbers of the specimen "modern man" have not lost a propensity for awe, for the uncanny, for all those possibilities that are legislated against by the canons of secularized rationality' (Berger 1970: 39), unease about apparently inexplicable phenomena can often assume curiously superstitious dimensions. In other words, the process of rationalization has only gone part of its way, so that there remain large areas, and usually ones of momentous import, which are left unresolved only to make themselves felt with paralysing force in moments of crisis. It is because of the prevalence of these areas and biases that King can use the following terms to describe a level-headed (and, given the type of novel he writes, inevitably doomed) young lady's confrontation with the unknown (in *'Salem's Lot*):

> She had always consciously or unconsciously formed fear into a simple equation: fear = unknown. And to solve the equation, one simply reduced the problem to simple algebraic terms, thus: unknown = creaky board (or whatever), creaky board = nothing to be afraid of. In the modern world all terrors could be gutted by simple use of the transitive axiom of equality. Some fears were justified, of course (you don't drive when you're too plowed to see, don't extend the hand of friendship to snarling dogs, don't go parking with boys you don't know . . .), but until now she had not believed that some fears were larger than comprehension, apocalyptic and nearly paralysing. The act of moving forward at all became heroism.
>
> (King 1976: 293)

I shall be discussing just how King's style of writing manages to tap and play on these areas of uncertainty below. At this stage, my main concern is to isolate precisely what lies behind the concept of evil in King's evocation of terror. He seems to suggest that, if evil is virtually synonymous with chaotic madness, it has been accommodated into a comprehensible workaday equation in the contemporary (more or less rational) mind because it is rarely encountered in its undiluted form. As the alcoholic priest reflects in the same novel,

> EVIL did not wear one face but many, and all of them were vacuous and more often than not the chin was slicked with drool. In fact, he was being forced to the conclusion that there was no EVIL in the world at all but only evil – or perhaps (evil). At moments like this he suspected that Hitler had been nothing but a harried bureaucrat and Satan himself a mental defective with a rudimentary sense of humour – the kind that finds feeding firecrackers wrapped in bread to seagulls unutterably funny.
>
> (ibid.: 164)

But, of course, the inexplicable virus of undisguised evil does manifest itself in the various archetypes portrayed in King's writing, and when this happens it is only those characters whose imaginations allow them to 'lay aside' the 'ossified shield of "rationality"' (ibid. 1982a: 109) who are able to recognize and accept it for what it is and hence stand a chance in fighting it. The mixture of metaphor and 'reality' inherent in this whole approach bears stressing, since it tends to relegate the whole issue to a realm of 'fantasy' which accommodates essentially insubstantial mental projections as physical realities, but does not do so in clearly religious or theological terms. One can argue that this is an extension of Matthew Arnold's prognosis in *Culture and Anarchy* that the role of religion was to be taken over by literature. The inexplicable and extraordinary constantly step into the commonplace world of routine 'reality' in King's novels, but it is clear that such encroachment is little more than an exercise in imaginative gymnastics. This is borne out in many of the figurative expressions King uses to describe his mode of writing – e.g. 'It's like that painting by Magritte, you know, with the steam engine coming through the fireplace. Nothing in that room is important. But because the steam engine is coming through the wall, *everything* in that room is important' (Herbert, H., 1983). Given the predominance of actuated imagery in this approach, it is only logical that evil in King's writing should reveal itself in terms of figures deriving mainly from popularized literary sources (Frankenstein's monster, Dracula, Mr Hyde). Before looking more closely at the implications of the linguistic processes in operation here, we shall therefore need to explore King's handling of these figures, or 'lusher concepts of evil', further.

UPDATED IMAGES OF THE SUPERNATURAL

The vampire is the central figure in *'Salem's Lot* (King 1976), closely modelled, as King acknowledges, on Bram Stoker's Dracula. The inexplicable and supernatural dimensions of this incarnation of evil are stressed, and King plays a lot on the vulnerability of a society which claims to have discarded superstitious practices and then finds itself faced with a 'real' threat which can only be subjugated with anachronistic weapons and icons (the cross, holy water, the consecrated host, the stake through the heart). But again, as in the case of the monster in *Cujo*, King stresses the 'almost familiar' features of this figure, his consanguinity, as it were, with the down-town mortals on whom he feeds. His existence, in effect, depends on the presence of a primeval wickedness (or 'aggression') which is asserted to lurk in men's hearts. As the foreign vampire explains to one of his many victims, ' "The folk here are still rich and full-blooded, folk who are stuffed with the aggression and darkness so necessary to . . . there is no English for it. *Pokol*; *vurderlak*; *eyalik*" ' (ibid.: 246). The shadow of the werewolf (the 'beast within') can in fact be seen to lurk behind that of each of the archetypes which King chooses to explore. This applies also to the figure of the ghost:

> What is the Ghost, after all, that it should frighten us so, but our own face? . . . . We fear the Ghost for much the same reason we fear the Werewolf; it is the deep part of us that need not be bound by piffling Apollonian restrictions. It can walk through walls, disappear, speak in the voices of strangers. It is the Dionysian part of us . . . but it is still us.
>
> (ibid. 1982a: 290)

It is worth noting that this conception is not exclusive to King. One of the most successful, and (as popular bestsellers go) highly accomplished, horror novels to appear in recent times, Peter Straub's *Ghost Story*, piles its Gothic horrors precisely around this notion, and insistently refers to Narcissus 'gazing at his image in the pool' and 'wearing out his innocence' because of the 'morally fatal glamour' which lives in the 'blackness' his image reflects (Straub 1979: 233, 342).[4] The notion in fact forms part of a long (and at times much exploited) tradition within the horror genre. One of its more influential exponents was Sheridan Le Fanu, whose typical plot, as Punter puts it, 'is one in which the protagonist, whether deliberately or otherwise, opens his mind in such a way as to become subject to haunting by a figure which is unmistakably part of his own self' (Punter 1980: 232).

Most of the arguments developed up to this stage have hinged on the contention not only that the fictions of the imagination reflect and address the modes of thought and feeling that orient our actions, but that they are also extensively conditioned by the cultural content of the society in which we live. Chapter 1, it will be recalled, considered some of the implications of Thomas's argument for a functional basis of beliefs in spirits and ghosts – i.e. that such figures 'personified men's hopes and fears, making explicit a great deal which could not be said directly' and that they were also a useful sanction for social norms (Thomas 1973: 717). In similar vein, Prickett has noted how the monsters of the Victorian imagination assumed palaeontological proportions as a result of geological discoveries and speculation, particularly as these were brought to public attention through Benjamin Waterhouse Hawkins's 'wildly inaccurate' representations of the great saurians in the life-size concrete models at the Crystal Palace. 'Images of horror which had always leaned towards the slimy and scaly became more specifically reptilian' (Prickett 1979: 83), so that John Martin's and (later) Gustave Doré's illustrations of *Paradise Lost*, for instance, reinterpreted Milton's demonic monsters as dinosaurs, while Tenniel gave Carroll's Jabberwocky (in 1871) 'the leathery wings of a Pterodactil and the long scaly neck and tail of a sauropod' (ibid.). According to Prickett, 'the Victorian age needed its concrete monsters if it was to keep at bay others, much less controllable' (ibid.: 95). But the prevalence of these types of monsters in the Victorian imagination also reflected a deep discomfort and uncertainty about mankind's position within a natural world which, 'red in tooth and claw', now appeared to be shrieking against the creed of humanity's pride of place in the great chain of being. The personifying functions which are allotted to fictional monsters, ghosts, and bogies in the popular culture of our age derive largely from the heritage of those uncertainties. One of the greatest sources of contemporary fears is lodged firmly within what we have come to think of as our psyche, and many of the primeval monsters of the Victorian imagination can now be said to have pitched their tents in the dark cellars and alleyways which the twentieth century has popularly come to associate with the human unconscious. As part II will illustrate more fully, popular renderings of Darwinian and Freudian theories of evolution and the unconscious form but a part (albeit momentous) of the variegated forces of influence giving rise to these concepts. It is worth recalling here that Jung too spoke of the human psyche as incorporating a 'shadow' – i.e. the sum of those personal characteristics that the individual wishes to hide from others and from himself, and which become more active and evil-doing the more one strives to hide them. There have also been a variety of literary and cinematic contemplations of the concept of the 'double' – ranging from Poe's *William Wilson* and Wilde's *Picture of Dorian Gray* to Hoffmann's *The Devil Elixirs* and the 1913 and 1926 films of *The Student of Prague*.[5] In his psychoanalytic study of the double, Rank also drew attention to a link between fear and hate of one's double on the one hand, and narcissistic infatuation with one's own image and self on the other (Rank 1971: 70–1). Similarly, as Prawer points out, Kierkegaard too spoke of the common dread 'of something unknown, something on which one dare not look, a dread of one's own being', and Nietzsche (supremely) speculated about the moral suppression of feelings that leads to their return in 'hideous disguises' and 'uncanny vampire forms' (Prawer 1980: 122).

The reinterpretative updating of 'supernatural motifs' and 'lusher concepts of evil' also draws heavily on the unease frequently generated by the advances of modern technology. One clear aspect of this process can be seen in those works of horror fiction which make the evocation and expression of such unease the focus of their explorations – an aspect eloquently examined by Prawer's *Caligari's Children* (1980), and exemplified in creatures like the mutinous HAL 9000 in Kubrick's *2001: A Space Odyssey* or the berserk computer which manages to rape and inseminate a helpless Julie Christie in *The Demon Seed*. There is also a proliferation of fictional machines which somehow assume or are possessed by magical and uncontrollable powers – as is the case in Stephen King's short story 'The mangler' (King 1978: 90–106), which tells of a laundry machine possessed by a bloodthirsty demon, or in his novel *Christine* (ibid. 1983) about a 1958 Plymouth Fury car with evil powers. Such nightmarish visions of animated heavy metal reflect more than what Prawer (writing about the continued appeal of and endless variations on Mary Shelley's *Frankenstein*) calls 'a fear of science, fear of the control of natural forces, without adequate corresponding control of the soul and psyche' (Prawer 1980: 128). The machines, like Frankenstein's monster in fact, usually possess uncannily human characteristics, and, in a period when mental and behavioural processes are frequently discussed and conceived of in terminology deriving from various branches of technology, distinctions between humans and machines can at times appear elusive.

I have already touched on some of the implications of the mechanical and electrical imagery which recurs in James Herbert's accounts of human motivation. There are similar linguistic tendencies in King's work too, suggesting an inclination to conceive of human nature in mechanical terms. In *The Shining*, for instance, it is not just the residual emotions of past inhabitants of the 'haunted' hotel which are viewed as forming a 'psychic battery' (King 1982a: 297) or a 'clockwork mechanism' (ibid. 1977: 252) waiting to be 'charged' or 'wound up' by the 'shine' of the protagonists. The characters themselves too are frequently described in terms and standard clichés which betray the same tendency:

It had nothing to do with willpower, or the morality of drinking, or the weakness or strength of his own character. There was a broken switch somewhere inside, or a circuit breaker that didn't work.

(ibid.: 109)

A pulse began to beat in the clockspring of veins at Jack's right temple.

(ibid.: 381)

He could be a calm, undemanding figure in the classroom, but when the right set of competitive stimuli was applied (like electrodes to the temples of Frankenstein's monster, Jack thought wryly), he could become a juggernaut.

(ibid.: 111)

That last quotation underlines both one of the key sources of dissemination of this mode of thinking at a popular level, and also the blurring of distinctions occurring here between humans and the activated artefacts of modern technology. Central to this association is the equivocal view of emotions and the unconscious as being essentially Dionysian, potentially beyond control and outside the realms of civilized comprehensibility. Men, the thinking here goes, are like machines because there are periods when they seem unable to exercise restraint over the 'ghosts' of irrationality within them, becoming, at times quite literally, no more than engines of destruction activated by demons of madness which have learnt a smattering of Freud and dabbled in technology. As noted above the progeny of this concept of madness as a threat to order is as old as it is complex. One need only think of the ancient belief that madness (like epilepsy) indicated demonic possession, whose symptoms were often 'scarcely capable of being differentiated from those of religious ecstasy' (Thomas 1973: 580), and the related Romantic notion of 'divine madness'. In his essay on the 'Uncanny' (which often seems to have served as a hornbook for horror writers with learned pretensions), Freud refers to Jentsch's suggestion that 'the uncanny effect' can be caused, among other things, by 'epileptic fits, and . . . manifestations of insanity, because these excite in the spectator the impression of automatic, mechanical processes at work behind the ordinary appearance of mental activity' (Freud 1919a, 1955 edn: 240–1). Where at one time madness suggested possession by transcendent spirits, the emphasis in modern versions falls on the 'automatic' and 'mechanical' aspects, with many overtones and much of the terminology of popularized science. In line with the implications of the hydraulic and electrical imagery in operation in this notion, the modern version of 'exorcism' is deemed to require the periodic draining out or discharge of irrational tendencies through the sewage pipes of the imagination if they are not to grow into torrents which will burst the dams of civilized 'sanity' and acceptable social behaviour. The literal application of these metaphors in fictional contemplations of human motivation betray elements of superstition in their very use of pseudo-scientific language. To vary the analogy, the ancient gods of superstition, which in earlier ages were believed to be amenable to propitiatory ritual sacrifices, now assume the shapes of 'internal' fiends and monsters of madness, of 'ghosts' within a complex human machine, which can only be kept in a relatively harmless slobbering state by periodic feeding with sacrificial portions of 'civilized' and controlled behaviour through the mindless flings of a gruesomely morbid imagination.

THE SHINING AND THE FANTASTIC

It will be worth looking more closely at a single novel to get a clear idea of how these notions can form an integral discursive component of a bestseller. King's own account of how he first conceived of the plot of The Shining is interesting, among other things, for the way he uses the terminology of galvanism to link the workings of human memory and the emotions with an updated version of ghostly hauntings. He had been interested, he recounts, by

> a speculative article which suggested that so-called 'haunted houses' might actually be psychic batteries, absorbing the emotions that had been spent there, absorbing them much as a car battery will store an electric charge. Thus . . . the psychic phenomena we call 'hauntings' might actually be a kind of paranormal movie show – the broadcasting back of old voices and images which might be parts of old events. And the fact that many haunted houses are shunned and get the reputation of being Bad Places might be due to the fact that the strongest emotions are the primitive ones – rage and hate and fear.
>
> (King 1982a: 297)

This idea, King continues, 'suggested a vague but intriguing referent in [his] own experience; that the past is a ghost which haunts our present lives constantly', so that 'with [his] rigorous Methodist upbringing, [he] began to wonder if the haunted house could not be turned into a kind of symbol of unexpiated sin' (ibid.). And thus, in *The Shining*, the Christmas-past ghost of original sin and the Christmas-present spectre of bogus science and naked apes join forces.

The plot of *The Shining* is straightforward and standard enough. Desperate for a job after his dismissal from a school where he had attacked and almost killed one of his students, Jack Torrance assumes the duties of winter caretaker at the Overlook Hotel in the Colorado mountains. The hotel, of course, has 'a bad reputation' among the inhabitants of the nearest town (ibid. 1977: 402), and its name and high position suggest that, like the similarly placed vampire mansion in *'Salem's Lot*, it too has spent many years looking down at all the 'peccadilloes and sins and lies' of the people living beneath it, 'like an idol' (ibid. 1976: 131). Needless to say, it has a gory and shady past, and the previous year's caretaker is reported to have killed his wife, two daughters, and himself while the family was snowed up at the hotel. Jack Torrance himself has a shady history of alcoholism (which he seems to have contained) and a violent temper which he has not always been successful in controlling. His 5-year-old son Danny possesses psychic powers which neither he nor his parents understand fully, and which also involve horrific but cryptic 'precognitions' of the dangers the family is to face at the hotel. In the course of the novel, the child's psychic gifts, together with his father's meaner 'instincts', become 'a small silver key' (ibid. 1977: 324) which winds up the deadly 'clockwork mechanism' of the residual emotions lurking in the hotel, or, in another recurring image, the 'charge' which powers the hotel's 'battery' of horrors. The hotel's past, like that of the protagonists, haunts the present in a steady crescendo of intensity and malevolence until (inevitably perhaps) the novel ends with a Grand Guignol explosion which destroys the building along with the now thoroughly possessed Jack Torrance.

Summarized that way, the novel has little to distinguish it from the profusion of haunted-house stories and films which the media cough up with almost compulsive regularity. There are obvious similarities, for instance, to Dan Curtis's 1976 screen version of Robert Marasco's *Burnt Offerings* and to Stuart Rosenberg's 1979 box-office success *The Amityville Horror*, to name but two examples about which King himself speaks with varying degrees of approval (King 1982a: 163–70, 432,

463). They often involve the gradual 'taking over' of one of the characters by the haunted house and its evil past – much like the 'taking over' of the good dog by the madness of rabies in *Cujo*, or that of the inhabitants of 'Salem's Lot by the virus of vampirism. The motif of possession links this type of narrative to works which exploit the notion of supernatural possession more directly – William Friedkin's *The Exorcist* (1973), with its detailed and nauseating portrayal of a teenage girl masturbating with a crucifix, rotating her head, and vomiting in the priest's face, being the most obvious example. But there are also clear echoes of Alfred Hitchcock's highly influential *Psycho* (1960), based on Robert Bloch's novel of the same name. It is worth pausing over that echo, not simply because Hitchcock's film has been so consistently imitated in the period after its production, but also because of what it reveals about contemporary versions of 'possession' and its amalgamation of Jekyll–Hyde/werewolf motifs with fears about mental imbalance and madness.

Throughout his writings, King frequently refers to Shirley Jackson's novel *The Haunting of Hill House* (first published in 1959 and used by Robert Wise as the basis of his film *The Haunting* in 1963). King is particularly impressed by, and often quotes from, the opening of Jackson's novel:

> No live organism can continue for long to exist sanely under conditions of absolute reality; even larks and katydids are supposed, by some, to dream. Hill House, not sane, stood by itself against the hills, holding darkness within; it had stood so for eighty years and might stand for eighty more. Within, walls continued upright, bricks met neatly; floors were firm, and doors were sensibly shut; silence lay steadily against the wood and stone of Hill House, and whatever walked there, walked alone.
>
> (quoted in King 1976: 13; 1977: 281; 1982a: 300)

King discusses this passage at some length in *Danse macabre*, noting how the 'insanity' of Hill House is linked to its lack of dreaming, and pointing to the similarity between its looking all right on the surface (unlike proverbially dilapidated haunted houses) and the apparent sanity and congeniality of the main character in *Psycho* (King 1982a: 301). The idea that appearances can be deceptive is common and old enough, of course, and as a motif it is patently at home in the literature of terror. But the link between insanity, lack of imagination (dreaming), and evil also bears directly, to labour a point, on the notion of internal darkness or 'beast within' which is assumed to become dangerous if it is repressed too rigidly. This is clearly suggested by the architecture of Hill House, which, like the social behaviour of the Norman Bates character in *Psycho*, is 'upright', 'firm', and 'sensibly shut'. In *The Shining*, King also makes frequent allusion to Edgar Allan Poe's 'Masque of the Red Death', with its account of nobles locking themselves away from a mysterious plague gripping their country and finding (at the unmasking which takes place on the stroke of midnight) that the Red Death is lodged in their midst. In terms of narrative, King plays on this image with skill, creating suspense and tension as a seemingly possessed clock (representing, not particularly subtly perhaps, the deadly 'mechanism' of the hotel) prepares to strike the hour of midnight and throw reality into its own fatal dimensions of time. But the choice of the image and the uses made of it are significant, as is the novel's frequent inversion of Carroll's wonderland into 'a land full of sick wonders' (King 1977: 305), reached through mirrors and a 'round black hole' (ibid.: 125, 304) which lead 'deep down in yourself in a place where nothing comes through' (ibid.: 419).

Early in the novel, the old negro cook at the Overlook realizes, just before he departs with the rest of the summer staff to leave the Torrances alone for the winter, that the young Danny is exceptionally gifted as a 'shiner': "What you got, son, I call it shinin on, the Bible calls it having visions, and there's scientists that call it precognition. I've read up on it, son. I've studied it. They all mean seeing the future"' (ibid.: 85). Another explanation of the child's 'shining' is offered by a young doctor, whom the Torrances visit before the snows set in, in terms of 'inductive reasoning and subconscious logic' (ibid.: 192). With the boy's mother, we are meant to realize that this explanation is 'glib' − 'it tasted more like margarine than butter' (ibid.: 148). But the doctor also associates it with an overstrong imagination: 'Children have to grow into their imaginations like a pair of oversized shoes,' he explains (ibid.: 144). In this respect, the doctor's account is close to, but also crucially different from King's own conception of the workings of the imagination as expounded in *Danse macabre*. King there speaks of the imagination not as something one grows into, but, in tones echoing Mario Praz's (1933) account of Romanticism, as an important faculty which adults learn to 'cage in' all too effectively. 'If you view imagination as a mental picture of a hundred different forms,' he argues, 'then one of the forms is that of a rampaging gorilla, a creature that is dangerously and totally out of control' (ibid. 1982a: 141–2). 'Children understand that this face of their imaginations must be caged,' but, while some adults 'seem to build Chase Manhattan Bank-type safes', children's 'cages are of necessity more flimsy than those their elders build' (ibid.: 143). He also insists that children 'are better able to deal with fantasy and terror *on its own terms* than their elders are' (ibid.: 123; his italics), because since the distinctions they make between make-believe and 'real things' are not so clear-cut as those made by adults, they are better able to live with monsters of irrationality whose incomprehensibility is but one aspect of a generally unintelligible world. In other words, if this reading of King's account is correct, children's imaginations are more psychotic than psychic – and, as we have seen, King believes that periodical psychotic flings are salutary. The trouble with adults, the argument suggests, is that they generally lose contact with the woe and wonder of incomprehensible irrationality. They assume that everything forms part of a logical pattern and 'cure' their childhood fears through the 'ossification of the imaginary faculties' (ibid. 1976: 253), only to find themselves tumbled back into a state of childish helplessness when the uncannily irrational makes itself felt. When this happens, as it regularly does in King's novels, the shock is so great that it proves fatal, since their 'rational' minds cannot solve 'apocalyptic' equations (cf. ibid.: 293 quoted on p. 52) or accommodate the irrational – they would have a heart seizure if Magritte's steam-engine came through their fireplace, while their imaginative (i.e. irrational) children might find the occurrence disturbing but soon get over it. The 'insoluble equations' which 'paralyse' King's characters usually involve phenomena which appear to belong to a realm outside normal, 'natural' experience, though in fact they are quite familiar in the 'make-believe' world of figurative language.

In his influential study of the 'fantastic' as a literary genre, Todorov describes in useful terms what processes are in operation when that which has always been assumed to be unreal suddenly appears to step into our cognitive world of everyday reality:

In a world which is indeed our world, the one we know, a world without devils, sylphides, or vampires, there occurs an event which cannot be explained by the laws of this same familiar world. The person who experiences the event must opt for one of two possible solutions: either he is the victim of an illusion of the senses, of a product of the imagination – and the laws of the world then remain what they are; or else the event has indeed taken place, it is an integral part of reality – but then this reality is controlled by laws unknown to us. . . . The fantastic is that hesitation experienced by a person who knows only the laws of nature, confronting an apparently supernatural event.

(Todorov 1973: 25)

Todorov further argues that 'the fantastic implies . . . not only the existence of an uncanny event, which provokes a hesitation in the reader and the hero; but also a kind of reading, which . . . must neither be "poetic" nor "allegorical"' (ibid.: 32). The supernatural, he suggests, 'often appears because we take a figurative sense literally' (ibid.: 76–7). In other words, the 'equation' facing the characters and readers of stories like those of Stephen King is only 'insoluble' and unnerving because common-sense distinctions between fantasy and reality have been blurred and all modes of discourse and perception are interpreted in purely literal terms – much in the manner of one version of childhood thinking, in fact. This is why, as Sartre argues (and as we saw in chapter 1), 'the horrible is not possible in the deterministic world of the usable', and why King can speak of his task as involving the 'lulling' of his readers into 'that state of believability where the ossified shield of "rationality" has been temporarily laid aside' (King 1982a: 109). According to Todorov, the 'fantastic' often involves the realization of 'the literal sense of a *figurative* expression' (Todorov 1973: 79) and 'the supernatural may sometimes originate in a figurative image, may be its ultimate extension' (ibid.: 77):

> If the fantastic constantly makes use of rhetorical figures it is because it originates in them. The supernatural is born of language, it is both its consequence and its proof: not only do the devil and vampires exist only in words, but language alone enables us to conceive what is always absent: the supernatural. The supernatural thereby becomes a symbol of language, just as the figures of rhetoric do, and the figure is . . . the purest form of literality.
>
> (ibid.: 82)

The unwinding of events in *The Shining* provides a clear example of the manner in which the literality of language can be used to create hestitation and to ascribe uncanny supernatural dimensions to irrationality and to the yield of repression. It is worth considering

63

a few examples of this process in some detail in order to establish how this 'mode of seeing' is related to the mechanistic versions of human nature discussed above.

MADNESS AND MAGIC

Early in the novel, the old negro Hallorann, who sports a bit of 'shining' in his own right, reflects on his attempts to discover whether Jack Torrance 'shines' as well:

> He had probed the boy's father and he just didn't know. It wasn't like meeting someone who had the shine, or someone who definitely did not. Poking Danny's father had been . . . strange, as if Jack Torrance had something – *something* – that he was hiding. Or something that he was holding in so deeply submerged in himself that it was impossible to get to.
>
> (King 1977: 88; his pauses and italics)

Later, as Torrance's wife hears him typing away at the play that he hopes will make him a successful writer, she reflects how

> her husband seemed to be slowly closing a huge door on a roomful of monsters. He had had his shoulder to that door for a long time now, but at last it was swinging shut.
>
> Every key typed closed it a little more.
>
> (ibid.: 121)

But this, we are meant to realize, is not quite right. A key image which drives this home is established in the early sections of the novel. At one point, while he is working on the roof of the hotel, Jack Torrance accidentally uncovers a wasps' nest and is stung. He spends about half an hour reminiscing about important episodes in his life when he had lost control of himself and had acted in a violently dangerous manner, particularly in relation to a stuttering student whom he had caught slashing his car tyres and had almost killed in a burst of mindless fury. His reflections give hints of seething or repressed envy on his part for the boy's good looks and rich background, but Torrance does not acknowledge this consciously. As a 'college-educated man' and aspiring writer, he starts to think of the wasps' nest as a 'cameo of reality':

> He felt that he had unwittingly stuck his hand into the Great Wasps' Nest of Life. As an image it stank. As a cameo of reality, he

felt it was serviceable. He had stuck his hand through some rotted flashing in high summer and that hand and his whole arm had been consumed in holy, righteous fire, destroying conscious thought, making the concept of civilized behavior obsolete. . . . Passively, with no say, you ceased to be a creature of the mind and became a creature of the nerve endings; from college-educated man to wailing ape in five easy seconds.

(ibid.: 110)

The implicit assumption in that passage (as in some of the examples from Herbert examined in chapter 2) that human nature is built on a clear polarity of 'civilized behavior' and 'nerve endings' is again worth underlining. Some further implications and issues raised by this assumption will be explored in some detail in part II, particularly in terms of its historico-cultural derivation and the uses which have been made of it in accounting for the fascination of horror. What should be noted at this stage is the manner in which King stresses both the arbitrariness with which 'the concept of civilized behavior' can be made obsolete, and also the individual's helpless lack of say in this matter.

The associations with which Torrance's mind imbues the wasps' nest somehow proceed to 'animate' it, so that its literary and figurative associations become part of the novel's world of reality, with horrifying consequences. There is of course no direct indication at this stage that this is what is taking place, but the events which follow depend, in terms of the novel's internal logic, on this initial amalgamation of 'reality' and linguistic fancy. Torrance fumigates the nest and, when he is convinced that all the wasps have been killed, gives it to his son to keep next to his bed. That night, Danny has one of his frequent nightmares – which again turns out to be a premonitory vision of himself being chased by a demented figure carrying a roque mallet and bent on his destruction. The pursuer is eventually discovered to be the boy's father, but his identity is not clearly revealed at this stage. Instead, dream and 'reality' coalesce just before the unmasking in a horrifying *coup de théâtre* as the wasps' nest suddenly comes to vicious life – a life, the text suggests, somehow linked with or deriving from the father's ill-controlled and seething furies:

There was a tiger in the hall, and now the tiger was just around the corner, still crying in that shrill and petulant and lunatic rage, the

65

roque mallet slamming, because this tiger walked on two legs and it was –

He woke up with a sudden indrawn gasp, sitting bolt upright in bed, eyes wide and staring into the darkness, hands crossed in front of his face.

Something on one hand. Crawling.

Wasps. Three of them.

They stung him then, seeming to needle all at once, and that was when all the images broke apart and fell on him in a dark flood and he began to shriek into the dark, the wasps clinging to his left hand, stinging again and again.

(ibid.: 131)

The generation of uncertainty and horror here is clearly linguistic in origin. An image has come to vicious ('literal') life, but that 'life' and its terms of signification are determined by and exist exclusively within the cocoon of language in which they are expressed. This, of course, is magic. 'That was when all the images broke apart': ostensibly this is meant to be taken as an empirical indication of time – there is no uncertainty of tense or modalization. It refers to the 'moment' when the 'reality' of the wasps' life was asserted ('they stung him then'), but our perception of that 'moment' not only is heavily conditioned by its appearance in a fantastical sequence (which of course also enhances its shock value) but also occurs in a context dominated by a series of variously loaded metaphors whose terms of signification are left vague. The 'images' which 'broke apart' are presumably a reference to the 'tiger on two legs' and the activated figure of the wasps 'seeming to needle all at once'. The close proliferation of dream, figurative, and 'real' waking images has the effect of placing them all on the same level of indeterminate 'reality'. The images 'break apart' to introduce a further rhetorical figure ('fell on him in a dark flood') and the child begins to shriek 'into the dark' (of the bedroom? of the 'flood'?) in such a way that his shriek and fear come across as more than a pained and shocked response to the wasps' stinging (an 'event' which in its turn also originated in a linguistic image). Given the type of novel it is, the reader also assumes that this particular sequence of uncanny manifestations is just an initial assertion of the hold of the fantastic (or the irrational) over 'reality' and that the dream images too will eventually come to vicious 'life' in a more direct fashion.

King is very much aware of the importance of getting his readers to acknowledge the possibilities of 'seeing things differently', and to recognize the frequent unreliability of perception. This is of course part of the method of creating a sense of uncertainty and raising doubts about what can be taken to constitute reality. There are frequent thematic references in *The Shining*, for instance, to the perceptual processes involved in watching 3-D movies (ibid.: 340); to the manner in which distance, light, shadow, and 'the viewer's imagination' can cause a clipped hedge to be 'seen as' (in Wittgenstein's famous phrase) a rabbit's face (ibid.: 204); and to 'games' involving pictures in which 'a jumble of blacks and whites' can also be seen to form the pattern of a face (ibid.: 279), or in which 'if you strained and squinted, you could see . . . the thing you had taken for a cactus at first glance was really a brave with a knife clamped in his teeth' (ibid.: 194). The implications of these processes are again taken to their literal extreme, so that one of the characters begins to wonder whether 'there is such a thing as a "real" world' (ibid.: 340), while the child protagonist nervously reflects (in relation to the picture-game 'Can you see the Indians?') that 'it was the ones you couldn't see that would sneak up behind you, tomahawk in one hand and a scalping knife in the other' (ibid.: 194). In one sequence, Jack Torrance desperately tries to shut out the possibility of seeing a doorknob to a locked room turn because such perceptual evidence would confirm the presence of the bloated 'ghost' of a long-dead woman, and thus wreak havoc with his conception of reality and prove him mad·

> But below the tumble of his chaotic thoughts, below the trip-hammer beat of his heart, he could hear the soft and futile sound of the doorknob being turned to and fro as something locked in tried helplessly to get out, something that wanted to meet him, something that would like to be introduced to his family as the storm shrieked around them and white daylight became black night. If he opened his eyes and saw the doorknob moving he would go mad. So he kept them shut, and after an unknowable time, there was stillness.

(ibid.: 255)

Through its concern with the implications of modes of perception, the passage touches on common fears about sanity in situations involving the type of 'fantastic' encounters described by Todorov (as quoted on pp. 62–3). Jack Torrance insistently opts for the first of Todorov's solutions in these situations, i.e. he takes the 'events' to be products of the imagination. This is in effect what they are, but in the context of the novel, as we have seen, imagination and reality are one and the same. Further, the alliterative echoes ('tumble of his chaotic thoughts', 'triphammer beat of his heart', 'turned to and fro') suggest that the reverberating sounds originate in Torrance's mind. This impression is reinforced by the insistence on there being 'something locked in', which Torrance hears '*below* the tumble of his chaotic thoughts', and which recalls the earlier references to the 'something' which he 'was holding in so deeply submerged in himself' (ibid.: 88) and to the 'roomful of monsters' behind the door his wife had imagined him to be pushing shut (ibid.: 121). Once again, rhetorical images have been given a literal realization – in this case, the images and the use made of them derive from the Freudian notion of the 'return of the repressed'. But, in the context of the novel, the notion and its attendant images are projected as forcefully physical realities. Thus, the 'ghosts' leave very tangible pieces of evidence of their physicality – the child, for instance, has been almost strangled by the ghostly lady and his neck remains bruised, his T-shirt damp from her clammy grasp. The reader is therefore led to the conviction that there is not only something inadequate about the types of rationalizations of the situation which are ascribed to Torrance (they too, presumably, are meant to taste like margarine in the novel's system of logic), but that to rationalize in this manner is to indulge in dangerously irresponsible behaviour. If Jack Torrance refuses to accept the existence and threat of these supernatural manifestations as real, the narrative insistently implies, it is because he has caged the very real gorilla of his passions too forcibly, and is now being used by the powers locked in himself and in the hotel. In the wasps sequence discussed earlier, the uncanniness of the wasps' 'regeneration' is considered at some length: Torrance tries desperately to find a rational explanation but the 'facts' cannot be fitted into the realms of logic (ibid. 136), precisely because they have no place there.

Within the linguistic context of the novel, 'events' can be manipulated and described in such a way that the apparently supernatural manifestations can be conveyed both as being objectively 'real' and as having links with the 'ghosts' of Torrance's past and the 'demons' of his inner nature. Thus, shortly after his son is stung by the wasps, Torrance covers the wasps' nest in the boy's room with a pyrex bowl, only to find it a few minutes later to be crawling with many more wasps. He takes it outside, convinced that the cold would kill the wasps by morning, shuts the door firmly on them, and 'after a moment's thought he locked it, too' (ibid.). During all this,

> One thought played over and over in his mind, echoing with
> (*You lost your temper. You lost your temper.*
> *You lost your temper.*)
> an almost superstitious dread. They had come back. He had killed the wasps but they had come back.
> In his mind he heard himself screaming into his frightened son's face: *Don't stutter!*
>
> (ibid.: 135; King's italics)

The screamed order not to stutter is of course the 'unexpiated' residue of Torrance's feelings and behaviour towards the student he had once resented and attacked, and it is precisely these feelings and the demon madness at their roots which, even as Torrance makes a 'firm and hard and sure' resolve to hold his temper in future (ibid.: 136), are suggested to act as one of the charges to the 'battery' of lingering past emotions within the hotel:

> He stood in the darkness for a moment, thinking, wanting a drink. Suddenly the hotel seemed full of a thousand stealthy sounds, creakings and groans and the sly sniff of the wind under the eaves where more wasps' nests might be hanging like deadly fruit.
> They had come back.
>
> (ibid.)

The standard rhetorical trope punctuating this passage is worth noting. Also, the lurking sounds described here owe their uncanniness to the suggestion, lodged in the choice of words, that elements which are normally impersonal and inanimate have assumed a volitional (and malevolent) life of their own ('stealthy', 'groans', 'sly'). But all this is also clearly associated with the character's thoughts and latent desires. Later in the novel, when the hotel's 'battery' is fully 'charged', we are told of old Hallorann (who is attempting to come to the family's rescue) that 'He was surrounded by a red force that might have been memory. He was drowning in instinct' (ibid.: 389). The prevalence of modifiers in both passages ('seemed', 'might be', 'like', 'might have been') maintains an element of initial hesitancy and ambiguity on which the reader's reactions are meant to hinge. As Todorov argues,

Without these locutions, we should be plunged into the world of the marvellous, with no reference to everyday reality. By means of them, we are kept in both worlds at once. The imperfect tense . . . introduces a further distance between the character and the narrator, so that we are kept from knowing the latter's position.

(Todorov 1973: 38–9)

Given the importance which I have attached to the task of identifying and analysing the assumptions and presuppositions informing percepts and concepts, it should perhaps be pointed out at this stage that, though King's text appears to offer conflicting interpretative claims, the attitude underlying much of the writing is heavily influenced by popularized Freudian perspectives. Thus, the young doctor who examines Danny early in the novel gives a telescopic résumé of Freudian thinking in terms highlighting the importance of censor and symbol:

'There seems to be a buffer somewhere between the conscious and the subconscious, and one hell of a blue-nose lives in there. This censor only lets through a small amount, and often what does come through is only symbolic. That's oversimplified Freud, but it does pretty much describe what we know of the mind's interaction with itself.'

(King 1977: 145)

As we have seen, the text is constantly referring to the interaction of Jack Torrance's mind with itself in terms of the attempts he makes to repress his meaner 'instincts', and of the manner in which this repression leads to their festering and growing in strength until they manifest themselves as activated symbols. While Torrance explains to his wife that 'Freud said that the subconscious never speaks to us in literal language. Only in symbols' (ibid.: 264), the text projects these symbols as literal realities and objectively physical phenomena. There are also many allusions to the manner in which these repressed 'instincts' result in 'impulsive' acts which at times appear to be uncannily motivated by unknown external forces and which progressively accumulate towards the final catastrophe and Torrance's complete possession by the hotel and/or the 'madness' within him. Thus, Torrance's obsession with the hotel's gory past is punctuated by a series of 'impulsive' acts, and, appropriately enough, it all starts in the hotel's basement:

He had gone down in the basement to knock the press down on the boiler and then, *on impulse*, he had taken the flashlight.

(ibid.: 152)

Quickly, *without thinking why he might be doing it*, he stuffed the scrapbook under a pile of bills and invoices.

(ibid.: 165)

. . . he *unconsciously* retreated a step, *unable to help himself*.

(ibid.)

He was going to start back, but then *some impulse made him change his mind*.

(ibid.: 204) (my italics)

Again, the emphasis is on the absence of conscious choice: the machinery of impulse dominates the character's actions.

The 'ghosts' of the hotel also consistently make their appearances at those moments when Torrance's repressed 'instincts' make themselves felt. Thus the child's horrific encounter with the putrid lady who had once killed herself in one of the hotel's bathrooms takes place while his mother is asleep and while his father has dozed off in the basement and is having a nightmare involving recollections of the time when he had broken his son's arm in a drunken rage, and a hallucinatory encounter with his own alcoholic father who urges him to kill his son: '"*No!*" he screamed back. "You're *dead*, you're in your *grave*, you're not in me at all!" Because he had cut out all the father out of him and it was not right that he should come back' (ibid.: 227; King's italics). The physicality of the ghosts, then, is a projection of inherited tendencies and an embodiment of the cursed thoughts that nature gives way to in repose – '(until i let go and sleep . . . and when i do that if i do that)' (ibid.: 179). Again, when Torrance himself goes to check out the 'haunted' room, it is at those moments when his irrational 'irritation and even real anger' (ibid.: 251) towards his son come to the fore that the ghostly appearances make themselves seen and felt. When his anger subsides to be replaced by 'sympathy for his son and terror for himself', the ghosts too recede: 'His anger at Danny evaporated, and as he stepped forward and pushed the shower curtain back his mouth was dry and he felt only sympathy for his son and terror for himself. The tub was dry and empty' (ibid.: 252). The linguistic trick which links the dry mouth to the dry tub is obvious enough. The text also suggests that sympathy and terror, an ability to suspend the 'lead weight' of disbelief (ibid. 1982a: 120) and allow oneself 'total emotional involvement' (ibid.) with the illogical, can partially lay down the ghosts of irrationality. Sure enough, soon after the passage just quoted, Torrance's temper raises its head again, and it is precisely at this point that 'the bathmat on the floor' (which should not be there) 'caught his attention' (ibid. 1977: 252–3).

HELPLESSNESS AND CIVILIZATION

What we have here, then, is an extension of the theory of 'animistic beliefs' which Tylor (in his 1871 *Primitive Culture*) argued to be at the basis of magical behaviour, and which was (later) variously applied to childhood, totemism, taboo, and 'the uncanny' in Freudian psychology. Freud's postulate about 'the omnipotence of thought' is here transformed into the omnipotence of impulsive feelings and aggressive instincts. More benign emotions and rationally civilized attempts to control these dread fiends are assumed to have but limited impact since 'the strongest emotions are the primitive ones – rage and hate and fear' (ibid. 1982a: 297). It is only by periodically giving these emotions 'free rein . . . or no rein at all' (ibid.: 203), the extension of this belief insists, that one can hope to remain sane. The only civilized sanity available to us, King seems to suggest, is one which has learnt to accept its own basis in insanity and impulsive destructiveness. As we have seen, the origins and evidence for this standpoint are lodged firmly in the nuances and literality of language, and in a basically infantile interpretation of perceptual impressions. Freud argued that one of the features 'closely allied to belief in the omnipotence of thoughts' incorporates an 'infantile element . . . which also dominates the minds of neurotics' and involving 'the over-accentuation of psychical reality in comparison with material reality':

> an uncanny effect is often and easily produced when the distinction between imagination and reality is effaced, as when something that we have hitherto regarded as imaginary appears before us in reality, or when a symbol takes over the full functions of the thing it symbolises.
>
> (Freud 1919a, 1955 edn: 244)

It is on this very process that the terrors generated in the works of an uptown horror writer like Stephen King depend.

The assumed helplessness of 'civilized' human beings in relation to their 'primitive emotions' and the essentially mechanistic conception of the psyche which is at the basis of this notion raise issues which highlight the importance of language and narrative (or, in Ricoeur's phrase, fictional redescription – Ricoeur 1978: 6) in our attempts to understand and come to terms with ourselves and our environment. It bears stressing that to make such an assertion is not the same as pointing to what King calls 'the regularity with which myth swallows truth' (King 1982a: 67). To briefly indicate the complexity of the forces of influence which need to be recognized as giving shape to this particular redescription of reality and the concept of man to which it gives rise, it is only necessary to draw attention to the mystifying confusions which arise in a culture where distinctions between people and the products of their labour are obscured because the abstract and often arbitrary values socially ascribed to the products are assumed to be objective and intrinsic. It was Marx who, in his famous analysis of what he termed 'the fetishism of commodities', underlined the social implications of this process and compared it to the mental and perceptual attitudes which prevail in 'the misty realms of religion', where 'products of the human brain appear as autonomous figures endowed with a life of their own, which enter into relations both with each other and with the human race'. 'It is nothing but the definite social relation between men themselves,' Marx insisted, 'which assumes here, for them, the fantastic form of a relation between things' (Marx 1890, 1976 edn: 164–5).

The magical attitudes in operation here, therefore, have social origins and repercussions which are only superficially (to say the least) confronted by token exhortations to 'keep your love alive and see that you get on, no matter what' (King 1977: 446). The prevailing assumptions of many of these popular works of horror fiction convey as inevitable a picture of helplessness which is based on the uncritical transference of pseudo-scientific images whose premises, as I shall argue in the chapters which follow, are set on very suspect ground. What makes the mode of dissemination of these attitudes in this type of cultural product insidious is that the presuppositions themselves are rarely stated explicitly and are thus generally simply taken for granted. What is spelled out can be questioned; what is assumed, especially from a position of unchallenged legitimacy, will tend to be swallowed whole and unawares.[6] It is not simply a case, therefore, of the horror genre and its contemporary presuppositions being 'swallowed whole' by young people, 'overgrown schoolboys' and other readers because of the 'deep depression [they] feel about themselves', as King suggests in one of his interviews (Herbert, H. 1983). Rather, depression can be generated and encouraged by the furtive and insistent projection of ill-conceived pictures of reality which (as I have argued to be the case with both James Herbert and Stephen King) combine helpless unease with vacuous optimism.

It has been the aim of this and the preceding chapters to identify some of the assumptions informing these pictures of reality and to bring them to the fore, where they can be questioned and examined in the context of the prevailing attitudes from which they derive. To state that these works of popular fiction belong firmly to the commercial culture of our age, therefore, is not simply a matter of pointing to their existence and success as bestsellers within the industrial mammoth of the mass media. The prevailing assumptions they make about unrestrained and unrestrainable 'natural' aggression call for much more detailed consideration. Such assumptions use what Raymond Williams calls the characteristically selective image of 'the burden of the "beast brain"' to interpret violence in twentieth-century societies, and then project this image as a '"more profound" alternative . . . to political, economic and historical investigations' (Williams 1980: 101–2). The assumptions in operation in these bestsellers, then, derive from and continue to form part of a conception of reality which is also at the core of what Williams designates as the dead social theory 'of that system that promised us order and progress and yet produced the twentieth century' (ibid.):

> Instead of facing that fact, in all its immense complexity, the rationalisers and the natural rhetoricians have now moved in to snap at and discourage us: not now to ratify an imperialist and capitalist order, but to universalise its breakdown and to persuade us that it has no alternatives, since all 'nature' is like that. In this respect they are worse than their predecessors and must be more resolutely driven off.
>
> (ibid.: 102)

In the chapters which follow, I shall be examining some of the origins and implications of these assumptions by looking more closely at the social and psychological theories underlying more academically oriented explanations of the appeal and functions of horror and violence in contemporary culture.

Part II

ACADEMIC PERSPECTIVES

Science frees us in many ways . . . from the bodily terror which the savage feels. But she replaces that, in the minds of many, by a moral terror which is far more overwhelming.

(Charles Kingsley, *Sermon, The Meteor Shower*, 1866)

Chapter 4

CATHARSIS
AND THE MYTH
OF THE BEAST

Placed on this isthmus of a middle state,
A being darkly wise, and rudely great:
With too much knowledge for the sceptic side,
With too much weakness for the stoic's pride,
He hangs between; in doubt to act, or rest;
In doubt to deem himself a god, or beast.
(Alexander Pope, *Essay on Man*)

Science is nothing but trained and organized common sense, differing from the latter only as a veteran may differ from a raw recruit: and its methods differ from those of common sense only as far as the guardsman's cut and thrust differ from the manner in which a savage wields his club.

(Thomas Huxley, *The Method of Zadig*, 1894)

INTERJACENCE

Part I set out to place the phenomenon of horror fiction within the context of a wider cultural debate by aligning the perspectives and values underlying a number of contemporary exponents of this genre with some of our century's concerns and ways of seeing. I have emphasized the social dimensions of this type of fiction, addressing it as an institutionalized technique of discussion which reflects and embodies a system of possibility for knowledge. This emphasis has involved the identification of a set of parameters underlying horror fiction's modes of functioning (its dependence on tradition and genre associations; its magically oriented linguistic structures), and the suggestion that it is these parameters which make it possible for

77

contemporary horror stories to act as exercises in ideological reassurance and also as self-referring exploitations of personal and social unease. In any work of horror fiction, these parameters (or formal rules of discourse and language) to a large extent determine and maintain a specific world view – a field of knowledge which acts as a kind of map against which author and audience measure various possibilities of experience. It is also on the basis of this field of knowledge that projected eventualities are evaluated as real or fantastic, as credibly threatening or else reassuringly outside the realms of practical possibilities. In analysing a phenomenon like horror fiction, then, we are concerned with systems of meaning and cognitive processes. To adapt Spengler's terminology, we are dealing with 'a culture-language' which makes it possible for us to have a 'world-consciousness', and thus to possess 'an "outer world" that reflects and attests our proper existence' (Spengler 1932: vol. 1, 55).

It is on the basis of these considerations that this chapter directs itself to the analysis of a series of very influential academic claims about the appeal and functions of fictional horrors and violence in contemporary culture. Many of the meanings and values encoded in these claims are very close to those underlying the more popular (customary) assertions made by exponents of the horror genre as exemplified in part I of this book. The point of focus here, therefore, will be that of evaluating and accounting for the symbolic universe and overarching reality definitions which are implicit in claims to the effect that fictional horrors appeal to, exercise, and help discharge the sadistic or 'bestial' urges which are alleged to reside in humans.

ACADEMIC VERSIONS OF THE CREED OF CATHARSIS

Many attempts have been made in educated circles to account for the fascination of violence, and for the fact that millions of people frequently engage in the types of discussion of horrific possibilities of experience which are offered and encouraged by horror fiction. Perhaps the most popular and influential explanation (at least with defenders of the horror genre) is the psychodynamically based assertion that 'vicarious experience' of aggression provides a relatively harmless release for pent-up aggressive instincts, and that it can thus be of therapeutic benefit in the socializing process. Exponents of this view often appear to assume the existence of a direct (virtually magical) link between the violations encoded in mass-media images and a set of allegedly seething instincts, emotions, and autonomic nervous reactions which are claimed to reside in those who decode such images. There is a tendency among such explanations to isolate horror fiction's seemingly growing preoccupation with scenes of graphic violation, and to take the prevalence of such scenes to indicate the *raison d'être* of, and thus describe and account for the social functions performed by, all types of marketed representations of violence and horror.

The reasoning behind psychoanalytically based claims about the cathartic properties of fictional violence is well caught in Winnicott's influential assertion that 'if society is in danger, it is not because of man's aggressiveness but because of the repression of personal aggressiveness in individuals' (Winnicott 1958: 204). As Brown elaborates, 'normal children and adults are normal because they express their aggressiveness as it arises within bounds acceptable to society (or at least not wholly unacceptable)' (Brown 1963: 154). According to this model of human nature, 'it is never any use trying to get rid of anything in human psychology', so that the energy which is contained in 'murderous impulses, dishonest desires, perverse sexual compulsions and a host of other objectionable feelings' must be 'expressed in some way or other' (Storr 1962: 14). The lengths to which the assumptions underlying this model have been stretched are strikingly reflected in Zinberg and Fellman's claim that

> War, among its many other meanings, provides whole populations with scenes and stories of destructiveness which may provide some sense of relief for one's own destructive impulses, along with, as well as in seeming contradiction to, the horror that war provokes.
>
> (Zinberg and Fellman 1967: 535)

According to these writers, 'war has always served as an effective outlet' for what they term the 'irreducible' and 'quintessential' destructive impulses ingrained in the nature of man (ibid.: 533). The same functions are allegedly also performed by organized sports (which 'serve as models of destructiveness successfully controlled'), by the political and economic systems, and by the mass media – 'in their offers of fiction tales of morbidity and in news accounts with their curious mixture of fictional and factual details of horror' (ibid.: 538). These 'forms of destructiveness' or 'sublimations of wishes directly to destroy' (ibid.) are argued by these writers to provide for participants and onlookers alike 'the satisfaction, the release that follows the discharge of tension from a dammed-up need' (ibid.: 536).

Claims about the cathartic or therapeutic properties of fictional violence often also associate the exercising of the aggressive instincts which are allegedly released by contact with such fiction with the process of growing up. At the base of such accounts is the assumption that 'naturally' chaotic and/or destructive impulses will develop into criminality or neuroses if they are not expressed in socially acceptable outlets. Healthy growth is here understood to involve development from a childhood marked by uncontrolled and upsetting urges and fantasies to a balanced and sanified adulthood involving the sublimation of such urges through socially sanctioned (and even creative) outlets. According to Brown, for instance, children who are continually and intensely absorbed in horror-producing scenes in comics and on television are engaged in 'a form of self-therapy' in that they are 'unconsciously trying to resolve [their] delinquent tendencies by working them out vicariously' (Brown 1963: 154). According to this broadly psychoanalytic viewpoint, what makes for healthy growth or normal development is the establishment of an evenly balanced tension between innate (and largely 'primitive') impulses and the restrictions imposed by social constraints. In psychodynamic terms, this theoretical framework makes it possible to analogically conceive of horror fiction as one of the means of 'discharging' (as in electricity) or 'draining' (as in plumbing) excesses of built-up psychic energy in order to maintain healthy equilibrium.

One manner in which psychoanalytic writers apply this conceptual framework is interestingly spelled out by Pickard:

> The whole business of learning to manipulate the environment of objects and people in order to satisfy as many wants as possible is the child's adjustment to outer reality. It is a laborious and often painful process, because he is driven forward by imperious inherited drives and driven backward by frustrations too strong for him to surmount.
>
> (Pickard 1961: 49)

'Outer reality' is thus made synonymous with frustrations, unless it is 'manipulated' in such a way as to satisfy a mass of somewhat tautologically conceived 'imperious inherited drives' by which the child is 'driven forward'. According to Pickard, play and story-telling constitute an important bridge between spontaneously chaotic or frighteningly violent drives and fantasies on the one hand, and adjustments to 'outer reality' on the other. In similar terms, Storr argues that the facts that 'children's games and fairy stories are shot through with aggressive and often bloodthirsty imaginings', and that 'children are in constant competition with each other and also with parents' are both manifestations of children's 'efforts to compensate for, and to overcome their sense of weakness' (Storr 1962: 15). It is worth noting that 'innate' dispositions are in these accounts frequently associated with undesirable qualities. Thus, Pickard speaks of an 'innate' type of anger in terms which project it as far fiercer and more horrible than the type of anger which has been in contact with 'outer reality' and rational control:

> Children are innately capable of anger; this anger can appear in the earliest months; during anger, thought is fantastically horrible and far more fierce than during anger in adults. If we accept these findings of modern research, then some of our difficulties are cleared away. The argument that we have to condition children to horrors is now seen as fallacious; there is no question of introducing them to horrors, because the horrors already known to them are far in excess of anything we experience as adults.
>
> (Pickard 1961: 6)

The immediate inspiration here is Melanie Klein's account of the part played in children's development by what she described as 'phantasy' and unconscious anxiety. In one of the résumés of Klein's arguments, Segal cites the following instance by way of illustration:

> When at the height of oral ambivalence, the child penetrates in his phantasy and attacks the mother's body and its contents, her body becomes an object of anxiety, which forces the child to displace his interest from her body to the world around him. Thus, through symbolisation his interest in his mother's body begins to extend to the whole world around him. A certain amount of anxiety is a necessary spur to this development. If the anxiety is excessive, however, the whole process of symbol-formation comes to a stop.
>
> (Segal 1973: 5)

Childhood phantasy is therefore asserted to be not only spontaneously violent, but also salutarily so; while coming to terms with 'outer reality' is claimed to involve being 'spurred' by the anxiety generated by violent phantasies into directing that violence into respectable channels. Although this account is more complex and challenging than unqualified assertions about the necessity of occasionally allowing free rein to the 'beast within', its underlying premises are based on the same assumptions and polarities. It is also worth noting that psychoanalytic interpretations of this process of development through symbolization at times assume fantastical proportions in their own right:

> A hungry, raging infant, screaming and kicking, phantasises that he is actually attacking the breast, tearing and destroying it, and experiences his own screams which tear him and hurt him as the torn breast attacking him in his own inside.

> (ibid.: 13)

The imagery here, and indeed the whole conceptual framework, derives from the Cartesian division between mind and matter, and the related concept of isolated ids and egos residing 'inside' our bodies and having to come to terms with 'outer' reality. The (as yet uncivilized) child is conceptualized as predominantly manifesting and being ruled by the more 'primitive' or 'animal' side of the psyche – i.e. that deriving from the heritage of the 'beast'.

Besides the key role played by psychoanalysis in the propagation of this view, a related contemporary rendering of its underlying assumptions which has received wide publicity and popularity is what may be broadly described as the 'human zoo' picture of civilized society – particularly as developed in the ethological perspectives of Niko Tinbergen and Konrad Lorenz, popularized by Desmond Morris and Robert Ardrey, and dressed in the more recent scientific jargon of 'sociobiology' and 'selfish genes' by (to name the major exponents) Richard Dawkins and Edward Wilson. The emphasis here too falls on innate drives which are viewed as our evolutionary heritage and which are said to be frustrated by the structure of modern society in a manner which creates a need for new expressive outlets. These outlets are claimed to assume various guises – e.g., respectably, of competitive sports and the 'rat race'; less respectably, of the 'ritualized aggression' of, say, gang warfare and football hooliganism. By extension, this conceptual model can be seen as a basis for justifying an obsession or fascination with fictional violence in the sense that such fascination can be claimed to constitute no more than an expression of what Lorenz calls 'a measure of aggression drive' which was allegedly bred into man in prehistoric times by intra-specific selection and 'for which in the social order of today he finds no adequate outlet' (Lorenz 1966: 209). A somewhat extreme (though anything but unrepresentative)[1] example of this type of extension is provided by Ardrey as part of his strident contention that 'man is a predator whose natural instinct is to kill with a weapon' (Ardrey 1961: 353), and that 'no instinct, whether physiological or cultural, that constituted a part of the original human bundle can ever in the history of the species be permanently suppressed or abandoned' (ibid.: 11). From this perspective Ardrey explains the appeal of violence at the cinema:

> The film-maker knows: it is the blazing six-shooter that the audience must see. The film-maker knows: violence, not sex, is the essence of box-office. Whether the audience be New Yorkers or New Guineans, Latins or Londoners, white or yellow or deepest Bantu brown, whether it be gathered in a Broadway, Leicester Square, Champs-Elysées, or Kurfuerstendamm cinema palace, or around the tailboards of an aspirin truck in the heart of the Amazon: whatever be the qualities or circumstances of that hypnotised, anonymous cinema community, its stripped-down, uninhibited, unselfconscious members may be cheated of the seduction scene, of the banquet orgy, or of the speech delivered from the monument; but they will not be cheated of that moment when the six-shooter blazes or the cannon speaks or the bomb, long-awaited, goes off. Hollywood knows more about the inner nature of *Homo sapiens*, viewed as a species, than any political, philosophical, or scientific school on earth. Hollywood is Hollywood, scorned and envied, feared and censored, because it has made minimum use of the romantic fallacy in its negotiations with mankind.
>
> (ibid.: 225–6)

Though Ardrey is frequently and vehemently disdainful of what he understands to be the psychoanalytic standpoint in this respect, his account of the 'inner nature of *Homo sapiens*' ('stripped-down, uninhibited, unselfconscious') juxtaposes instinct and repression along a pattern which also forms a central component of psychoanalytic thought. This model of human nature, it will be recalled, also informs much of the content and language of popular horror fiction, which in its more prominent contemporary forms promulgates (and also expects its readers to have cognisance of) a related set of polarized images and assumptions about human beastliness and civilized rationality.

Contemporary notions of what constitutes the 'animal side' (or basis) of our nature have therefore been heavily influenced by the findings and interpretations of studies of animal behaviour – particularly as these have been popularized in the images associated with catch-phrases like Morris's 'naked ape' and 'human zoo', or Ardrey's 'territorial imperative'. There have also been a series of much publicized physiological experiments involving electrical or chemical stimulation of the brain, which were claimed to demonstrate innately physiological causes of aggressive behaviour in that normally docile animals (and humans) could be induced to act in extraordinarily violent manners when certain parts of their brains were 'stimulated'. Thus, Jose Delgado (at Yale University) implanted sensitive radio receivers in various parts of the brains of cats, monkeys, rats, and other species in order to test the 'neural basis of aggression' and the extent to which behaviour could be modified through what he termed the 'physical control of the mind'. Smith, King, and Hoebel similarly experimented with neurochemical stimulation and claimed to have found 'evidence for a cholinoceptive mechanism' in the 'lateral hypothalamic control of killing'.[2] These and similar studies have been asserted to prove the existence of instinctive aggressive dispositions and even an 'innate killing response' which can be 'triggered' by electrical or neurochemical stimulation. In the case of 'higher mammals' (notably primates), these 'instinctive aggressive patterns' have been argued to be more influenced by experience because of greater cortical control. Thus, it was found that, when the hypothalamus of monkeys was stimulated, their response (attack or flight) depended on their position in the status hierarchy of the colony to which they belonged. Following Delgado, Hilgard et al. explain this phenomenon in the following terms:

> The hypothalamus may send a message to the cortex indicating that its 'aggression center' has been activated, but the cortex, in choosing the response it will initiate, considers what is going on in the environment and its memory of past experiences.
>
> (Hilgard et al. 1979: 321)

According to these accounts, human beings are 'like the lower animals' in having 'the neurological mechanisms that enable them to behave aggressively' (ibid.). However, normal individuals (i.e. those who do not have 'a high incidence of neurological defects') also have a certain amount of 'cognitive control' over 'the activation of these mechanisms' (ibid.). Thus, 'the frequency with which aggressive behaviour is expressed, the forms it takes, and the situations in which it is displayed are determined largely by learning and social influences' (ibid.). In human beings, therefore, there is asserted to be a more pronounced duality of forces determining behaviour. As Eysenck and Nias put it,

> Just as the voluntary activities of man are organised and controlled by the neocortex, so his emotional reactions are controlled by the 'visceral brain', situated in the limbic system. We thus have two largely separate and independent systems controlling behaviour, the old-fashioned, primitive, but very powerful emotional-conditioned system, and the new-fangled, recent, cognitive system.
>
> (Eysenck and Nias 1980: 45)

Spelled out in this manner, these ideas may not seem to be so fundamentally different from the presuppositions informing the concept of innate depravity and the Jekyll–Hyde polarities of inherited drives and acquired social habits. There are two implications which can be drawn from psycho-physiological accounts like those outlined above, and which (I wish to suggest) have helped indirectly in the propagation of some of the major assumptions underlying the creed of catharsis. In the first place, the assertion that humans share with 'lower animals' a physiologically based orientation to aggression is not far from designating the more deep-rooted parts of our nature ('old-fashioned, primitive, but very powerful') as essentially prone to a type of violence which points to the resilience of an irrational beast within. In the second place, the suggestion that the neocortex can give a specific direction to the expression of 'activated neurological mechanisms' is also not very far (at least in its underlying premises) from the claim that it is possible to give vent to aggressive or even destructive impulses in safe and socially acceptable outlets. It is important to stress that writers like Eysenck and Nias would reject suggestions that images of sex and violence on the mass media serve a cathartic function, preferring an account which emphasizes the conditioning and reinforcing properties of exposure to such fare. As they put it,

> Conditioning is far more powerful, and far more closely integrated with the rest of our personality and conduct than most people

realise; we are part animal, part socialised human being, and the process of socialisation itself is in part based on conditioning paradigms testifying to our animal origin.

(ibid.: 54)

What I am suggesting here is that the Jekyll–Hyde polarities endorsed by accounts of this persuasion have also helped to reinforce some popular and deep-seated assumptions about the animal side of human nature and about civilized ('newfangled, recent') methods of living and coping with it. The model of human nature underlying this and the other accounts considered in this section is basically Cartesian: it juxtaposes the rational mind against the drives and tendencies of the flesh. Violent or cowardly dispositions are thus projected as deriving from the animal or more primitive part of human nature, while more socially acceptable characteristics become the province of a rational mind which is conceptualized as being historically more recent and as having the task of balancing, directing, controlling, or placating the chaotic dictates of the 'beast within'. Why these contrasting values should be allocated in this manner is a question which raises a number of historical issues that require some elaboration. In order to gain a clearer perspective on contemporary renderings of the theory of catharsis, it will therefore be worth our while to consider briefly some representative instances in the history and development of the concept of the 'beast within'.

IRRATIONAL BEASTS AND THE ONUS OF EVIL

The belief that human beings are rotten at the core, that there is a beast within us which causes us to commit evils that our rational selves blush to think of, holds very wide currency in the popular imagination. The progeny of this belief is as varied as the attitudes and ideologies to which it has given rise. A lot of its impact derives from renderings and misrenderings of the Christian doctrine of original sin, and its tendency to project images of clearly polarized forces of evil and good lodging within the human mind (or soul) is also a focal point in Christian teaching about sin and grace. In the Epistle to the Romans, for instance, the Apostle Paul explains the fact that he finds himself doing that which goes against the law (which he designates as 'spiritual') by asserting that 'if I do what I do not want to do, it is no longer I who do it, but it is sin living in me that does it'

86

(Romans 17: 20). St Paul speaks of himself as serving what he describes as the law of God with his reason, and as serving the 'law of sin' in his 'unspiritual self':

> For in my inner being I delight in God's law; but I see another law at work in the members of my body, waging war against the law of my mind and making me a prisoner of the law of sin at work within my members.

Because of its relative clarity as an explanation of contradictory feelings and behaviour, the conceptual image of externalized good and evil cohabiting in man's nature has had a profound influence on our understanding of ourselves. The manner in which these forces at various points in history became personified as, say, guardian angels and patron saints on the one hand, and tempting devils and fiendish spirits on the other, is a further example of the influence and appeal of clearly schematized categories in this relation. The notion of the beast within (or of a recalcitrantly sinful nature lodged somewhere in the members of our body) also helps to lift from the individual's shoulders the burden of responsibility for disreputable behaviour, as well as for mankind's appalling record of war and destruction.[3] Noting what man has done to beast (physically as well as conceptually) in the pursuit and vain evasions of an understanding of the roots of human nature, Midgley argues that the use of the 'beast within' as a scapegoat for human wickedness has led to some bad confusion not only about beasts but also about men:

> If the Beast Within was capable of every iniquity, people reasoned, then beasts without probably were too. This notion made man anxious to exaggerate his difference from all other species and to ground all activities he valued in capacities unshared by the animals, whether the evidence warranted it or no. In a way this evasion does the species credit, because it reflects our horror at the things we do. Man fears his own guilt and insists on fixing it on something evidently alien and external. Beasts within solve the problem of evil. This false solution does man credit because it shows the power of his conscience, but all the same it is a dangerous fib.
>
> (Midgley 1980: 40)

According to Midgley, because the beast within has been set in opposition to the rational soul, 'fear of and contempt for feeling make up an irrational prejudice built into the structure of European rationalism' (ibid.: 43–4).

It is worth stressing that this prejudice forms part of a conceptual framework which also informs many of the assumptions underlying contemporary claims about the cathartic functions of fictional horrors – as illustrated, for instance, in Robert Ardrey's account of 'the inner nature of *Homo sapiens*' (cited on p. 83) or in Stephen King's assertions about the necessity of occasionally 'lifting a trapdoor in the civilized forebrain and throwing a basket of raw meat to the hungry alligators swimming around in that subterranean river beneath' (King 1982a: 205). The tenor and resilience of such claims also owe a great deal to the fact that in the course of the nineteenth century the concept of the beast within came to assume 'scientific' standing through the incorporation of a set of uncertainly worked out notions about man's evolutionary origins.

The complex interweaving of social, moral, and biological consider-ations which marked the early development of evolutionary theory is perhaps most strikingly caught in Darwin's exclamation (entered in one of his notebooks) that 'the mind of man is no more perfect than instincts of animals. . . . Our descent, then, is the origin of our evil passions!! – The Devil under form of Baboon is our grandfather!' (cited in Sulloway 1979: 242). William James's *Principles of Psychology* (1890) similarly reflects the manner in which prominent educated enquiries into human nature and behaviour in the latter part of the nineteenth century appropriated the comparatively recent discover-ies and speculation about evolution in such a way as to assimilate them into a particular conceptual framework (embodying, for our purposes, the creed of innate depravity) and then proceeded to reapply this framework (now 'scientific') to the interpretation and reaffirmative explanation of social reality and human motivation.[4] James speaks of 'the fascination which stories of atrocity have for most minds' as deriving from a combination of 'the hunting and the fighting instinct', both of which (he insists) have a 'remote origin in the evolution of the race' (James 1890, vol. 2: 411–12). According to James, the 'ferocity with which otherwise fairly decent men may be animated', and the 'carnivorous self-consciousness' which is easily 'agreeably tickled' by the notion of violence, can 'only be explained from *below*' – as 'an impulse aboriginal in character, and having more to do with immediate and overwhelming tendencies to muscular discharge than to any possible reminiscences of effects of experience, or association of ideas' (ibid.: 412–14):

> If evolution and the survival of the fittest be true at all, the destruction of prey and of human rivals *must* have been among the most important of man's primitive functions, the fighting and the chasing instincts *must* have become ingrained. Certain perceptions *must* immediately, and without the intervention of inferences and ideas, have prompted emotions and motor discharges; and both the latter must, from the nature of the case, have been very violent, and therefore, when unchecked, of an intensely pleasurable kind. It is just because human bloodthirstiness is such a primitive part of us that it is so hard to eradicate, especially where a fight or a hunt is promised as part of the fun.
>
> (ibid.: 412)

James thus accounts for the fascination of violence and for what he terms 'the pleasure of disinterested cruelty' (experienced for instance while reading about shocking atrocities in newspapers) by ascribing historical and scientific standing to the notion of innate depravity:

> In many respects man is the most ruthlessly ferocious of beasts. As with all gregarious animals, 'two souls', as Faust says, 'dwell within his breast,' the one of sociability and helpfulness, the other of jealousy and antagonism to his mates . . . . Hence the gory cradle, the *bellum omnium contra omnes*, in which our race was reared; hence the fickleness of human ties, the ease with which the foe of yesterday becomes the ally of today, the friend of today the enemy of tomorrow; hence the fact that we, the lineal representatives of the successful enactors of one scene of slaughter after another, must, whatever more pacific virtues we may possess, still carry about with us, ready at any moment to burst into flame, the smouldering and sinister traits of character by means of which they lived through so many massacres, harming others, but themselves unharmed.
>
> (ibid.: 409–10)

The reference to Hobbes's view of man's condition 'in the state of nature' (the '*bellum omnium contra omnes*') is worth underlining for what it suggests both about the tradition of thought to which the ideas expressed here belong, and also about the changes which took place in the presentation and understanding of the creed of innate depravity.

The state of nature which Hobbes describes in chapter 13 of *Leviathan* is one based on logical considerations. As Krook has pointed out (Krook 1959: 123), Hobbes's image of the 'nasty, brutish, and short' condition of life outside the commonwealth is not presented as a historical hypothesis about the original state of primitive man. It is, rather, a logical construction, an analytical diagram of human nature in a hypothetical condition of life. Hobbes's account of the *bellum omnium contra omnes* is therefore a projection of a condition of life which is logically (not historically) antecedent to the condition of commonwealth – it is defined by the total absence of civil laws and of a properly constituted power to make laws and maintain them. The account of human destructiveness and of the 'war of all against all' presented by James, on the other hand, is offered as historical and scientific fact. Primitive man, James is insisting, *was* nasty and brutish: his survival depended on it, and as his descendants we have inherited his nasty and brutish (even bestial) traits. Civilization for James, as for many of his intellectual contemporaries, has involved a movement away from this type of brutishness, so that we can now distinguish between the 'child of nature' (in whom 'the hunting instinct' is dominant) and a type 'now becoming frequent' (in whom this instinct is 'not exercised at all') (James 1890, vol. 2: 415). James is intent on stressing the necessity of inhibiting (as he terms it) and eventually replacing the hunting instinct with more sociable (or cerebral) impulses. But his entire approach rests on a conviction of the prevalence and innateness of pointless destructiveness and bloodthirstiness – a conviction both expressed in and deriving from a picture of the natural world of animals and 'primitive people' which has a complex and value-laden progeny, and which has repeatedly been set in emphatic (and self-satisfied) contrast to 'advanced' (i.e. superior and virtuous) rationality.

This picture has since been frequently challenged as outmoded and misleading. At its root lay the assumption that human nature (like the version of evolution on which its underlying premises were based) is constituted according to what Geertz has termed the 'stratigraphic' conception of the relations between the biological, psychological, social, and cultural factors in human life:

In this conception, man is a composite of 'levels', each super-imposed upon those beneath it and underpinning those above it. As one analyses man, one peels off layer after layer, each such layer being complete and irreducible in itself, revealing another, quite different sort of layer underneath. Strip off the motley forms of culture and one finds the structural and functional regularities of social organisation. Peel off these in turn and one finds the underlying psychological factors – 'basic needs' or what have you – that support and make them possible. Peel off psychological factors and one is left with the biological foundations – anatomical, physiological, neurogical – of the whole edifice of human life.

(Geertz 1975: 37)

This conception, which Geertz notes to have been characteristic of the anthropology of the late nineteenth and early twentieth centuries, is based on an account of racial history involving a series of clearly demarcated moments that do not, in fact, seem to have existed. As Geertz points out, the transition to the cultural mode of life took the genus *Homo* several million years to accomplish, and involved a long, complex, and closely ordered sequence of marginal genetic changes. Man's socio-cultural way of life is not skin-deep, with an ape close behind: it goes to the bone:

As our central nervous system – and most particularly its crowning curse and glory, the neocortex – grew up in great part in interaction with culture, it is incapable of directing our behaviour or organising our experience without the guidance provided by systems of significant symbols.

(ibid.: 49)

Thus, if human beings could be magically deprived of their culture – in itself a contradiction in terms, since we are 'incomplete or unfinished animals who complete or finish ourselves through culture – and not through culture in general but through particular forms of it' (ibid.) – what we would be left with would not be Mr Hyde or

the clever savages of Golding's *Lord of the Flies* thrown back upon the cruel wisdom of their animal instincts; nor would they be the nature's noblemen of Enlightenment primitivism or even, as classical anthropological theory would imply, intrinsically talented apes who had somehow failed to find themselves. They would be unworkable monstrosities with few useful instincts, fewer recognisable sentiments, and no intellect: mental basket cases.

(ibid.)

Yet the paradigm of human nature involving clearly separable 'primitive' and civilized/cultured components continues to maintain a certain hold on the popular imagination under a number of more or less camouflaging guises. The model was given a great deal of prominence in the educated accounts of society propounded at the turn of the century under the influence of social Darwinism, as well as in more popular writings. Thomas Huxley, for instance, equated civilization with ethics:

> Society differs from nature in having a definite moral object; whence it comes about that the course shaped by the ethical man – the member of society or citizen – necessarily runs counter to that which the non-ethical man – the primitive savage, or man as a mere member of the animal kingdom – tends to adopt. The latter fights out his struggle for existence to the bitter end, like any other animal; the former devotes his best energies to the object of setting limits to the struggle.
>
> (Huxley 1894: 203)

The image of human nature projected here finds its fictional and popular embodiment in Stevenson's *Strange Case of Dr Jekyll and Mr Hyde* (first published in 1885), where goodness is civilized, and mindless destructiveness is primeval and buried deep 'inside' – the 'animal within . . . licking the chops of memory [when] the spiritual side [is] a little drowsed' (Stevenson 1885, 1978 edn: 65). Similarly, at the height of public alarm over the Jack the Ripper murders, *Punch* magazine carried a grotesque cartoon personification of criminality, in which the ante-civilization aspects of this monster ('ruthless, furtive, unerect') were also stressed:

> There floats a phantom on the slum's foul air,
>   Shaping, to eyes which have the gift of seeing,
> Into the spectre of that loathly lair.
>   Face it – for vain is fleeing!
> Red-handed, ruthless, furtive, unerect,
> 'Tis murderous crime – the nemesis of neglect!
>   (*Punch* 29 September 1888)

Criminality had thus been designated as the antithesis of civilized rationality, and as deriving, therefore, from a set of feelings and irrational (insane) tendencies with 'scientifically' identified primitive origins. Man's basic instincts and passions had become the source of all evil, and were identified by influential psychologists like G. Stanley Hall as the vestiges of 'prehuman or animal traits', incorporating 'some of the aggressiveness of the carnivora and the timidity and deceit of creatures long preyed upon' (Hall 1904, vol. 2: 60). As a result of these designations, some of the fears associated with the threats of criminality to the social order could be partially placated, since criminals could now be patronizingly 'understood', as well as being seen to be susceptible to treatment and control by the forces of law and order. But the common heritage represented by the image of the 'beast within' also raised doubts about the individual's own sanity and his/her ability to control the potentially criminal (or cowardly) tendencies to which human flesh was heir. In other words, now that it had achieved 'scientific' standing and a certified pedigree, the beast within called for even more constant and rationally planned vigilance.

It was largely as a result of the growing influence of psychoanalytic thinking in the early twentieth century that this vigilance came to be seen as also requiring the civilized members of industrialized societies to occasionally give expression to their 'smouldering and sinister traits of character' in socially sanctioned (cathartic) outlets in order to prevent them from bursting into less acceptably civilized flames.

THE PSYCHOANALYSIS OF MR HYDE: CATHARSIS AND DRAMA IN FREUDIAN THEORY

Though the theoretical formulations of the nature and origins of aggression and violence assume different and less overtly evolutionary emphases in the psychoanalytic perspective, concepts very similar to those discussed above form a central component of the speculative instruments with which Freud explored what he termed the 'wolfishness' of human intra-specific relations. According to Freud, 'men are not gentle creatures who want to be loved', but 'creatures among whose instinctual endowments is to be reckoned a powerful share of aggressiveness' (Freud 1930, 1963 edn: 48). All human existence, in Freud's view, is based on a struggle between the instinctive side of man's nature and his more civilized inhibitions. Thus, in one of his late lectures, he described the endeavours of civilization and 'the first task of education' as being determined by the requirement that 'the child must learn to control his instincts', so that 'education must inhibit, forbid and suppress' (ibid. 1933, 1973 edn: 184). At the same time, 'precisely this suppression of instincts involves the risk of

93

neurotic illness', so that 'education has to find its way between the Scylla of non-interference and the Charybdis of frustration' (ibid.). Yet, Freud points out, even if education 'discovers the optimum and carries out its task ideally', the most it can hope for is 'to wipe out one of the factors in the aetiology of falling ill – the influence of the accidental traumas of childhood'. Freud is insistent that education 'cannot in any case get rid of the other factor – the power of an insubordinate instinctual constitution' (ibid.: 185).

According to Freud, then, 'a powerful share of aggressiveness' is one of man's 'instinctual endowments', and this is an aggressiveness which will 'manifest itself spontaneously' (revealing 'man as a savage beast to whom consideration towards his own kind is something alien') when '*the mental counter-forces which ordinarily inhibit it* are out of action' (ibid. 1930, 1963 edn: 49, my italics): 'instinctual passions are stronger than reasonable interests. Civilization has to use its utmost efforts in order to set limits to man's aggressive instincts and to hold the manifestations of them in check by psychical reaction-formations' (ibid.). There are clear similarities between this juxtaposition of 'instinctual passions' and 'reasonable interests', and the Jekyll–Hyde/primitive–civilized polarities encoded in the late nineteenth-century images of human nature discussed in the preceding section. It is also worth noting that the same type of argument can be made for related psychoanalytic accounts of the different layers of the human psyche. Jung, for instance, is insistent that 'outwardly people are more or less civilized, but inwardly they are still primitives', and that 'the conflict between the two dimensions of consciousness is simply an expression of the polaristic structure of the psyche, which like any other energic system is dependent on the tension of opposites' (Jung 1956, 1972 edn: 149). More specifically, Freud's emphasis on the importance of 'psychical reaction-formations' echoes William James's symptomatic insistence on the importance of developing sociable impulses to replace primitive ones. Freud and his followers thus worked from a perspective which was inevitably influenced by the complex interplay of social, moral, and biological considerations which gave the nineteenth-century rendering of the divided self its peculiar shape. It was because of that influence, and the desire, among other things, to place the horrors of human destructiveness highlighted in the 1914–18 war within cognizable categories, that Freud endorsed Plautus's assertion that 'man is a wolf to man', and (in one of his most celebrated passages) described the evil that men do in terms of the 'instinct' of 'cruel aggressiveness':

> their neighbour is for them not only a potential helper or sexual object, but also someone who tempts them to satisfy their aggressiveness on him, to exploit his capacity for work without compensation, to use him sexually without his consent, to seize his possessions, to humiliate him, to cause him pain, to torture and to kill him. *Homo homini lupus*. Who, in the face of all his experience of life and of history, will have the courage to dispute this assertion?
>
> (Freud 1930, 1963 edn: 48)

The emphasis in Freud moves away from a direct consideration of evolutionary issues to an account of motivation and a model of the human psyche which, by lodging the 'instinctual passions' associated with the beast firmly within a systematized concept of the unconscious, incorporate such considerations as tacit and unquestioned assumptions. Freud's conception of instinct can in this sense be seen as an extension of a late nineteenth-century understanding of evolution in which chaotic and destructive feelings are associated with an irreducible layer of 'primitive' irrationality, while rationality is projected as the exclusive province of civilization. According to Freud,

> Man's archaic heritage forms the nucleus of the unconscious mind; and whatever part of that heritage has to be left behind in the advance to later phases of development, because it is unserviceable or incompatible with what is new and harmful to it, falls a victim to the process of repression.
>
> (Freud 1919b, 1955 edn: 203–4)

Freud himself never made any claim to having discovered the unconscious. What he did offer as his contribution was having 'discovered . . . the scientific method by which the unconscious can be studied' (cited in Jahoda 1977: 16). The existence of levels of motivation and feeling outside (or 'below') conscious awareness had not only been discussed and given artistic expression in philosophical and literary works dating from antiquity, but (as Ellenberger and Sulloway have shown) the intellectual climate of the late nineteenth century vibrated with explorations of its nature and significance. Nietzsche, supremely, conceived of the unconscious as an area of confused thoughts, emotions, and instincts, at the same time as an area of re-enactment of past stages of the individual and the species.

Freud himself noted how what he termed Nietzsche's 'guesses and intuitions often agree in the most astonishing way with the laborious findings of psychoanalysis' (*Freud, Standard Edition*, vol. 20: 60); but claimed to have avoided reading Nietzsche's works for a long time in order to keep his mind free of external influences. However, as Ellenberger points out (Ellenberger 1970: 277), at the time of Freud's early maturity it was not necessary to have studied Nietzsche to be permeated with his thought, seeing how much he was quoted, reviewed, and discussed in every journal and newspaper. Like Freud, Nietzsche had viewed words and deeds as manifestations of unconscious motivations and the conflict of instincts. The unconscious as conceptualized by Nietzsche is (as in Freud's account) the realm of wild, brutish instincts which derive from earlier stages of the individual and of mankind, and which, finding no permissible outlet in civilized society, are expressed in passion, dreams, and mental illness. The fact that these ideas carry strong echoes of some of the notions discussed in the preceding section of this chapter underlines the manner in which scientific speculation and interpretation are inevitably influenced by the ideological perspectives and world views which permeate the intellectual and popular climates with and within which they inter-react. The discovery of what Freud described as the scientific method of studying the unconscious was part of these inter-reactions. This is a point which is often missed in the popular image of Freud as the isolated Viennese doctor who serendipitously hit upon the profound nature of the unconscious through his work with cases of hysteria among the wealthy Viennese Jews at the turn of the century, and who then proceeded to undertake the daring and lonely task of tapping his own unconscious through a long and arduous self-analysis and the interpretation of his own dreams. Given the mythical associations which have grown around this account, it will be useful to review its accuracy and implications in terms of how the development of Freud's ideas and their impact on present-day thinking were influenced by the context in which he worked.

Freud's collaboration with Josef Breuer (which culminated in the publication of *Studies on Hysteria* in 1895), like his period of studies under Charcot in Paris, is generally agreed to have been instrumental in giving a direction to the formation of his theories. One of the most extraordinary and seminal of the cases of hysteria treated by Breuer was that of Anna O. – identified by Ernest Jones in 1953 as Bertha Pappenheim, who in later life became an important pioneer in the women's movement and anything but an advocate of psychoanalysis (Sulloway 1979: 57). Hysteria as a clinical malady has, significantly enough, in the course of the twentieth century become a relatively rare curiosity, and it has generally come to be associated with the rigid middle-class mores of the context in which Breuer and Freud's patients (mostly women) lived. For all this, its origins and symptoms were both bizarre and disturbing. Breuer's prolonged treatment of Anna O. involved tracing every remembered occurrence of each of her symptoms in turn till the events surrounding the first occurrence were recalled and, to Breuer's initial surprise, 'when they were brought to verbal utterance the symptoms disappeared' (Freud and Breuer 1895, 1955 edn: 34). It is of significance that Breuer classified this treatment (which though dramatic was not complete or entirely successful) as 'cathartic'. Sulloway (using Dalma and Hirschmueller as his sources) points out in this relation that the Aristotelian concept of dramatic catharsis had been a long concern of Jacob Bernays, the uncle of Freud's future wife, and that in Vienna, as elsewhere, the subject was much discussed among scholars and in the salons, and even assumed for a time the proportions of a craze. According to Hirschmueller, for instance, by 1880 Bernays's ideas had inspired some seventy German-language publications on catharsis, and this number more than doubled by 1890. As Sulloway remarks,

It seems very possible that an intelligent girl like Anna O. might have been acquainted with the subject and have unconsciously incorporated this knowledge into the dramatic plot of her illness. And the connection between catharsis in its theatrical and medical senses was certainly not lost upon Bernays and others.

(Sulloway 1979: 56–7)

Sulloway finds it extremely difficult to believe that Breuer and Freud were not acquainted with Bernays's ideas while they were developing their theory of hysteria, and notes how, a year after *Studies on Hysteria* appeared in print, 'Breuer, who had a special interest in Greek drama, discussed Bernays' views in a letter to Theodor Gomperz' (ibid.). In the case of Freud too, to borrow a phrase from Jerome Bruner, 'his love for Greek drama and his use of it in his formulations are patent' (Bruner 1979: 153).[5]

Whether or not one accepts Freud's later claim that Breuer discontinued the treatment and further exploration of the implications of hysteria because of discomfort over the 'transference relationship' and an unwillingness to come to terms with the sexual etiology of neurosis,[6] it is clear that Breuer's 'cathartic' approach and his identification of the instigating forces in Anna O.'s malady were of profound influence in the formulation of the theories on which he and Freud collaborated. Freud himself proceeded to examine the implications of feelings like those of Anna O. and the way in which they revealed a conflict between internal and external reality. He determined, as Jahoda puts it (Jahoda 1977: 28), 'to understand the meaning of symptoms in the light of a patient's private world', and proceeded to construct a complex (and in many ways revolutionary) system of viewing and studying human nature. Jahoda designates this development as a 'change from catharsis to the uncovering of the repressed via the study of meaning' – a change which, she claims, 'marks the true beginning of psychoanalysis', in that 'Freud wanted to discover the concrete content of the repressed, make it available to the patient's consciousness so that it could be accepted or rejected in a rational manner' (ibid.). But the types of interpretation which prevail in any particular study of meaning will be directly related to the interpreter's individual experience (in this case, among other things, Freud's work with pathological cases), and – partly through that experience – to what Fiske and Hartley call 'the broad principles by which a culture organises and interprets the reality with which it has to cope' (Fiske and Hartley 1978: 46). Those principles are reflected in the myths which operate as organizing structures within an area of cultural intersubjectivity, and which 'are themselves organised into a coherence that we might call a mythology or an ideology' (ibid.). Thus, the polarization of rationality and feelings remains a central component of Freud's 'uncovering of the repressed via the study of meaning'. Similarly, Freud's model of what Jahoda terms 'the concrete content of the repressed' is in many ways an elaborate reworking of the images implicit in the concept of catharsis, and an extension of the myths of 'beasts within' and inherited 'smouldering and sinster traits' which figured so prominently in the common experience of the period in which he worked. Since it is largely Freud's model which lies at the base of many contemporary claims about the 'expression' of normally repressed instincts through the 'vicarious experience' of aggressive acts and violence in, say, horror fiction, it will be useful to look closely at a sample of Freudian analysis in order to establish these connections more clearly.

Civilization and its Discontents offers an interesting example of the manner in which Freud's (culturally inspired) understanding of what is involved in the repression of instinct is reapplied to the consideration of cultural issues. At one point in the essay, Freud describes what he terms 'the genesis of conscience' by speculating about the manner in which a child is obliged to renounce the satisfaction of the 'considerable amount [of] revengeful aggressiveness' which 'must be developed in the child against the authority which prevents him from having his first, but none the less his most important, satisfactions' (Freud 1930, 1963 edn: 66). In Freud's view, 'every piece of aggression whose satisfaction the subject gives up is taken over by the super-ego and increases the latter's aggressiveness (against the ego)' (ibid.), so that 'in the formation of the super-ego and the emergence of a conscience innate constitutional factors and influences from the real environment act in combination' (ibid.: 67). Freud associates this process of individual development with its 'phylogenetic model' in that, he argues, 'the father of prehistoric times was undoubtedly terrible, and an extreme amount of aggressiveness may be attributed to him' (ibid.: 68). The child in Freud's account 'finds his way out' of the 'economically difficult situation' created by the demand for 'instinctual deprivation' with the help of 'familiar mechanisms' (ibid.: 66):

> By means of identification he takes the unattackable authority into himself. The authority now turns into his super-ego and enters into possession of all the aggressiveness which a child would have liked to exercise against it. The child's ego has to content itself with the unhappy role of the authority – the father – who has been thus degraded. Here, as so often, the 'real' situation is reversed: 'If I were the father and you were the child, I should treat you badly.' The relationship between the super-ego and the ego is a return, distorted by a wish, of the real relationships between the ego, as yet undivided, and an external object.
>
> (ibid.)

Freud's account of the genesis of conscience, it should be noted, carries strong echoes of late nineteenth-century accounts of 'the gory cradle in which our race was reared' and of assertions to the effect that (as Huxley put it) 'ethical nature, while born of cosmic nature, is necessarily at enmity with its parent' (Huxley 1894: viii). What is different and more striking in Freud's account is the handling of the imagery which he employs both to express these ideas and, by amalgamating them to other operative concepts, to extend their resonance. Working within and giving direction to the carefully worked out logic and drama of Freud's analysis of suppression (itself highly reminiscent of Nietzsche's *Genealogy of Morals*) are a set of images and speculative instruments which assume and project instinct as functioning according to what Bruner calls 'the necessity of the classical mechanics' (Bruner 1979: 157). But the images and assumptions interact in a manner which is innovatively and memorably rich in dramatic overtones. Thus Freud's account involves the concept of a 'considerable amount' of aggressive energy, which is attributable to alleged philogenetic antecedents – like a stream to a spring – and which flows inexorably on until it comes up against a dam of suppression, at which point it follows 'familiar mechanisms' and breaks out in a displacement elsewhere. The child in the example cited is visualized as following the same type of processes as those implied in the application of the principle of catharsis to psychopathological cases. There is a build-up of unacceptable aggressiveness which must find expression. 'Identification' with the authority figure (i.e. a feat of the imagination) makes it possible for that build-up of aggressive energy to be expressed through an outlet which is not blocked – the super-ego representing, in Freudian terminology, the 'internalized' morality or conscience of civilization. Hyde becomes Jekyll in order to survive. As a result of 'psychical reaction formations' (Freud 1930, 1963 edn: 49), the 'satisfaction' and expression of crudely brutish instincts is transformed into a process which is not only socially acceptable but even necessary for the upholding of civilized behaviour. This latter process is in its turn conceptualized as a type of force field or battery which derives its strength from a series of electrical charges: 'The beginning of conscience', Freud reasons, 'arises through the suppression of an aggressive impulse' and 'it is subsequently reinforced by fresh suppressions of the same kind' (ibid.: 67). As the damming of rivers transforms unharnessed hydraulic energy into serviceable electricity, so too the measured suppression of anti-social 'instincts' forces the energy behind those instincts to express itself in functionally more acceptable ways. But the source of that energy (call it the id) remains wild and distinct from the psychic forces which it feeds and by which it is in turn controlled (call them the ego and super-ego). If, because of environmental or 'innate constitutional' factors, the balance of power between these forces is not maintained adequately, the build-up of, say, aggressive energy might require new (acceptable) outlets of expression. New 'identifications' may be called for, which, for our purposes, might be argued to include the 'vicarious satisfactions' provided by messages about violence, or the distanced thrills evoked by images of horror.

This mode of thought, as Bruner points out, 'is not a theory in the conventional sense; it is a metaphor, an analogy, a way of conceiving man, a drama' (Bruner 1979: 158).[7] It is a mode of thought which embodies the scientism of its age as well as a deep current of romanticism: Freud, 'a child of his century's materialism . . . wedded to the determinism and the classical physicalism of nineteenth-century physiology so boldly represented in Helmholtz', also has a profoundly Romantic sense of the role of impulse, of the drama of life, of the power of symbolism (ibid.: 152). The impact of Freud's views on our ways of seeing ourselves and of designating reasons for our behaviour is therefore firmly grounded in the nature of his 'imagery of necessity':

> Success in transforming the common conception of man did not come simply from adopting the cause-and-effect discourse of science. Rather it is Freud's imagery, I think, that provides the clue to his ideological power. It is an imagery of necessity, an imagery that combines the dramatic, the tragic, and the scientific views of necessity. It is here that Freud's is a theory or a prototheory peopled with actors. The characters are from life: the blind, energetic, pleasure-seeking id; the priggish and punitive super-ego; the ego, battling for its being by diverting the energy of the others to its own use. The drama has economy and terseness. The ego develops canny mechanisms for dealing with the threat of id impulses: denial, projection, and the rest. Balances are struck among the actors, and in this balance are character and neurosis. Freud was using the dramatic technique of decomposition, where the actors are part of a single life – a technique that he himself had recognised in fantasies and dreams, one which is honoured in his essay, 'The poet and the daydream'.
>
> (ibid.: 156–7)

Freud's studies on hysteria, then, as much as the intellectual climate and the educated renderings of biogenetic evolution which prevailed in his day, had a profound influence on the manner in which he came to conceptualize the realm of the unconscious, and on the method in which he went on to become the most persuasive cartographer of that realm. Towards the end of his career, Freud noted how psychoanalysis had been discovered and developed as a method of treatment and 'in connection with sick people':

> but I did not want to commend it to your interest as a method of treatment but on account of the truths it contains, on account of the information it gives us about what concerns human beings most of all – their own nature – and on account of the connections it discloses between the most different of their activities.
>
> (Freud 1933, 1973 edn: 192)

What Freud is stressing here is the realization that the most important contribution of psychoanalysis and his life's work was less that of suggesting or providing therapy than of developing, extending, and making more malleable a specific set of speculative instruments for understanding ourselves: of offering a systematic ('scientific') but also imaginatively syncretic method of studying, 'seeing', and thinking about men and women and their (frequently unaccountable) behaviour. The pervasive influence of Freud's 'legitimate concept of unconscious mental activity', as Alasdair MacIntyre phrases it, is thus directly related to that concept's use as a descriptive tool: 'When Freud "explains" a dream, what he does essentially is to decode it. Seeing that something hidden is said in the dream is like seeing the hidden shape in a rebus or puzzle-picture' (MacIntyre 1958: 72–3). In the course of extending his contemporaries' concept of repression and the related images of innate and inherited bestial drives, Freud showed how (to borrow a phrase from Habermas) self-reflection could be made into a science – most famously, by devising a lexicography of human nature which worked from the premise that the reasons and meanings of behaviour are encoded in the symbols and 'slips' which manage to evade repression in the course of dreams and mental illness as well as in normal waking life.

The impact of the language of Freud's system on our ways of seeing was noted by Wittgenstein in his 1932–3 lectures, where he asserted that, in enabling us to discover the reasons (as distinct from the cause) for modes of behaviour, psychoanalysis provides a representation of processes by doing what aesthetics does: it puts two factors together (Wollheim and Hopkins 1982: 9, 11). Unlike the investigation of a cause – which, according to Wittgenstein, 'is carried out experimentally' – the investigation of a reason entails as an essential part one's agreement with it, so that 'the subconscious is a hypothetical entity which gets its meaning from the verification these propositions have' (ibid.: 10):

> What Freud says about the subconscious sounds like science, but in fact it is just *a means of representation*. New regions of the soul have not been discovered, as his writings suggest. The display of elements of a dream, for example, a hat (which may mean practically anything) is a display of similes. As in aesthetics, things are placed side by side so as to exhibit certain features. These throw light on our way of looking at a dream; they are reasons for the dream.
>
> (ibid.)

During his conversations with Rush Rhees, Wittgenstein also argued that the reasons or 'explanations' proposed by Freud in his analysis are speculations of the type which 'many people are inclined to accept' (ibid.: 2). Freud's view that anxiety is linked to an organic compulsion to repeat, for instance, is 'an idea which has a marked attraction':

> It has the attraction which mythological explanations have, explanations which say that this is all a repetition of something that has happened before. And when people do accept or adopt this, then certain things seem much clearer and easier for them. So it is with the notion of the unconscious also.
>
> (ibid.)

The acceptance of these reasons, Wittgenstein argues, makes it easier for people 'to go certain ways: it makes certain ways of behaving and thinking natural for them' so that 'they have given up one way of thinking and adopted another' (ibid.: 3).

DRAMATIC PERSONIFICATION AND THE DEFINITION OF FEELINGS

Freud's influence on our ways of seeing, then, derives directly from the dramatic structure of his explanations, and from the fact that his representations were based on a set of interweaving popular and educated accounts of human motivation. The fact that such explanations and representations are cultural in origin and orientation points to the inadequacy of interpreting motivation and behaviour exclusively in terms of images which claim to identify 'natural' traits and dispositions lodged 'within' the human psyche. It is from an awareness of the cultural and discursive processes motivating and influencing such interpretative images (as well as conflicting ones) that one can begin to argue that human nature is inseparable from human culture, and that accounts which attempt to explain disturbing characteristics by claiming that 'that's the way of nature' are tautological or even pleonastic, and as such magical. A direct implication of all this is that if we wish to make adequate sense of the appeal of horror fiction we will need to explain its popularity in terms of the intersubjectivity of language and social processes. That intersubjectivity and the cognitive structures which are built in and which function within its contexts need to be recognized and worked into our account if we are to form a clear syncretic understanding of the phenomena we are considering.

According to Bettelheim,

> When all the child's wishful thinking gets embodied in a good fairy; all his destructive wishes in an evil witch; all his fears in a voracious wolf; all the demands of his conscience in a wise man encountered on an adventure – then the child can finally begin to sort out his contradictory tendencies. Once this starts, the child will be less engulfed by unmanageable chaos.
>
> (Bettelheim 1976: 66)

The trend of the argument is to juxtapose 'chaos' – which is assumed to be endemic, since it is conceived as deriving from what are alleged to be inevitably contradictory and potentially overpowering feelings – with the order of socially imposed structure. But catharsis is here presented as involving much more than a simple draining or discharging of 'inner' tendencies. The exercise Bettelheim is describing is one of giving the child tools with which to manage chaotic feelings by tying them to a local habitation and a name. Fiction is here claimed to have therapeutic qualities when it is stylized enough to 'embody' (allow the understanding and expression of) the 'contradictory tendencies' which threaten to engulf the child in 'unmanageable chaos'. Unlike more bland assertions about the 'vicarious satisfactions' provided through 'identification' in works of fiction, Bettelheim's argument underlines the metaphoric dimensions of fiction – its uses (and possible abuses) in the provision of clearly differentiated perspectives in the human quest for meaning. This is an important distinction, and it deserves some elaboration. As Harding has pointed out, the terms 'vicarious satisfaction' and 'identification' are frequently used in literary critical circles in manners which overlook their metaphoric dimensions. They have thus 'been taken literally without realisation of the extent of pathological disorientation that the supposed psychological process would imply' (Harding 1962: 143). It is as a result of this type of simplification that many popular claims about the cathartic qualities of fiction (horrific or otherwise) become no more than exercises in verbal magic, replete with the bogus technicalities of simple (and simplistic) but psychological-sounding explanations, and riddled with tautological references to 'the inner nature of *Homo sapiens*'. As Harding insists, what is frequently referred to as 'identification' can be more accurately (though less dramatically) described as an onlooker's imaginative or empathic insight into the experience of a character (fictional or otherwise) who is being actively observed from 'the receiving end of a conventional mode of communication' (ibid.: 140). Similarly, what is frequently described as 'vicarious satisfaction' or 'wish-fulfilment' can be more plausibly designated as 'wish-formulation or the definition of desires' in the course of 'the social act of affirming with the author a set of values':

> It seems nearer the truth, therefore, to say that fictions contribute to defining the reader's or spectator's values, and perhaps stimulating his desires, rather than to suppose that they gratify desire by some mechanism of vicarious experience. In this respect they follow the pattern, not of the dream with its hallucinated experiencing, but of waking supposition and imagining – 'Wouldn't it be wonderful if . . .' 'Wouldn't it be sad if . . .'.
>
> (ibid.: 144)

I have spent so much time placing psychoanalytic theory in its context within the history of ideas because it is my contention that we can only make logical and constructive sense of contemporary versions of the creed of catharsis within the frame of this context. I have stressed the idadequacy of designating violent or destructively 'bestial' behaviour as 'natural' by pointing to the fact that the values and associations which have grown around such images have been culturally determined. I have identified the impact of the theory of evolution as an important starting-point for various assertions to the effect that the 'destructive basis' of human nature (previously described either in spiritual or else in purely logical terms) could be accounted for on historical or scientific grounds. In the course of becoming part of customary and popular discourse, the new images and symbols which have grown with and out of this development have merged quite readily with older prejudice and uncertainty. They have now become so widespread that, more often than not, little need is felt to examine their underlying assumptions or to question the viability of the significance they ascribe to motivation and behaviour. By examining some of the more forceful and influential of the seminal statements about the 'gory cradle' in which our race was claimed to have been reared, the preceding pages have pointed to the limitations of those assumptions in terms of the questionable nature of many of the claims they made in relation to science and history. Arguments about the need for 'cathartic release' of aggressive impulses have frequently been used to justify some very disturbing fictional and not-so-fictional elaborations of sadistic violence. The modes of discourse with which these arguments have been associated have also, however, contributed towards some of the more searching reflections on human nature conducted in our century. Right or wrong, the interpretations and metaphors which have grown around and from these assumptions and orientations continue to inhere in the fabric of contemporary culture and in customary conceptions of what constitutes reality. On these grounds, I have argued that the interpretative issues raised by more refined psychoanalytic perspectives (and most notably those of Freud himself) have had a profound influence on our ways of seeing, and on our methods of personifying and dramatizing our feelings in order to account for our (at times illogical) behaviour.

The focus of the preceding discussion has thus been on those ideas explored, developed, or simply assumed by Freud and his followers which have had a profound impact on popular conceptions and attitudes, particularly as these are reflected and compounded in cultural phenomena like contemporary horror fiction. Recent and more refined psychoanalytic approaches, it bears noting, have in many cases moved well beyond some of the more simplistic orientations discussed in the course of this chapter. These developments, however, do not appear to have filtered down to a popular level, and it is precisely those aspects of psychoanalytic thought which present exponents would consider outdated that continue to inhere in the fabric of popular culture and in 'common-sense' assumptions about what it means to be human. What I have argued is that this influence can be explained and accounted for in terms of the fact that the psychoanalytic perspective is itself a powerful example of the dramatizing and interpretative process which psychoanalysts assert to underlie human action. As such it has supplied (or refined and/or disguised in some cases) some of the most pervasively influential metaphors which continue to inform and give direction to our century's attempts to understand itself.

This argument raises questions about the cultural implications of phenomena like horror fiction which we shall need to consider more closely. Chapter 6 of this book will attempt to grapple with some of these issues by aligning approaches suggested and developed in the psychoanalytic perspective with a number of philosophical and cognitive psychological orientations. Before that, however, I propose to identify and discuss the implications of some further points of convergence between popular and academic assumptions about the nature and uses of horror. The next chapter thus examines a series of influential assertions about the effects and consequences of mass-marketed images of violence and fear. My point of focus will be the extent to which dramatizing tendencies and methods of making sense through metaphor influence and direct contemporary reactions to horror fiction.

Chapter 5

CLOCKWORK COPY-CATS AND THE STUDY OF HORRIFIC INFLUENCES

'Ah, it is the fault of our science that it wants to explain all; and if it explain not, then it says there is nothing to explain. But yet we see around us every day the growth of new beliefs, which think themselves new; and which are yet the old, which pretend to be young – like the fine ladies at the opera.'

(Dr Van Helsing, in Bram Stoker's *Dracula*)

'I can bring you proof that the superstition of yesterday can become the scientific truth of today.'

(Dr Van Helsing, in Tod Browning's 1931 film version of *Dracula*)

ORIENTATION

Reports in the popular press frequently give the impression that there exists a more or less direct link between criminal behaviour and the depiction of violence on the mass media – that if one takes the trouble to look beneath the floorboards, as it were, one will find that the perpetrators of the most heinous crimes have been reared on a steady diet of horror stories, 'TV violence', and 'video nasties'. The present chapter proposes to look closely at the logic and evidence underlying such assumptions. This will involve a fairly detailed consideration of the intellectual lineage and conceptual frameworks informing a number of experimental studies which have been claimed to prove a wide range of cause-and-effect relations between the representation of violence and its perpetration. Explanations of such connections frequently hinge on an understanding of human behaviour which held great prominence in the social sciences from the 1950s to the early 1970s, and which places various degrees of emphasis on the impact of conditioning. Relatively updated versions of such accounts vary in orientation from insistence on imitation and role-modelling, to a focus on desensitization, disinhibition, arousal, and (more recently) mainstreaming and the cultivation of fear. The present chapter is intended to analyse and contextualize some of the most prominent and influential of these theories and studies, with the aim of placing the assertions which they are supposed to back in a coherent perspective.

It is worth noting at this stage that popular claims about the horrific effects of 'exposure' to the representation of violence are frequently linked with suggestions that 'mass-media violence' and horror fictions appeal to or draw out what are variously referred to as our 'basest passions', our 'bestial tendencies', or our 'animal nature'. These suggestions are clearly implicit, for instance, in the *Daily Mail*'s assertion (on 4 August 1983) that the people responsible for the 'video nasties' are 'men who grow rich on bloodlust'. Such claims suggest a curious conceptual hybrid, in that (in more educated or academic discourse) the view that it is the observation of violence which makes people aggressive, and the contention that such activity appeals to depraved or beastly aspects of our nature, form part of two conflicting versions of how we function as human beings. To state this differently, popular concepts of what happens to people who watch a lot of 'violence on the media' derive from a complex mixture of assumptions. On the one hand, these assumptions form part of the web of notions underlying the myth of the 'beast within' – i.e. the designation of all criminal, violent, and destructive as well as cowardly behaviour as resulting from an inherited component of innate depravity or 'animal instincts'. On the other hand, there is also a quite different set of assumptions informing these popular concepts, and these are assumptions which coincide in a number of significant respects with the philosophical principles underlying positivist, behaviourist, and neo-behaviourist accounts of the mechanisms propelling behaviour – i.e. that humans are 'bundles of perceptions' which start life as a *tabula rasa*. At various points during the present century, these conceptual frameworks have formed the basis of very heated controversy and debate among academic and professional communities, and it is interesting to find them happily amalgamated in popular translations. The pages which follow are partly intended to account for this amalgamation.

I want to suggest that attempts to apply the notions of learned aggressiveness and learned anxiety to media studies have been as influenced by the purpose of confirming established attitudes and supplying reassurance about unpleasant phenomena as has been the discursive mode of the innate aggressiveness/cowardliness model. It is partly because of this community of usually unidentified purposes that there is a tendency for images like those of the beast within and of an impersonally conditioning environment (or a mechanically 'de-sensitizing' or 'polluting' mass media) to merge quite readily in the popular consciousness. This is a merger which can be argued to betray a widespread desire to believe in the power of extraneous forces on to which can be attributed (in the jargon of cognitive social psychology) the locus of control responsible for the undeniable existence of human destructiveness and for frequently unnerving 'negative emotions'. Conflicting theoretical models thus return to points of intersection in popular discourse, and in the customary habit of reappropriating legitimized views and systematized speculative instruments (even when these are in methodological conflict with each other) in order to reaffirm established values, or else derive reassurance in the face of disturbing phenomena.

In part I of this book, I pointed to a number of examples of horror fictions which characteristically presented some of the most horrific of human destructive pursuits as originating from a beastly heritage and functioning in a mechanistic fashion – once the switch has been flicked, as it were, the mechanisms controlling and determining the beastly side of human nature are assumed to be as regular and unstoppable as wound clockwork. In chapter 4, I stressed how contemporary versions of the catharsis explanation of the appeal of horror fiction have been influenced (through popularizations of Freud's work and thence of the notions which had formed unques-tioned presuppositions underlying his work) by attempts to account for human motivation in terms which made use of a mixture of speculative tools derived from, on the one hand, dramatic/Romantic literary traditions and, on the other, rigid nineteenth-century notions of mechanics. One of the things I wish to draw out in this chapter is the manner in which behaviourist and neo-behaviourist theoretical perspectives and studies have also, ironically, lent respectability to an aspect of the conceptual framework out of which contemporary horror fictions are compounded. By providing an air of academic respect-ability to the assumptions underlying the notion that mindless destructiveness is unstoppable once set in (mechanical) motion, researchers working from behaviourist and neo-behaviourist perspectives can be said to have also played an important role in the establishment and consolidation of the (magically oriented) frames of reference within which contemporary horror fiction continues to function. The exercise of mapping out the fields of discourse surrounding contemporary horror fiction and the roots of its success, therefore, requires a consideration of the ways in which this theoretical perspective has interacted with popular and 'common-sense' assumptions in the formation of contemporary notions of what it means to be human.

The next section proposes to trace some of these points of intersection by considering why a number of academic and professional explanations have readily found their way into popular discourse and come to form part of a fairly widespread ('common-sense') understanding of the impact of 'mass-media violence'.

POPULAR CLAIMS ABOUT HORRIFIC INFLUENCES

The most popular explanation of the alleged link between viewing violent material and acting violently is what has been termed the 'copy-cat' phenomenon. Thus, during the height of concern over the 1981 race riots in inner British cities, a number of very specific accusations were directed against television broadcasters on the basis of claims of this nature. Among those who apparently gave credence to these claims was Margaret Thatcher, who in a speech at the Parliamentary Press Gallery at London's Caledonian Club reportedly suggested that the media may have been one of the causes of these troubles (Tumber 1982: 8). The suggestion was in fact endorsed in the Scarman Report into the Brixton disorders of 10–12 April 1981 (published in November of that year). According to Lord Scarman,

> The media, particularly the broadcasting media, do in my view bear a responsibility for the escalation of the disorders (including the looting) in Brixton on Saturday 11 April and for their continuation the following day, and for the imitative element in the later disorders elsewhere.
>
> (Scarman Report, 1981: 111, para. 6.39)

More zealously, in the *Daily Mail* of 14 July 1981, Mary Whitehouse described how she had sent telegrams to the television networks asking them if they would please consider whether the televising of acts of vandalism and violence did not contribute to the spread of riots by creating excitement, encouraging imitation, and actually teaching the techniques of violence. Thirteen years earlier, in an article which appeared in *Viewer and Listener* (June 1968) and headlined 'Violent world of TV makes murder climate', Mrs Whitehouse had similarly asserted that the assassination of Robert Kennedy was directly related to 'the amount of violence shown on American TV screens'. 'Violence on television', Mrs Whitehouse proclaimed, 'is bound to play its part and a very vital part in the creation of an increasingly violent society' (cited in Tracey and Morrison 1979: 83–4). The evidence to back claims of this nature, according to Mrs Whitehouse, is to be found not so much in empiricist and rational methods of research but in 'common sense' – a term which she equates with 'the sum total of human experience', and which 'teaches us, both in the home and in the school, that example is the most powerful educator' (Address to the Royal College of Nurses, 5 April 1970; cited by Tracey and Morrison 1979: 84).

For all her insistence on the primacy of 'common sense' in this sphere, Mrs Whitehouse's assertions about the power of example find backing (and possibly ultimate inspiration) in an impressive array of data and reports of experimental studies conducted (mostly) by adherents of various factions of learning and social learning theory in the social sciences. It is more frequent, in fact, to find scientific evidence cited (or distorted) in the interest of giving the claims of Mrs Whitehouse's type of 'common sense' greater punch and respectability. Thus, the popular press gave very wide publicity in 1983 to Dr Clifford Hill's interim report to the British Parliamentary Group Video Enquiry – a committee which had been set up in response to the large number of reports in the British press insistently linking the viewing by children of 'video nasties' with violent behaviour. The report (entitled *Video Violence and Children*) made loadedly selective use of incomplete statistics collected by researchers at Oxford Polytechnic to link the easy access to what were described as ultra-violent and horrific videos (the 'video nasties') with rising statistics for crimes of violence. Like the final report (edited in 1985 by Geoffrey Barlow and Alison Hill under the same title) Dr Hill's interim report effectively demanded reform of the Obscene Publications Act in Britain as a means of prosecuting the makers and distributors of violent films more successfully. The researchers at Oxford Polytechnic were understandably angered and embarrassed by the use made of their figures (particularly in relation to a small sample of 6-year-old children), but the popular press was intensely interested.[1]

The figures, after all, appeared to confirm a long and steady stream of claims to the effect that, as the *Daily Mail* of 30 June 1983 put it, a 'rape of our children's minds' was being conducted by these 'soul-soilers that deaden decency and encourage depravity'. The 'soul-soilers' of the 1980s, of course, were the 'video nasties', but very similar popular accusations had been levelled against 'TV violence' in the 1960s and 1970s, against 'horror comics' in the 1950s, and against the depiction of violence in movies and talkies in the decades preceding that. And it is not just 'scientific evidence' which tends to get cited whenever it can be made to reinforce claims of this type. The news of the world provides another source, so that sections of the press frequently report acts of violence in a manner which suggests that such acts are self-evident illustrations of the ('common-sense') veracity of the claims they make in the course of their explanation of the way we live now. On 7 July 1983, for instance, the *Daily Mail* carried a story headlined 'Cruel movies fan hacks four to death', in which an escaped prisoner in California was reported as having murdered four people 'after watching violent video films'. According to the writer, this was a case to be taken as a warning which 'underlines the importance of the *Daily Mail*'s campaign for urgent government control on video nasties in this country'. Six days later (i.e. on 13 July 1983, when the *Mail*'s campaign was still in full swing), the same paper carried a front-page story in which it recounted how 'Kenneth Smart, 23, murdered his best friend after seeing horror films in which his peculiar sexual fantasies were acted out'. The horrific street massacres which occurred within weeks of each other in Australia and Britain in 1987, when two separate gunmen went on shooting sprees in Melbourne and Hungerford, gave rise to similar reporting and to popular generalizations about the impact of the type of film-fare and screen heroes which had allegedly inspired these 'Rambo killers'.

Tudor has also noted how, from the first spread of the cinema, public discussion as well as academic studies of this medium were dominated by questions about effects. As was the case at other historical points and in relation to other media, the major focus of attention here was the growing child who was at that period 'rapidly substituting the cinema for more traditional sources of socialisation' (Tudor 1974: 92). Thus, between 1929 and 1932, the Payne Fund financed a series of ambitious researches on the effects of motion pictures upon youth in the United States, and to this was applied the newly respectable weaponry of experimental, statistical, and survey analysis – tools which have since then remained the hallmarks of most research into effects. The results of the Payne studies were published by W. W. Charters (the research chairman) in 1935 as *Motion Pictures and Youth*, and their popularization (which spoke of 'our movie-made children') appeared to confirm the worst expectations of worried parents – much in the manner, in fact, of later popularizations of research on the effects of newer media like comics, television, and videos.

A number of writers in this field have argued that the tendency to denounce the mass media for their allegedly awesome power and bad effects derives from a culture complex which perpetuates a legacy of fear. DeFleur and Dennis (1985: 293), for instance, note how the growth of mass communications, like other social changes, stimulated anxiety in most industrialized societies – an anxiety which received much publicity as the media themselves published and gave prominence to the charges against first the penny press, then movies, and then radio and television (DeFleur and Dennis 1985: 293). Other critics (e.g. Rowland 1983: 22) have noted how, in industrialized countries, concern over the social impact of the media of mass communication appears to have become confused in the public mind with worries of an economic nature. The fact that the influence of the media became a serious and hotly contested public issue after the First World War can thus be argued to suggest the extent of (possibly unacknowledged) public concern over economically related social problems at the period when film and radio started spreading rapidly. Because they were more universally accessible than earlier means of communication, and because they could be generally seen to be having an impact on national and economic matters, these media soon came to be associated in the public mind with a complex array of cultural and political dislocations which were disturbingly difficult to analyse and come to terms with. The anxieties aroused by these dislocations, as well as the simplistic popular associations made in their regard, were also reinforced by claims made by various professionals and social scientists in their frequently uneven attempts to account for the ailments of society. Pearson cites many examples of this type of claim – including an assertion made by a psychiatrist in 1938 that 'seventy per cent of all crimes were first conceived in the cinema', and a magistrate's declaration in the same year that 'these lads go to the pictures and see dare-devil things, and they are imitating them' (Pearson 1984: 93–4).

Claims and associations of this nature have not, of course, been exclusively inspired by moral panics confined to any one period of social concern, nor have they been applied uniquely to any one medium of communication. Four decades after the psychiatrist and magistrate just cited made their assertions about the cinema, members of the medical profession were making almost identical accusations against television. In his speech before the House Subcommittee on Communications (Los Angeles, 17 August 1976), Dr Thomas Elmendorf declared that

> For a considerable proportion of American children and youth, the 'culture of violence' is now both a major health threat and a way of life.
> We of the medical profession believe that one of the factors behind this violence is televised violence. Television has become a school of violence and a college for crime.
>
> (in Rodman 1984: 67)

There is, in fact, 'a tired historical lineage of doom-laden pessimism' (Pearson's phrase) behind complaints of this nature. Thus, a social psychology textbook published in France in 1898 (written by Gabriel Tarde and entitled *Etudes de psychologie sociale*) noted how there had been a growth in the popularity of newspapers in France between the 1860s and the 1890s, and declared that the emphasis on reports of crime during that period had stimulated a sharp rise in juvenile delinquency, as well as encouraging immorality, crime, and alcoholism among adults (cited in DeFleur and Dennis 1985: 294). As early as 1751, Henry Fielding's *Enquiry into the Cause of the Late Increase of Robbers* had identified 'too frequent and expensive Diversions among the lower kind of People' as one cause which 'hath almost totally changed the Manners, Customs and Habits of the People, more especially of the lower Sort' (cited in Pearson 1984: 97). As Pearson puts it, the complaints about 'video violence' which became fashionable in the 1980s form part of

> a long and connected history of fearful complaint and controversy on these matters, stretching back in a direct line for more than a century and a half. A history, moreover, in which each succeeding generation has understood itself to be standing on the brink of some

radical discontinuity with the past, and in which the rising generation has been repeatedly seen as the harbinger of a dreadful future.
(Pearson 1984: 102)

Popularized experimental investigations have on many occasions
reinforced and given respectability to 'common-sense' fearful complaints about horrific influences, and thus to the assumptions on
which such complaints are based. In providing this type of reinforcement and by supplying ammunition for censorship campaigners, such
investigations have also become (conservative) agents of reassurance,
in the sense that they are seen to provide 'scientific' confirmation to
established and popularly entrenched ways of seeing and reasoning.
It will perhaps be worth our while here to look closely at the
conceptual frameworks underpinning the 'scientific evidence'
allegedly supplied by such investigations. This contextualization will
be used as a basis from which to consider some examples of studies
claiming to prove and explain cause-and-effect processes of media
influence. Since such studies appear to share a number of assumptions with popular reactions to the fictional and horrific representation of violence, we shall need to consider the implications of this
community more closely.

BEHAVIOURISM AND THE 'DISPASSIONATE OBSERVATION' OF EFFECTS

The most consistent and influential exposition of the contention that
behaviour is determined almost exclusively by environmental influences has in our century come from adherents of behaviourist and
neo-behaviourist theory. At the root of this theory lies Locke's image
of the *tabula rasa*, which visualizes the new-born as a blank slate on
which the finger of experience progressively writes its shaping contribution. It is thus among behaviourists that the theory of innate
aggressiveness (or of innate anything, for that matter) has been most
forcefully and passionately rejected.

Because of the predominant influence of dogmatic behaviourism on
the development of scientific psychology as an academic discipline,
most of the efforts of experimental social psychologists to analyse the
influence of the mass media were for a long time structured according
to an essentially behaviourist understanding of what constitutes
scientific observation. Studies based on this understanding were seen

as forming part of a venture which would provide what one of behaviourism's chief exponents termed 'an account of the essential features of culture within the framework of a natural science' (Skinner 1953: 419). This enterprise started from the premise that scientific psychology was an infant discipline which would only reach maturity if it followed the methods and applied the rhetoric of the physical sciences. In its classical form, therefore, behaviourism sets about its professed business of 'dispassionate observation' by excluding from its consideration any facets of behaviour which, in Skinner's terms, 'lack the dimensions of physical science' (ibid.: 31). These 'dimensions' are in their turn gauged by the extent to which the facets of behaviour in question can be measured, tested for statistical regularities, predicted, and measured again. An important moulding influence on this model was J. B. Watson's proclamation that psychology must concern itself only with 'stimulus and response', and that it 'must discard all reference to consciousness' in order to become 'a purely objective, experimental branch of natural science' (Watson 1913: 158). In similar tones and working from similar assumptions, Skinner has asserted that all phenomena associated with human consciousness (such as mind or ideas) are non-existing entities, 'invented to provide spurious explanations' (Skinner 1953: 30). In these terms, questions of motivation and intentions are bypassed (and frequently ignored) by classical behaviourists.

Much has been written (and many battles fought and won) in reaction to these tenets, and some very powerful attacks have been levelled against behaviourism because of the myopic limitations it imposes on considerations of human and social issues. I should perhaps stress that my return to this intellectual battleground here is not intended as a simple attempt to shoot further artillery at defeated (though still active) combatants. My contention is that the influence of the behaviourist theoretical framework can still be traced in academic as well as popular ('common-sense') assumptions about media influence. The logic underlying approaches and studies influenced by behaviourism – and particularly where this influence has passed through the generally more humanly faced neo-behaviourist revisionism of social learning theory – has to be taken into serious account in any attempt to chart out the complex economy of discourses surrounding a phenomenon like contemporary horror fiction.

The behaviourist attempt to use the methods and rhetoric of the physical sciences as a model for the study of human behaviour has resulted in a tendency for psychologists reared in this conceptual framework to express themselves in a special jargon which makes their learned papers read rather like publications in physics. Rom Harré has described the tendency as an affectation involving a ritual of public display not unlike that manifested in the wearing of different types of costumes to suit specific occasions and in order to project desired images of oneself. This convention, Harré points out, is 'a harmless enough affectation if recognized as an aspect of personal display', but it becomes seriously misleading if the rhetoric is taken at face value, since it suggests that the cognitive processes by which men control their actions are really the workings of causal mechanisms. This, Harré insists, 'is wholly to mislocate these processes, concealing the fact that social action and the ways it is decided on are part of the moral order' (Harré 1981: 224).

The convention, in effect, constitutes another version of the dramatizing tendency which chapter 4 of this book asserted to underlie the orientations, contributions, and insights of the psychoanalytic model. What the behavioural psychologist dramatizes is not so much the nature of the account which he is retelling, but his own role as the dispassionate and reliably objective observer and narrator. For this role to be convincing, it is necessary for both narrator and audience to work from a common ground of presuppositions, the most basic of which is that of accepting that such a role is scientifically possible and valid. To use a literary analogy, they need to accept the narrative's setting as providing its own terms of reference. It is the (at least temporary) acceptance of these terms as absolute which makes for enough suspension of disbelief to allow the narrative to become self-contained and self-referring, and thus to remain unaffected by issues which have been left out of its specified province of concern. The process and paradigms involved are not unlike those underlying the genre conventions which, as was argued in part I of this book, allow horror fiction to function on a magical level. It is this preliminary and tacit process of dramatic negotiation which makes it possible for the behaviourist to assume the stance of the dispassionate observer who can (reassuringly) redescribe human experience and behaviour in mathematically predictable and controllable ways.

There are two risks run by researchers who work within the boundaries of this conceptual framework. The first is that of confusing accuracy in the mathematical calculations which they have adopted with strength of empirical verification in the field of study to which the mathematical method is being applied. The second is that of forgetting the existence of the confines within which the method functions and assuming that the universe of scientific enquiry ends at the conceptual borders of its chosen realm of investigation. Breaking out of the boundaries imposed by the model should imply recognizing behaviourism as constituting (like psychoanalysis) what Ricoeur calls 'fictional redescription' (Ricoeur 1978: 6). It is an account and a model which, as with the functioning of metaphor in the arts, works as a speculative instrument and brings about (in Max Black's terms) 'a wedding of disparate subjects, by a distinctive operation of transfer of the *implications* of relatively well-organised cognitive fields' (Black 1962: 237). The proponents of such models cannot be described as merely offering formulas and theories in fancy dress, or as comparing two domains from a position neutral to both. Rather, they use language appropriate to the model in thinking about the domain of application. They work 'not *by* analogy, but *through* and by means of an underlying analogy' (ibid.: 229). It is therefore important for us to identify clearly what that analogy involves, and to understand the nature of the assumptions and presuppositions which make it possible, if we are to evaluate the scientific standing of the studies, claims, and conclusions which are based on it. This, in effect, means asking whether the use of specific analogical models helps us see new connections, or whether it does little more than compound popular misunderstanding and the confusion of values by simply dressing them up in scientistic jargon. On these terms, if we are to adequately assess the validity and implications of the man–machine analogy as it has been applied to the study of horrific influences, we shall first need to look more closely at how and why a set of terms and concepts originally developed to describe mechanical (and man-made) devices came to be considered appropriate for the study, control, and explanation of human behaviour.

Though behaviourism and psychoanalysis appear to be radically opposed in the models they project to explain human behaviour and action, they do share a number of important assumptions about the roots of human nature. This community of assumptions is also partly responsible for the fact that, as I suggested above, images and arguments deriving from these contradictory perspectives have merged so readily in the popular consciousness (where academic refinements and abstracted nuances are ignored, and where it is crude presuppositions which tend to be used in the process of giving meaning to experience). Behaviourist and neo-behaviourist theoretical perspectives do not negate or even ignore the existence of an animal component to human nature. It is the interpretation of what it means to be animal that differentiates this conceptual framework so radically from psychodynamic and socio-biological perspectives. The immediate sources of the behaviourist theory of psychology, in fact, were studies in animal psychology, particularly as developed in the conceptual framework of E. L. Thorndike's 'law of effect'. Rejecting the tendency of researchers into animal behaviour of his period to depend on anthropomorphic explanations (involving the hypothesis that animals can 'think' or recall previous situations), Thorndike set out to explore the possibility of a more purely mechanical explanation of animal adaptability. The approach, then, was initially intended as a corrective to the simplifications which had become prevalent among Darwinians anxious to 'upgrade' the lower animals in the interests of their theory. But the simplicity and mechanical uniformity of the 'law of effect' – i.e. that animals learn responses which lead to rewarding consequences, and drop those which do not[2] – also suggested a method of systematizing the study of human behaviour in mathematically predictable terms. John Watson's theoretical formulation of the creed of behaviourism thus rejected the study of consciousness (which had introspection as its method of investigation) partly on the grounds that such an approach excludes any possibility of conducting accurate studies of animals, infants, and mentally disturbed people. The observation and measurement of responses to stimuli, and of how such responses can be modified (conditioned) and reinforced, on the other hand, could be applied to any living organism. By conceptualizing all living organisms as machines in a universe governed exclusively by mechanical and physiological laws, this application of the theory of conditioned reflexes reduced the study of human behaviour to proportions which (according to Watson's formulation) could be observed, were repeatable by others, and yielded data that could be recorded by instruments. But the model of behaviour underlying this approach remains fundamentally that of evolutionary natural selection. Thus, in the course of attempting to answer the question 'Why is a reinforcer reinforcing?', Skinner has argued that 'the connection between reinforcement and satiation must be sought in the process of evolution' since 'we can scarcely overlook the significance of the primary reinforcers', and 'an individual who is readily reinforced by such events [as are obviously connected with the well-being of the organism] will acquire highly efficient behaviour' (Skinner 1953: 83).

According to Eysenck and Nias, 'we are part animal, part socialised human being, and the process of socialisation itself is in part based on conditioning paradigms testifying to our animal origin' (Eysenck and Nias 1980: 54). These 'conditioning paradigms' are in their turn interpreted in different ways by different researchers, but in broad terms the mechanistic view which is in operation here constitutes a speculative instrument which marries the tenets of evolutionary natural selection to the Cartesian concept of nature as a machine which can be explained (and thus controlled) in terms of the arrangement and movement of its parts.[3] The 'beast within', in this version, is thus understood to be mechanically operated. In applying this conceptual framework to the question of 'mass-media violence', Eysenck and Nias assert that 'the media produce their effects on human conduct through the use of conditioning mechanisms', so that 'the usual habit of many writers in this field of treating the media in strictly rational terms . . . is strictly inadmissible' (ibid.: 46). Emotional reactions, Eysenck and Nias explain, are unlike 'the voluntary activities of man' (which are 'controlled by the neocortex') because they are 'mediated by a semi-separate nervous system, the autonomic system' (ibid.: 45). These Jekyll–Hyde polarities are thus appropriated and modified to fit a conceptual model which emphasizes conditioning and reinforcement, both in explanations of how modes of behaviour develop and also of how they can be changed. Eysenck and Nias thus insist that 'not sweet reasoning, but proper methods of conditioning have any chance of changing our conduct' (ibid.: 46). This, in their view, is because 'both sexual activity, and aggression and violence, are deeply rooted in the more primitive system of the paleocortex, and become attached to certain objects or situations through processes which may defy thought and cognitive control' (ibid.: 45).

The values which underscore this conceptual framework are also worth underlining. This, as one of Skinner's later titles (1973) has it, is a conceptual realm 'beyond freedom and dignity' – and hence beyond accountability. If an abstractly conceived and impersonal 'conditioning environment' determines the course of our behaviour, and extinction or survival are exclusively dependent on mechanical responses to stimuli and on a capacity to be reinforced, then we are not only helpless, but reassuringly beyond real responsibility. This is a particularly critical case where 'sexual activity, and aggression and violence' are in question, since Eysenck and Nias's argument suggests that we have little control (exposed to a predetermined and conditioning environment as we are) over which 'objects or situations' these proclivities will 'become attached to'. It is in its resolution of this potentially worrying state of affairs that the behaviourist account begins to lean most heavily towards a magical type of thinking. The explanatory role once performed by concepts and abstractions like 'chance', 'fate', 'destiny', 'the divine will', 'heavenly bodies', and 'the stars' has here been passed on to a suitably mathematized and 'scientifically' perceived conditioning environment. It is this environment, the behaviourist insists, which can and should be controlled and changed so as to make for the conditioning of more desirable modes of behaviour. When behaviourists speak of changing the environment, however, it is a very local environment which tends to be envisaged, since within the confines of their account the norm of objectivity is inevitably determined by the status quo. The process of socialization thus here becomes synonymous with learning to respond according to the requirements of that norm, and, when things go wrong, what the behaviourist perspective offers are suggestions about the reconditioning of those who have deviated from that norm: the appropriateness and moral justness of the norm itself remain unquestioned. In the last resort, then, the behaviourist perspective creates a climate of (popular and educated) opinion which feels both reassured about the ultimate rightness of the status quo and also comfortable that there are scientific methods of accounting for and correcting any undesirable deviations from the norm dictated by that rightness.

I am not taking issue with specific and local applications of all this. If one's aim is that of 'rectifying' deviancy, then conditioning and behaviour modification techniques do, of course, work and they have been effectively applied to a number of therapeutic purposes. But on a wider (socially and politically viable) scale, the tools which the behaviourist offers for the interpretation and control of experience depend for their efficacy on an understanding of the environment which only makes sense within the terms of reference which created this understanding in the first place. One of the central presuppositions behind these terms is the view of nature as a purely mechanistic process of evolutionary natural selection. Like the functioning of shock–horror effects discussed in the first part of this book, this account is only convincing within the confines of its own self-generated and self-referring cocoon of language and logic. Its standing as a purely objective branch of natural science ultimately depends on the creation and acceptance of an elaborate system of representation, even though, ironically, symbolic activities are excluded from its province of 'scientific' study. To return to the literary analogy suggested above, not only has the dramatization of human experience proposed by this narrator dressed as learned scientist failed to deepen our understanding of that experience, it has also become an agent abetting the confusion of values. At the root of the confusion lie the narrator's belief in the costume as an absolute, his refusal to consider the implications of the fact that his stance and explanations have an important symbolic dimension, and his inability to recognize the fact that as an influential (meaning making and interpreting) agent he is also helping to modify the nature of the human reality which he claims to observe dispassionately.

The next section considers how many of these unrecognized assumptions and loaded dramatic stances continue to underlie those modificatons of behaviourist theory which have more recently been applied to the investigation of horrific influences.

SOCIAL LEARNING THEORY AND SOCIAL NORMS

Adherents of the neo-behaviourist theory of social learning insist that the emphasis placed in other schools of thought on an aggressive instinct as the root of violent behaviour is not only misplaced and misleading, but also socially disruptive. For the same reasons they also refute the view of aggression as a reactive process. One of the most influential expositions of this latter view was the 'frustration–aggression hypothesis', which (as framed into a theory by Dollard *et al.* in 1939) stated that aggression is always a consequence of frustration and, conversely, that the existence of frustration always leads to some form of aggression. On the evidence of research findings like those of Bandura and Walters (1959) on the influence of child-training practices and family interrelationships in the development of aggression, the frustration–aggression hypothesis has been dismissed as a 'fragile' explanation which is 'less often advanced in serious studies of aggression than it is in popular and ideological writings' (Selg 1975: 36). The popularity of this hypothesis has been attributed by social learning theorists to the fact that it 'allows every one of us to play the amateur psychologist' (ibid.). The implications raised by the stance of exclusive expert assumed in this dismissal will be discussed shortly. What I wish to stress first is the fact that the views that aggression is either instinctive or reactive are both denounced by social learning theorists as unscientific excuses which actually foster and reinforce the existence and growth of aggression itself. Aggressive behaviour, the neo-behaviourist claim goes, is an effect of adverse conditioning within the process of socialization. Among the forces which are asserted to influence this process is the entertainment industry, which is said to associate the depiction of anti-social modes of behaviour with rewarding and attitude-reinforcing states of being, and hence to condition people into considering such behaviour as desirable and worthy of imitation.

Unlike classical behaviourism, then, social learning theory concedes that 'a theory of human behavior . . . cannot afford to neglect symbolic activities' since 'the capacity to use symbols provides humans with a powerful means of dealing with their environment' and 'the capability for intentional action is rooted in symbolic activity' (Bandura 1977: 13). This is all very commendable, but, when one looks more closely at the theory and its experimental applications, one finds that the references to 'intentional action' and 'symbolic activity' amount to little more than pious gestures in a basically mechanistically oriented model. The theory works from a perspective which assumes what is presumably meant to be a syncretic (or at least conciliatory) standpoint:

> In the social learning view, people are neither drive by inner forces nor buffeted by environmental stimuli. Rather, psychological functioning is explained in terms of a continuous reciprocal interaction of personal and environmental determinants. Within this approach, symbolic, vicarious, and self-regulatory processes assume a prominent role.
>
> (ibid.: 11–12)

The key term here is 'interaction' – a concept which (as it is used in this context) abstracts the interweaving complexities of biological, psychological, social, and cultural processes into 'a process of reciprocal determinism'. Within this abstracted process, 'behavior, other personal factors, and environmental factors all operate as interlocking determinants of each other', so that the 'relative influences' which they exert 'differ in various settings and for different behaviors' (ibid.: 9–10). There is an almost clockwork neatness about all this which is somehow too pat.

124

Social learning perspectives frequently tend to abstract concepts like 'socialization', 'aggression', and 'interaction' in a manner which makes their application to practical situations both methodologically limited and conceptually confused. To imply that serious studies of the causes and consequences of aggression function on a level which is untouched by popular and ideological ideas (Selg 1975: 36) is not only to assume the impossible (i.e. that studies of human and social behaviour and interaction can be conducted in a culture-free vacuum) but also to set up an absurdly limiting set of parameters within which these 'serious studies' can function. If the 'process of socialization' is taken to signify no more than 'learning the ways and becoming a functioning member of society', and 'interaction' is neatly taken to designate 'a process of reciprocal determinism', then to speak of 'conditioning' within these 'processes' is to say very little indeed. Such an account, in fact, can only begin to have applicability outside the confines of its limited and abstracted terms of reference when the forms of the society which determine any particular socialization and which allocate the functions of control and communication have been precisely specified. In this connection, Raymond Williams has noted that what is given theoretical priority in studies based on this perspective is what the 'process of socialisation' has in common in many different societies. Such an emphasis is misleading because what in practice defines the real process are precisely the cultural specifics of any named society – the radical differences of 'ways' and 'functioning', and the highly differential character of being a 'member' of the society. 'The abstract notions of "socialisation" and "social function"', Williams points out, 'have the effect of conferring normality and in this sense legitimacy on any society in which a learning and relating process may occur' (Williams 1974: 120). When this is so (and in spite of pious gestures like those of Bandura), it becomes impossible to recognize intention in any full sense, let alone study it.

Bandura's assertion that, in the social learning view, 'symbolic, vicarious, and self-regulatory processes assume a prominent role' (Bandura 1977: 11–12) in real terms amounts to little more than saying that the concept of the conditioned reflex needs to be extended to incorporate these 'processes', which in their turn will need to be abstracted and systematized in order to fit the mould of the cognitive model into which they are to be assimilated. In other words, far from challenging the presuppositions which the preceding section

125

identified as informing the tenets of classical behaviourism, the social learning perspective tacitly embraces them. In the social learning view too, emotions become 'attached' to 'objects and situations' through 'a process of conditioning' – with the qualification that the 'attachment' of these surfaces is now asserted to be mediated by the 'interacting' properties of other quantifiable 'processes' ('symbolic', 'vicarious', 'self-regulatory').

Working within the parameters outlined above, social learning theorists have made a number of very influential assertions about the nature of (abstracted) society and about how individuals progress through the (generalized) socialization process. These assertions have been backed by an impressive number of experimental investigations of a wide range of social issues. Quite prominent among such investigations have been studies which focus on the effects that 'mass-media violence' is claimed to have on the attitudes and behaviour of individuals who are 'exposed' to it, as well as on the society in which such fare becomes a widespread mode of entertainment. It is to an analysis of representative examples of such investigations that we now turn.

It bears stressing that the discussion which follows is not intended as a uniform (and simplistic) rejection of all claims made by experimental psychologists working within the social learning perspective. Indeed, even the less challenging of these claims are often so self-evidently correct that they amount to little more than truisms dressed up in scientistic jargon. Nor do I wish to give the impression that I am simply and anachronistically attacking a straw man by picking on outdated and superseded approaches – when a number of more recent investigations (as I in fact argue on pp. 144–5) have taken account of and overcome these limitations. The discussion, rather, examines these experimental studies as dramatized narratives, with the aim of underlining the functions they perform as dramatic agents of reassurance. The focus is on the methodological limitations of studies which (precisely because they bear striking similarities to popular preconceptions about horrific influences) have been widely popularized and quoted to back 'common-sense' claims. In other words, having outlined the assumptions underlying the conceptual framework within which these claims and studies work, I propose to place them back in their cultural context by considering them from outside the confines within which they function. This (to adapt Harré's analogy) will involve looking more closely at the pattern, cut, and material of the costume of learned scientist which frequently provides spurious respectability to a number of popular preconceptions and moral panics about the effects of 'mass-media violence'.

STUDIES IDENTIFYING 'MEDIA VIOLENCE' AS AN INSTIGATOR OF AGGRESSIVE BEHAVIOUR

According to the American Department of Human Services, most researchers are agreed that 'the evidence accumulated in the 1970s seems overwhelming that televised violence and aggression are positively correlated in children'. Cataloguing suggestions from over thirty reports on major research projects on the effects of TV violence conducted during the preceding decade, the National Institute of Mental Health (NIMH) report identified four 'processes' which have been claimed to produce this relation: 'observational learning, attitude change, physiological arousal, and justification processes' (NIMH 1982: 38–40, 42–3). A similarly extensive list of research projects is quoted in the seventh edition of Hilgard *et al.'s Introduction to Psychology*, which insists that 'the majority of studies lead to the conclusion that viewing violence does increase interpersonal aggression, particularly in young children' (Hilgard *et al.* 1979: 327). Hilgard *et al.* also tabulate five ways in which 'exposure to filmed violence can elicit aggressive behaviour': 'teaching aggressive styles of conduct', 'increasing arousal', 'desensitising people to violence', 'reducing restraints on aggressive behavior', and 'distorting views about conflict resolution' (ibid.: 327–9). The theoretical foundation for the overlapping suggestions making up these categories is neo-behaviourist in orientation: all of them place their major emphasis on the key role played by the learning process, and most come with reports of empirical experiments whose findings are claimed to vindicate their suggestions (or else discredit those of others).

In this context, some curiously thought-out experiments have been conducted and systematized in the rarefied air of the laboratory in order to substantiate the 'scientific' or 'objective' basis for what amounts to sociological speculation, or else to elaborate or test a number of truisms. To take the most frequently cited example, the 'observational learning' variation of learning theory contends that children learn to behave aggressively from the violence they see on television in the same way that they learn cognitive and social skills from watching their parents, siblings, peers, teachers, and others. This contention in turn rests on the claim that rigidly controlled experiments in the laboratory have made it possible to predict that children who watch adults or peers behaving aggressively will behave aggressively in their turn when they find themselves in similar situations. The pioneering work here was mostly conducted by Albert Bandura and his associates in the late 1950s and early 1960s. Many of the experiments initiated by Bandura (e.g. 1965) involved various groups of children watching a 'model' (live or on film) furiously knocking a large inflated doll (the 'Bobo doll') in a manner which was claimed to have 'created a permissive atmosphere in which the child could not only learn novel forms of aggression but also perform them' (Belschner 1975: 90). By extension, it has been argued that 'in carrying extensive reports of horrible crimes, the mass media are not so much meeting an old need as creating a new one', in that 'by making us familiar with a host of vicious acts, they blunt our sensibilities and sense of compassion' (Selg 1975: 174).

It is worth noting that this understanding of 'sensibilities' and of the manners in which they can be 'blunted' parallels the more widely publicized claims of moral crusaders like Mary Whitehouse, as well as the criticism by scholars like David Holbrook of the 'cultural pollution' which is claimed to form part of the way we live now. But, as was pointed out by the Williams report on obscenity and film censorship (1981), it comes close to begging the question to offer as proof for claims with very wide social and moral implications the investigation of 'violence' towards a fantasy or surrogate object such as a doll. Similar objections have been raised by Brody (1977) and by Howitt and Cumberbatch (1975), who insist that it is quite unwarranted to extrapolate to social behaviour the way in which a child plays with dolls which are designed to invite knocking about. Bandura's studies involved presenting children with fairly novel kinds of toys: according to Howitt and Cumberbatch, if the children have prior experience of Bobo dolls, the amount of imitative behaviour is reduced. Further, if such behaviour was (as was claimed) adequate as a predictor of real-life aggression, the children classified as more aggressive might have been expected to attack the doll more readily than others. This was not the case in the studies reported by Bandura, and that fact would seem to point away from the conclusion that the findings may be generalized to real life.

As criticisms of methodology these arguments work within the same terms of reference as those which were used in the construction of the studies themselves. But it is also worth remembering that the studies and their attendant claims constitute exercises in the construction of meaning – they are redescriptions of (social and personal) reality developed in the course of attempting to make sense of that reality. On this level they have cultural and conceptual implications which deserve serious consideration, since, through their ability to compound or else modify (academic and popular) ways of seeing, they are inevitably assuming either the role of conservative guardians of preconceptions, or else that of agents of social change. The linguistic (and conceptual) trait of ascribing a very generalized and abstracted value to words like 'aggression' and 'violence' (as reflected in the Bobo doll redescription) thus has a number of social implications. These implications need to be placed in proper perspective, but before this can be done we need to look at some further examples of this type of study in order to trace more clearly the contours of their guiding metaphors and internal (linguistic) logic.

A series of studies which explicitly amalgamate the assumptions underlying emphases on instinctive aggression with the mechanistic orientations of behaviourism are those which work from a 'disinhibition' theoretical perspective. One of the major exponents of this view is Leonard Berkowitz, who has argued that the 'effects of viewing violence' are not determined by a simple process of imitation but rather by one involving the weakening of inhibitions and restraints which normally prevent the expression of already existing responses. In one experiment (Berkowitz and Green 1966), eighty-eight male students at the University of Wisconsin were 'angered' by an accomplice of the experimenters who, in judging their ability at a 'creativity'-type task, decided to give them a large number of shocks for a poor performance. When the students' and the accomplice's roles were reversed, it was reported that, among the subjects who received seven shocks, those who had just seen what was designated as a 'violent film' administered more shocks to the accomplice than did those who saw a 'neutral film'. The 'violent film' in question was a seven-minute boxing scene from the Kirk Douglas movie *The Champion*, while the 'neutral film' took the form of the Bannister–Landy sports track duel from the Commonwealth Games in one instance, and of documentaries about canal boats in England or about the travels of Marco Polo in others. Berkowitz insists that his experiments make it clear that 'an aggressive film can induce aggressive actions by anyone in the audience' (Berkowitz 1964: 187). He acknowledges that in most instances this effect will be short-lived and that 'the emotional reaction produced by filmed violence probably dies away rapidly as the viewer enters new situations and encounters new stimuli'. But it is precisely on the generalization of this temporary and allegedly momentous 'effect' that Berkowitz bases his contention that there is a 'major social danger inherent in filmed violence', and that 'the motion picture aggression has increased the chance that an angry person, and possibly other people as well, will attack someone else' (ibid.: 188–9). Here again there are serious methodological problems raised by the structure of the type of tests on which these claims are based. As with the Bandura studies, a number of critics have pointed to the limitations of an argument which applies to generalized social situations, or to theories about social–psychological patterns of behaviour, the 'findings' interpreted from inevitably artificial laboratory experiments of the kind which usually used college students as their subjects. The claims are large, but the evidence (particularly when it is stripped of its scientistic costume) is disappointingly weak-kneed. Let us consider the costume.

One serious flaw of the Berkowitz studies derives from a tendency it shares with many other experimental investigations of the effect of televised or filmed violence on viewers' propensities towards aggression – that of designating films as 'violent' or 'neutral' (whatever that may mean) in an abstract and arbitrary fashion. It has, in fact, been shown that most laymen would not label behaviour studied in these types of laboratory experiments as violent at all.[4] It is thus misleading to take the depiction of violent incidents in films or programmes at a common face value, since different people will perceive violent portrayals in different ways, and often according to the context in which they view them. The mode of perception will also, of course, inevitably influence what attitudes viewers will assume towards what they see, and hence how their behaviour may or may not be modified as a consequence of the viewing experience. The mode of perception varies according to determinants which include social norms and cultural expectations, personal values and current moods, and the context and tone of presentation, as well as the physical form of the violence itself. The abstracted use of terms like 'violence' and 'aggression', in other words, betrays the fact that, though these studies make very large claims about the nature of social functioning, they rarely take account of specific social realities. The whole pattern of reasoning, in fact, seems to be geared towards reducing behaviour and motivation to terms which are uniform and uncomplicated enough to allow for the setting up of statistical regularities that can give the reassuring impression that convincing explanations have been supplied, and that the generalization of concepts related to modes of social functioning has been vindicated. Acceptance of the vindication also involves accepting the premise on which it is based – that it is scientifically valid to explain human behaviour and social functioning in exclusively mechanistic terms since they are nothing but complex machines anyway. These are explanations, in other words, which lean towards a circuitous and magical pattern of reasoning. It is partly the familiarity and accessibility of this type of reasoning which help to make these studies so appealing to the popular imagination and which betray a tendency among this school of psychologists to follow (in Liam Hudson's phrase) 'any path that relieves the pain of thought' (Hudson 1975: 27). These accusations can be levelled even more forcefully at a variation of these types of studies which sets out to prove that it is 'physiological arousal' which acts as a bridge between media violence and aggressive behaviour.

In order to counteract the Freudian assumption (at the basis of most versions of the catharsis theory) that it is a state of constant repose which is strained for by all living organisms, it has been deemed necessary to provide statistical evidence to the effect that 'exposure' to filmed (or televised) violence in fact has a physiologically arousing effect. Thus, a number of psycho-physiological experiments have been conducted in which various emotional reactions were first 'induced' and then studied together with the accompanying physiological phenomena. Osborn and Endsley (1971), for instance, measured the changes in the electrical conductivity of the skin (the galvanic skin response, or GSR in jargon) of 4- and 5-year-old children who were made to watch 'violent' and 'non-violent' TV programmes. The measurements showed a significant increase in the GSR when 'violent' films were being watched, and this was taken to prove that children become much more emotionally aroused when they watch 'violent' than when they watch 'non-violent' programmes. Speisman et al. (1964) similarly detected increased heart rate and GSR in adults watching filmed scenes of violence; while Froeberg et al. recorded increases in the urinary excretion of adrenalin and noradrenalin under similar conditions. Some of the reasoning behind these experiments and the speculations to which they have been applied suggest incredibly straight-faced levels of banality – a characteristic which the experimenters fail to recognize because they have been carried away by the linguistic magic of the analogical model which they have adopted and which has come to determine their mode of reasoning. In Froeberg *et al.*'s experiments, for instance, 'twenty young female office clerks, acting as their own controls, were presented with a different film of 1½ hours' duration on each of several consecutive evenings' (Froeberg *et al.* 1971: 291). On the first evening they were shown 'bland natural-scenery films, produced by the Swedish National Railway Company'. The second programme consisted of 'Stanley Kubrick's tragic and agitating *Paths of Glory*'; while 'on the third evening, the stimulus was of a clearly *pleasant* character, a charming, comic film, *Charley's Aunt*, directed by Hans Quest'. Froeberg *et al.* report that, both during the second evening (when, in the questionnaires returned, 'the subjects reported feelings of anger and excitement') and during the third (when 'there was considerable laughter, and the subjects reported being very amused'), there was a significant rise in the urinary excretion of adrenalin and noradrenalin as tested in the subjects before, during, and after they viewed the films. This was taken to be 'a reflection . . . of the intensity, and not the quality, of affective arousal'. All this, in other words, is admitted to add very little to our understanding of how and why 'exposure' to violent and disturbing material differs from 'exposure' to other 'affectively arousing' fare (like comedy, adventure, or tear-jerking romance). This triteness of substance, however, is covered under heavy layers of scientific-sounding jargon. Here are Froeberg *et al.* describing how the 'feelings of calmness and equanimity' reported by the office clerks on the first evening were

> reflected on a biochemical level by a significant *lowering* of the catecholamine excretion during the film period, as compared with the control periods before and after . . . thus supporting the hypothesis of an interrelation between general emotional arousal and sympatho-adrenomedullary activity.

(ibid.)

On the basis of evidence from experiments of this nature, it has been possible for some researchers to argue that it is a 'stimulation hunger', or an urge for an 'adrenalin high' which forms the link between the watching and the acting out of violent behaviour. Thus, according to Tannenbaum (1980), since boredom and depression (caused by lack of stimulation, or 'adrenalin lows') are unpleasant states, people seek an optimal level of arousal; watching aggressive behaviour is arousing, but, since continued watching leads to desensitization, persons who are desensitized may act aggressively to raise their levels of arousal. As the NIMH report puts it, 'once the desired level is reached, aggression will continue, because the behavior most likely to be continued is the behavior readily retrievable from memory' (NIMH 1982: 40). The argument looks seductively self-evident. Its major fault is that it conveniently ignores the fact that the evidence on which it is based is actually unable to distinguish between reactions to different types of viewing experiences (amusing, exciting, attractively or disturbingly violent, frightening, heart-rending, etc.). All material which is 'affectively arousing' (according to that evidence) encourages 'sympatho-adrenomedullary activity'. In this case (and if one follows these researchers' lead in ignoring cognitive activities), 'exposure' to any type of 'affectively arousing' material should lead to a spiral of confused quests in which any mode of behaviour capable of producing 'adrenalin highs' could be expected to follow. Thus, whether one watches violent or amusing films becomes immaterial, since both can (interchangeably) lead one to behave in violent, foolhardy, dangerous, silly, or any other way which happens to correlate with 'sympatho-adrenomedullary activity'. The mechanistic assumptions made by the argument are on these terms misguided and misleading in their method of applying observation of chemical and physical reactions to the explanation of individual and social activity.

There have also been many observational and field studies testing for cause and effect correlations and explanations of media influence. The more recent of these surveys (though not, usually, their popularizations) have been more qualified than laboratory studies in the claims they have made about effects, and the NIMH report significantly concedes that 'the "clean" outcomes of laboratory experiments are rarely to be found in field studies' (NIMH 1982: 38).[5] However, the orientations, assumptions, and implications remain largely unchanged. Thus, to take a few noted examples, a longitudinal study conducted by Lefkowitz et al. (1977) used data collected over a ten-year period to argue that an early preference for 'TV violence' is related to later aggressiveness and that 'observational learning' provides the most plausible explanation of this relation. Other field studies have produced data which have been interpreted as agreeing

133

with this explanation. Belson's London-based survey (1978), for instance, reported that the watching of most types of 'TV violence' was related to violent acts in that a large group of adolescent boys who were interviewed declared themselves to be more likely to engage in 'serious violence' after 'watching violence on television'. This did not seem to be the case, however, when the 'violence' occurred in cartoons, comedy, science fiction, and sport. The implications of this important qualification do not appear to have been analysed in any detail, so that little sustained consideration was given in these (as in the laboratory studies exemplified above) to the implications of (genre-mediated) perceptual processes – i.e. to the manners in which social behaviour is influenced by ways of seeing and interpreting.

It will be useful at this stage to look more closely at the presuppositions underlying the apparently arbitrary ascription of values to terms like 'violence' or 'aggression' in experimental studies of the type exemplified here. Very large claims about patterns of social behaviour have been made on the basis of studies of 'aggression' which, given the vagueness and generality of the definition, can be made to include activities like the stealing of an apple from a fruit stall by a hungry boy (Belschner 1975: 65 ff.), hitting a large inflated doll (as in the Bandura experiments), giving electric shocks (Berkowitz), or giving what are tautologically described as 'aggressive responses' in a word association test (as in Feshbach's 1961 experiments on 'the stimulating versus cathartic effects of a vicarious aggressive activity'). The meanings which the terms 'aggression' and 'violence' can be made to assume become even more diverse when one considers other theoretical and popular perspectives than those represented here. But the diversity derives from unfocused thinking, rather than from consideration of specific situational differences and actors' interpretations. The practical implications of the generalizing pattern to behaviourist and neo-behaviourist assumptions about what 'violence' and 'aggression' involve are perhaps most tellingly revealed in the way these terms are frequently taken to be synonymous with 'anti-social behaviour', i.e. behaviour which goes against accepted social norms. Most of them, in other words, start from the assumption that 'violence' or 'aggression' by definition contradict the norms of accepted social behaviour, or at least that 'aggressive behaviour' is socially unacceptable. But, as Williams has noted (Williams 1974: 122–3), most of these studies were conducted at a time and in societies where engagement in violent action of a certain kind had been sanctioned by the norms of society, in the sense that political decisions taken within normal procedures had authorized the undertaking and continuation of violent activity (some of it of exceptional scale and intensity). In the same contexts and for equally discoverable social reasons, other types of violent practices (like 'violent protests' and armed robbery within the societies) had been identified and condemned. Viewed from the perspective suggested by this contextualization, these studies' shared tendency to assume that 'violence' can be defined in a blanket and abstracted manner as 'a breach of the socialization process' becomes not only methodologically limited but also riddled with political implications. As Williams points out, in the actual societies where the studies were conducted, the real norm would seem rather to be: 'unauthorized violence is impermissible'. By using such unacknowledged norms as the basis of their definitions, studies of this type are in effect doing no more than following the pattern set by the behaviourist mode of thought which was identified in the preceding sections of this chapter. They tacitly accept the status quo and project it as an absolute. In this sense, they make themselves conservative guardians and reinforcers of the very structures and interactive processes which they claim to observe and explain dispassionately.

In the course of his attempt at defining the neo-behaviourist concept of 'aggression', Schott declares that 'there cannot, in fact, be a fully satisfactory definition while we continue to borrow the vague and equivocal word "aggression" from common speech' (Schott 1975: 157). According to this perspective, while 'common usage can suggest the possible scope of a definition . . . science alone can give it an adequate sharpness'. The statement reflects the extent to which, in its paradoxical quest for 'objectivity' and repeatable empirical validation, this type of enquiry misses the crucial role played by 'common usage' in our customary and educated methods of ascribing meaning to behaviour, action, and interaction. These are processes which are controlled by social norms, and such norms, as Habermas points out (Habermas 1970: 92), are of a consensual nature and enforced through sanctions. Their meaning is 'objectified in ordinary language communication', and their validity is 'grounded in the intersubjectivity of intentions'. Further, ordinary-language terms bring with them a great variety of implicit theories which become obscured or perverted (but not dissolved) when they are replaced by scientistic jargon. To state all this bluntly, researchers into media influence are as affected by the traditions of thought underlying linguistic usage and common-sense assumptions as anybody else. To blame the unsatisfactory and loosely defined nature of the neo-behaviourist concept of 'aggression' on the fact that it uses a term borrowed from common speech is to betray a conception of psychology which has lost contact with the world as we ordinarily experience it – a world, in other words, whose myths ultimately provide the foundations for the conceptual frameworks around which these studies (as well as 'common-sense' proclamations) have been built. The behaviourist and neo-behaviourist method in this sense constitutes an unacknowledged attempt to dress up the assumptions underlying popular mythologies in elaborate costumes which turn out to be only superficially scientific. According to one definition (in behaviourist jargon) 'aggression is the delivery of noxious stimuli to an organism or to a substitute' (Selg 1975: 156). The sterilized blandness of this definition reflects little more than a characteristic tendency towards abstracting notions and divesting them of their specific meanings in the (misguided) hope of making them sound dispassionately scientific. The discursive system surrounding this mode of thought has become so self-enclosed and self-referring that researchers who endorse it become incapable of recognizing that they share some very basic values, assumptions, and prejudices with perspectives and hierarchies which they despise.

There have of course been quite a number of relatively recent studies which have focused on the manners in which the media influence social and cultural realities by affecting the ways such realities are perceived. I shall be looking more closely at some of the issues raised by such approaches in the next chapter, but I wish first to illustrate how even such apparently subtler investigations can at times be serving purposes similar to those of the studies discussed above when they continue to function within the conceptual parameters determined by behaviourist 'genre conventions' – i.e. when they assume methodological orientations whose analogical trends and underlying values have not been properly scrutinized and recognized. The next section, therefore, considers some of the issues raised by a series of field studies which have applied the social learning perspective to the question of horrific influences in a manner which emphasizes the role played by perceptual processes. These are studies which have attempted to prove empirically that media representations of violence encourage fearful attitudes and climates of opinion, and thus condition the ways individuals behave in social contexts.

'MAINSTREAMING' AND THE CULTIVATION
OF FEAR

In a series of studies spanning more than a decade, George Gerbner and his associates at the Annenberg School of Communications (University of Pennsylvania) argued that the overemphasis of violence on television drama gives viewers an exaggerated impression of the extent of threat and danger in society, and that these impressions cultivate fear and distrust of fellow citizens in real life (Gerbner and Gross 1976a,b; Gerbner *et al*. 1977, 1978, 1979). According to this 'cultivation hypothesis', people who involve themselves deeply in television's fictional world will develop beliefs that correspond to what is depicted in that world. After analysing large samples of prime-time and daytime television programmes (an exercise which they started in 1967), Gerbner and his colleagues decided that there were a number of significant differences between the world of television drama and the 'real' one. They noted, for instance, that the world of television has a preponderance of males, that it overemphasizes the professions and over-represents the proportion of workers engaged in law enforcement, and that around 70 to 80 per cent of all programmes usually contain at least one instance of 'violence'. Gerbner's argument is that television's misleading representations nurture erroneous perceptions of reality and hence influence (condition) patterns of behaviour. Thus, because of the overemphasis on violence, 'heavy viewing is associated with greater apprehension of walking alone at night in the city in general and even in one's own neighbourhood' (Gerbner 1980: 245).

Significantly, the understanding of 'violence' which was used in these analyses was based on a generalized definition chosen by the researchers themselves (rather than by the subjects of the survey). Incidents resulting in the infliction of injury or suffering were uniformly taken to constitute 'violence', irrespective of the context in which these incidents occurred. Gerbner *et al*. justified this generalization on the grounds that since 'there is substantial evidence that fantasy and comedy are effective forms in which to convey serious lessons . . . eliminating fantasy or comic violence, as well as violence of an "accidental" nature, would be a major analytical fault' (Gerbner *et al*. 1980: 12). The argument suggests important points of convergence between the assumptions underlying these studies of the 'cultivation' of fear and alienation among heavy viewers of television, and those informing the studies of 'observational learning' of aggressive behaviour discussed in the preceding section. On the basis of their research, Gerbner and his associates have argued for what is basically (and perhaps tautologically) an endorsement of social learning theory. They have thus contended that portrayals of violence on fictional television drama programmes provide demonstrations of the power structure of society, and that, through the differential involvement in violence and victimization of various character types, these programmes teach viewers to manage their behaviour according to erroneous interpretations of the risks and dangers of everyday life.

There has been a great deal of criticism of these studies, most of it based on empirical investigations which produced evidence conflicting with Gerbner's claims. Thus, Doob and Macdonald (1979) tested Gerbner's findings in Canada and found that when there is fear of crime it is not the pattern of television viewing but the actual amount of crime in a specific neighbourhood which is the determining factor. Hirsch (1980) and Hughes (1980) reanalysed the same data reported in Gerbner et al. (1977) and, by using simultaneous rather than individual controls for demographic factors like age, sex, and education, showed that the relationships claimed in the Gerbner studies did not hold up, or were even opposite to those found. Wober and Gunter introduced similar variations and personality measures to the Gerbner studies in surveys conducted in Britain and concluded that 'it may not be television which makes viewers wary of the environment, but that people who are not resolute stay in to watch television, and also express cautious attitudes' (Wober and Gunter 1982: 246). Gerbner and his colleagues have accounted for these inconsistencies by refining their cultivation hypothesis with the introduction of a new emphasis on what they term 'resonance' (Gerbner et al. 1980). According to this refinement, television's effect is strongest among viewers whose real-life situations are most closely parallel to those portrayed on television. As they put it,

> When what people see on television is most congruent with everyday reality (or even perceived reality), the combination may result in a coherent and powerful 'double dose' of the television message and significantly boost cultivation. Thus, the congruence of the television world and real-life circumstances may 'resonate' and lead to markedly amplified cultivation patterns.

> (ibid.: 15)

There is, however, a circuitous ring to these refinements which suggests that they amount to little more than conciliatory patching – of the type which covers gaping holes in the researcher's costume of learned scientist, but also allows for the carrying over of many of the limitations of the frames of reference and 'genre conventions' within which the studies were originally formulated. The exercise of nominally updating these preconceptions by dressing them up in more fashionably patched costumes, and thus keeping them supplied with covers behind which to hide, in effect postpones the possibility of such assumptions and preconceptions becoming transparent when their old clothes have worn away. Some of the most challenging criticism of these studies, in fact, has come from researchers who have broken out of the neo-behaviourist conceptual framework and pointed to the threadbare quality of many of Gerbner's claims when the habit of generalizing and abstracting terms like 'violence' is not adhered to, and when content analyses of TV programmes are conducted in more discriminatory (context- and content-specific) fashions. Zillman (1980) and Gunter and Wober (1983), for instance, have produced evidence to suggest that television may have a cultivation effect which is the reverse of that proposed in the Gerbner studies. These researchers noted that the dramatic story-lines of fictional TV programmes which feature conflict between the forces of law and order and criminal elements are typically resolved with the triumph of good over evil, and the eventual bringing to justice of law-breakers. On the basis of this interpretation of TV content, they argue that, if TV distorts reality at all, it is more likely to be towards feelings of greater security than of danger. Gunter and Wober are insistent that 'British viewers show no significant tendencies towards enhanced fearfulness or mistrust of the society in which they live simply as a result of the amount of television drama programming they watch' (Gunter and Wober 1983: 176). Gunter (1985) also argues that there are serious limitations in the structure of Gerbner's system of message analysis, in that ordinary viewers do not always perceive programme content according to the pattern established in these analyses. The Gerbner model, for example, would point to cartoon shows as containing four times as much violence as does any other type of programme; yet a sample of British viewers surveyed by Howitt and Cumberbatch in 1974 did not rate cartoons as being particularly violent. After studying what they term 'children's experience of three types of cartoon', Bjorkqvist and Lagerspetz similarly concluded that what determines whether scenes

139

of violence will lead to anxiety is not the amount of explicit violence shown, but 'the manner in which the violence is presented . . . dramatically, humorously, or with technical effects' (Bjorkqvist and Lagerspetz 1985: 90). Children's understanding of these effects and genre conventions – the level and type of moral judgements which they make in the process of viewing and interpreting them – were thus found to be of much greater determining importance than the amount of 'violence' which the researchers themselves identified in the films. Gunter further points out that 'even in TV programmes featuring human characters, violent portrayals may not be perceived as important or significant aspects of content' (Gunter 1985: 35).

As with many of the studies considered in the preceding section, Gerbner's claimed findings have been made the basis of some very large assertions about the nature of media influence and social functioning. Here again, when one looks at these assertions in the raw, as it were, they turn out to be tediously and scrawnily familiar. Gerbner's emphasis on 'mainstreaming', for instance, is in many respects an updated version of assertions about the media possessing 'brainwashing' or 'hypnotic' powers which are alleged to allow those in positions of authority to transform crowds of individuals into sheeplike masses – analogies which achieved great popularity when social scientists and other observers were attempting to account for the rise and continued popular appeal of autocrats like Hitler, or for the unchallenged power-base of despots like Stalin. Gerbner and his associates have also suggested that differences apparently due to cultural, social, and personality factors tend to diminish among heavy television viewers. Arguing that 'television dominates the symbolic environment of modern life,' they suggest that a 'mainstreaming' process cultivates 'a relative commonality of outlooks' among heavy viewers, irrespective of the levels of education or the economic standing of these viewers (Gerbner *et al.* 1980: 10–11). They thus claim that 'for heavy viewers, television virtually monopolises and subsumes other sources of information, ideas and consciousness', so that 'amount of exposure to television is an important indicator of the strength of its contribution to ways of thinking and acting' (ibid.: 10). On the basis of these interpretations, Gerbner compares what he terms the 'cultural production' of television with a number of industries which influence the environment by (among other things) polluting it with 'defective, unsafe, and even deadly products and by-products':

In cultural production, even more than in the tobacco, pharma-
ceutical, automobile, airplane, nuclear energy and other industries, the confusions and evasions can be quite prolonged. What the
cultural industries discharge into the climate of common consciousness is not some clearly identifiable and measurable pollutant, but
rather it discharges the environment itself, including most of the
norms, standards, and definitions by which its quality is supposed
to be measured.

(Gerbner 1980: 267)

In their evocation of Orwellian echoes and anxieties, these images of
'mainstreaming' and 'pollution of consciousness' betray a number of
further assumptions which this perspective (like other neo-
behaviourist approaches) shares with more popular and 'common-
sense' preconceptions – and which it also continues to compound and
reinforce. The environment, here again, is conceptualized as an
abstract entity with awe-inspiring potential over (ultimately passive,
reactive, and irresponsible) human learning, reasoning, and behaviour. It is in effect this conceptual framework which both inspires
and is in turn reinforced by Gerbner's rhetorical reduction of the
complex interpretative and socio-cognitive processes involved in the
watching and decoding of television messages to 'the climate of
common consciousness' on to which the 'cultural industries discharge
. . . norms, standards, and definitions'.

These generalized claims are thus tacitly endorsing long-
established fearful anxieties about the ways of the world as well as the
uncertainties generated by large-scale changes in those ways. In the
long run, such claims also reflect, reinforce, and justify the age-old
tendency of identifying transparently influential social phenomena as
the (scapegoat-like) sources of trouble. As I suggested earlier in this
chapter, the anxieties underlying such tendencies have more complex
sources than is acknowledged by their chosen and apparent points of
attack. It is worth noting in this relation how in their more consciously
metaphoric vein, Gerbner's claims about 'cultural pollution' betray a
tendency which is also shared by more popular expressions of communal anxieties – i.e. that of being conceptualized through images
and analogies which derive from other areas of social concern. Thus,
while earlier versions of the 'mainstreaming' notion referred to
'brainwashing' and 'mass hypnosis', the popular highlighting of
concern about the rise in drug abuse among the young in the 1960s

and after has been echoed in widespread claims about the mass media possessing 'drug-like qualities' which allegedly lead to addictive and passive modes of response and reaction. In *The Plug-in Drug* (1977), for instance, the professional writer Marie Winn attributed many of society's ills (including juvenile delinquency, drug abuse, and the drop in the national reading scores in America) to the 'potentially addictive qualities' of television viewing. Winn hypothesized that the presumed right-brain arousal of television may be weakening the verbal skills associated with left-brain activities. The fact that an argument of this nature appears to carry a lot of weight on a popular level presumably derives from its resonance (to borrow Gerbner's terminology) in a context where simple and simplistic solutions and preconceptions have repeatedly been given unwarranted respectability by being dressed up in scientistic jargon. However, proponents of arguments based on this type of evocative analogy have not been limited to the vociferously popular or the academically pretentious, and it would be a mistake to dismiss the logic and analogical trend of these explanations lightly – not least because even some of this century's most perceptive critics and researchers appear to have found their logic to be self-evidently correct.

According to Winn, because of the time children and adults spend watching television (instead of reading, writing, or actually exploring the environment), the medium can nourish a certain kind of 'cognitive passivity' which leads to a 'show me or entertain me' orientation that can have serious personal and social implications. A number of more weighty writers in this field have also spoken about a process of 'cognitive passivity' which is claimed to describe the relationships of TV audiences with the messages and signs of the medium. Thus, though they have doubts about Winn's more extravagant claims, Singer and Singer agree with her emphasis on the 'powerful implications of the television-viewing habit for the nature of consciousness' (Singer and Singer 1981: 3). In their view, television has 'special cognitive properties' in that it 'in a sense represents a form of vicarious play or fantasy' which is in marked contrast to the spontaneous play of children. Similar points were made in the 1960s by Bettelheim, who expressed concern about what he termed 'the real danger of TV', which he saw as residing less in 'the often asinine or gruesome content of the shows', and much more in 'this being seduced into passivity and discouraged about facing life actively, on one's own' (Bettelheim 1961: 51). The logic underlying such worries has a long lineage which includes (at times illustrious) proponents from a variety of academic disciplines. As early as 1930, for instance, F. R. Leavis was expressing concern about the cognitive implications of film and broadcasting because he considered them to have 'insidious', 'standardizing', and 'levelling-down' influences which 'involve surrender, under conditions of hypnotic receptivity, to the cheapest emotional appeals' (Leavis 1948: 149–50). In Leavis's view, 'broadcasting, like the films, is in practice mainly a means of passive diversion, and . . . it tends to make active recreation, especially active use of mind, more difficult'. It is perhaps particularly significant in this context that the creator of this century's most widely known vision of political and emotional 'mainstreaming' should also have spoken (in 1943) of 'the passive, drug-like pleasures of the cinema and radio' (Orwell 1970: 61). The analogies used in the formulation of each of these evocative assertions have identifiable sources in the social context of the periods when they were formulated and put in discursive circulation. They do not, however, add very much to our understanding of how the media may or may not be influencing perceptions and behaviour. The very evocativeness of the associations aroused by the analogies has in fact also contributed to some very basic confusions in popular as well as academic attempts to describe media influence, and also prejudiced the process of coming to terms with, understanding, and thus controlling the changing realities demanded by advances in communications technology.

The understanding of media messages (including horror fictions) which has been repeatedly stressed in this book is one which asserts that such messages consist of institutionalized techniques of discussion involving (frequently self-referring) genre conventions, patterns, and (in Barthes's terms) variously motivated or arbitrary connotations. According to this understanding, it is misleading to speak of 'passivity' in relation to the decoding of messages and the synthesizing of consciousnesses (Sartre's phrase) which make it possible for us to interpret and react to the images and ideas which are projected (encoded) for our consideration through different media of communication. This, of course, raises important methodological issues with regard to any attempt we may wish to make to analyse the cognitive and behavioural consequences of watching horror films or representations (gruesome or otherwise) of physical or other violence on any of the media. Our perceptions and understanding of events and actions as 'violent', 'horrific', or otherwise are important

determinants of how we react to them. The consequences of viewing
(i.e. interpreting) messages about acts and situations which can be
described by (morally loaded and complex) terms like 'violent' or
'aggressive' are thus, as has been widely recognized by many contemporary scholars, importantly mediated by socio-linguistic processes.
What that means is that if we are to begin to understand the processes
which may or may not trigger off imitation (or any other consequence) when we watch or read representations of violent actions on
the media, then we will need not only to take account of those
perceptions, but also to identify and untangle the webs of assumptions
out of which they are compounded. This, in effect, involves an
approach which makes more than token gestures towards acknow-
ledging the importance of 'symbolic activities', but which gives full
value to the symbols which give meaning to the activities in question.
Such activities, governed as they are by (in Habermas's phrase)
'binding *consensual* norms', are also and importantly of a context- and
actor-specific nature, since 'the validity of social norms is grounded
only in the intersubjectivity of the mutual understanding of intentions
and secured by the general recognition of obligations' (Habermas
1970: 92).

I am not suggesting that these considerations have never been
taken into account by experimental investigations into the effects of
representations of violence. Indeed, a number of recent researchers
have, in the course of their attempts to chart out the cognitive and
behavioural consequences of 'mass-media violence', paid a great deal
of attention to the implications of genre conventions, 'television
literacy', individual and personality factors, 'dimensional salience',
and methods and techniques of presentation. Though different terms
have been used, there have also been studies noting how effects are
importantly mediated by viewers' abilities to distinguish between
scenes and images which are, in Barthes's terminology, highly iconic
or motivated (i.e. made up of signs which come close to the ways in
which we normally see the world of everyday reality, and which are
thus interpreted as being 'realistic'), and scenes, stories, and images
which are presented in terms of signs which label them as 'fictional' or
'unrealistic'. A number of researchers in this field have also produced
some very challenging and optimistic analyses of the cognitive and
social psychological implications of the mass media by considering
their methods, characteristics and educational possibilities.[6]

Unfortunately, however, these are considerations which have not been given the importance they deserve in the majority of neo-behaviourist and popular claims about horrific influences which have been represented in this chapter. As a result of this omission – and a related refusal to consider intentions, motives, and purposes – the perspectives, attitudes, and values underlying many of the standpoints discussed in the preceding pages can be argued to have been inspired by anxieties and uncertainties which have little to do with scientific and objective observation, and which have led to investigations ranging from the reductionist to the tautological. In this sense, they can be said to share some of the characteristics of magical acts which, as Barthes puts it (Barthes 1973: 153), believe themselves even with causality because they have uttered the word which introduces it. Working from the perspective suggested by this consideration, I have also suggested that it is not only the processes and manners of being or not being affected by horrific influences which are mediated by symbolic and consensual norms. Playing the role of dispassionate scientist investigating such issues, and having popular and academic communities accept the costumes which go with this role as valid and adequate also, in their turn, depend on such negotiations of meanings. The constraining conventions and discursive frames within which the behaviourist and neo-behaviourist conceptual modes function can in this sense be said to be similar to the genre conventions that part I of this book argued to characterize the workings of horror fiction.

Throughout this book, I have repeatedly emphasized the importance and implications of the part played by the complex processes of interpretation which allow us to make sense of and understand the social conventions and institutionalized techniques of discussion out of which horror fictions and messages about violence are compounded. These processes of interpretation are heavily influenced by the mediating properties (socio-linguistic, semiotic) of the conventions themselves, as well as of other conventions and expectations with which they come in contact. In other words, it is not enough to take into account the connotations, attitudes, and values which the authors of such works project, claim to be appropriate, and invite us to share when they paint horrific pictures for our consideration. Popular and academic claims about the effects of horrific fictions and 'mass-media violence' have played a very prominent and controversial role in discussions about, and hence in the understanding of, such fare. As a result, the fields of discourse and the assumptions informing such claims can also be argued to have become important components of the mediating conventional expectations which we bring to any interpretation of horror fiction. The present chapter's focus has been inspired by this consideration.

In the next chapter I propose to place these assertions in sharper focus by examining some of the processes whereby the contemporary consciousness ascribes significance to itself and its environment, and hence how these cognitive processes are linked to the development of fear and uncertainty. This examination will be used as a basis from which to consider some of the links between perception and the myths of our times, particularly those encoded in the texts of horror fiction.

Chapter 6

CONSCIOUSNESS, FICTION, AND THE TERRORS OF UNCERTAINTY

'You believe in nothing but what consists with your own prejudices and illusions.'
(General Spielsdorf, in Sheridan Le Fanu's *Carmilla*)

PRELUDE: GAMES OF THE NAME

Horror fiction has been approached throughout this book as a genre which works within a set of conventionalized parameters, and thus within the form of a specific set of formal rules of discourse and language. These socio-linguistic structures have been argued to be determined and maintained by forces, attitudes, and processes that are more complex than is allowed for by the assumption that fictional horrors exist exclusively to satisfy or encourage a sadistic delight in bathing in gore. Indeed, the preceding two chapters have suggested that arguments which purport to be based on evidence supposedly justifying such assumptions are themselves (not unlike exponents of the horror genre) heavily influenced by the constraining discursive conventions within whose parameters they function. It follows from all this that, as has in fact been recognized by a number of critics and scholars, the horror genre is perhaps best understood as a language which is an expression (rather than a primary cause) of an undesirable or unsatisfactorily patched-up state of society.

In the course of the preceding chapters, I have placed much emphasis on the importance and implications of the manners in which meanings are habitually ascribed through analogical processes which often follow the patterns of theatrical dramatization and ritual. It bears noting that the metaphor of a theatrical play with a script and assigned roles for different actors and changing situations is one of the major analogies on which social scientists have built many of their attempts at explaining patterns of social behaviour. A second (related) analogy which has informed and influenced much social scientific thought and research is that of a game with rules which social actors learn to follow or negotiate.[1] By extension, play-roles/ rules analogies have also been applied to the study of literary and cinematic genres. The emphasis in the application of the roles analogy falls on the fact that genre writers have to work within clearly defined (script-like) conventions. Like theatrical or even musical performers, they can either produce humdrum and hackneyed renderings of the formula which they happen to be following, or else (if they are gifted) variations of interpretation which can be innovative and inspired. The notion that the institutionalized techniques of discussion which make up horror fiction can be understood as an elaborate game with clearly defined rules has frequently also been made the basis of explanations of the appeal of horror. In this context, one recurring analogical image used is that of amusement park rides, which provide thrills and the taste of danger but always within a reassuringly controlled and unthreatening context. There are rules to this game, in other words, which readers of mainstream horror fiction expect to be respected when they place themselves in the hands of the authors and entertainers who have offered to drive them safely through a series of adrenalin-raising thrills.

In the present chapter I propose to tackle some of the issues raised by the application of these analogies to the horror genre. This will involve a fairly complex route which will first try to trace the reasons why people should want to play the types of games proposed by horror fiction. As was illustrated in part I of this book, the emotions on which exponents of this genre focus, and which they help to put in discursive circulation, are usually related to fear and uncertainty, even when (as is usually the case in the lurid bargain basements of mass-marketed horror) the accent falls on revulsion and nausea. On this understanding, this chapter explores the contours and sources of human fears and communal uncertainties, the circumstances which cause them, and our ways of dealing with them – including that of building games around them so as to resolve, dissolve, or evade them. From here, I propose to consider how the game analogy has been applied to fiction, and then discuss some of the cultural and political implications of those contemporary variations of this 'game' which invite their participants to contemplate horrific possibilities of experience. On these terms, the chapter aims to consider some of the wider implications of contemporary horror fiction as an increasingly influential exemplar of the myths of our times.

At different points in the preceding chapters, various methods of ascribing meaning, of accounting for disturbing phenomena, or of dealing with uncertainty (by horror writers as well as academic researchers) have been described as working on a magical level. This term has been used to refer to the methods in which horror fictions as well as many scientific-sounding explanations very often work from foundations which are linguistically and conceptually self-enclosed. I have thus suggested that the apparent impact of such depictions or explanations derives from the fact that they function within clearly circumscribed conventions which they and their audience tacitly agree to consider absolute, and which allow for the creation and projection of meanings that are exclusively self-referring. It will perhaps be useful to open this chapter's discussion by considering how magical modes of perceiving and thinking relate to fear and uncertainty, in order to identify more precisely the ways in which horror fiction grows out of and reflects on the anxieties surrounding personal fears and communal uncertainties. This will involve a fairly detailed consideration of the cognitive and emotional processes which can be said to be operative when we ascribe meanings in the course of our attempts to make sense of ourselves and of our environment.

FEAR AND ITS MAGICAL ATTRIBUTES

Fear is an emotion that is distinguished from anxiety and from stress. One can speak of a spectrum of fear, usually aroused by real or imagined dangers, and which ranges from mild disquiet to raging terror. Responses to a terrifying object or situation have marked physiological characteristics which can manifest themselves either through a 'fight or flight' reaction (faster heartbeat supplying fresh blood to the muscles as a prelude to action), or through a state described in the phrase 'frozen with terror'. Both types of response can be said to be part of a defence mechanism and have been taken to imply the presence of genetically determined biases resulting in a preparedness to meet real dangers. But it is not just real dangers which can arouse fear, nor do fear responses work on a purely automatic basis. The interconnection between physiological arousal and cognitive appraisal in this context is reflected in the way that, just as it is possible for material which is not really threatening to give rise to the physiological responses normally associated with fear (when such material is erroneously interpreted as posing a threat), so too threatening material can be 'recoded' as safe with a consequent lowering of tension. Differences in what is appraised will thus lead to different emotional reactions, so that fear differs from anger, for instance, largely because seeing something as threatening differs from seeing it as thwarting, and these different appraisals have different consequences both physiologically and in the behaviour which may be their outcome.[2]

Many of the attempts to categorize the sources of fear have insisted that adult fears have their roots in childhood experiences. Studies of childhood and later fears have also emphasized a general tendency to fear the very strange, especially when it is closely related with the familiar, and various investigators have noted that a key factor influencing whether or not an object or situation will arouse fear is the amount of control which is felt in its relation. This has been noted to apply even in reactions to pain or to the prospect of pain. According to G. S. Hall's (oddly conceived but at times insightful) 'synthetic genetic study of fear', pain or its prospect necessarily leads to fear because it 'puts to life the question of its very survival or extinction, complete or partial' (Hall 1914: 152). Yet, among more recent researchers, and even among psychologists who continue to insist on innate and genetic bases of fear, the prospect of pain has been noted to produce surprisingly little fear as long as it is roused in circumstances under the individual's own control, in an expected form, and in a familiar situation.[3] Whether or not an individual will feel control over any given situation depends very much on what that situation means to him or her, and the types of meanings which are ascribed will in turn depend on the nature of the individual's knowledge and expectations about surroundings.

In his *Sketch for a Theory of the Emotions*, Sartre argued that we find our way around the world of everyday existence by making use of what he termed 'hodological maps'. These maps are mental constructs which are built in the course of experience and on which we come to depend heavily as we manoeuvre our ways through life – they allow us to chart out the paths which we need to follow in order to reach our goals. We make these 'maps' of the world for ourselves and in their light we see the world before us as if it were an artefact of our own. Sartre's 'hodological maps' are in this sense similar to Piaget's 'schemes', or to what more recent psychologists have called 'cognitive maps'. They are hypothetical (and analogically conceived) structures which are assumed to be stored in memory, and which are said to preserve and organize information collated in the course of our encounters with various events and experiences. These maps (or mental constructs) in their turn become tools which we use to make sense of (i.e. interpret) new experiences, encounters, and situations. The information contained in the maps is thus also assumed to be amenable to modification as a result of further experiences and encounters. Thus, according to Piaget's model of cognitive development, the cognitive system changes its internal structure by repeatedly attempting to accommodate and assimilate novel (previously unassimilated) environmental elements. New experiences can cause us to restructure details or even the pattern of our expectations if we become convinced that the elements previously charted on the map, as it were, do not correspond with newly perceived reality. Such experiences can of course also act as reinforcers of those expectations when they are perceived to fulfil and fit in with them. These mental constructs (models, maps, schemes) thus need to be as clearly defined as they are flexible, in order to allow those who use and depend on them both to make realistic sense of new experiences and encounters, and also to learn from them in such a way that further experiences can be interpreted more sharply and realistically. The flexibility should be of a kind, in other words, which allows for the realization that the mental constructs are not themselves all-embracing, and which thus makes allowance for realistic methods of coming to terms with unexpected (and as yet uncharted) encounters. When this flexibility is not available, or when it is of a type which is not rooted firmly enough in the world of the realistically possible, what is likely to happen is that the new experience will be misinterpreted or assimilated into a world view which is so self-enclosed and exclusively self-referring that it has lost (or not yet fully achieved, in the case of young children) contact with the world of reality which it is supposed to describe and chart out. It is such situations which give rise to the development of magical categorizing pegs for phenomena which baffle comprehension.

Sartre argued that there are occasions in life when the paths which we chart out to reach our various goals get blocked by obstacles which are too great. In these conditions, we often pretend that we can get what we need by 'magical means', rather than acting in a realistic, goal-directed manner. Emotions, in Sartre's view, are the manifestation of such pretence, so that fear (the emotion which fits his argument most convincingly, in fact) occurs when we stop thinking and acting realistically. As Sartre puts it:

> all ways out being barred, the consciousness leaps into the magical world of emotion, plunges wholly into it by debasing itself. It becomes a different world – a world which it constitutes with its own most intimate quality, with that presence to itself, utterly non-distant, of its own point of view upon the world. A consciousness becoming emotional is rather like a consciousness falling asleep.
>
> (Sartre 1971: 78)

It will be worth pausing here and looking at the cultural sources of Sartre's account, in order to identify more precisely what is meant by these 'magical means' of dealing with incomprehensible situations. The conceptual progeny behind this understanding of 'magical behaviour', in fact, is an interestingly mixed one. On the one hand, Sartre's thesis draws on an account of behaviour which interprets magic as an expression of 'animistic beliefs' and as a reflection of the notion of 'the omnipotence of thought'. This is an account which was originally forwarded in 1871 in Tylor's *Primitive Culture*, and which was subsequently and variously applied to the interpretation of childhood, totemism, taboo, and the 'uncanny' in Freudian psychology. Briefly defined, this view asserts that magical beliefs arise when no distinctions are made between physical realities and the products of the imagination, so that a person thinking magically will invest inanimate objects (for instance) with properties and associations which in fact remain lodged in the very mind from which they derive. It will be recalled that in chapter 3 I argued that this account underlies many of the magical effects evoked in the work of Stephen King. Another immediate influence on Sartre's account of the magical nature of fear was Malinowski, who (on the basis of his anthropological observations) argued that magic is 'to be expected and generally to be found whenever man comes to an unbridgeable gap, a hiatus in his knowledge or in his powers of practical control, and yet has to continue his pursuit' (Malinowski 1937: 75).[4] The fountainhead of magical belief, Malinowski, insisted, is to be found

> in those passionate experiences which assail [man] in the impasses of his instinctive life and of his practical pursuits, in those gaps and breaches left in the ever imperfect wall of culture which he erects

between himself and the besetting temptations and dangers of his destiny.

(ibid. 1926: 75)

Sartre can thus be argued to have imaginatively amalgamated the implications of two different anthropological accounts in order to suggest that magical reactions are as much a consequence of perceptual expectations (which are also crucially influenced by the cultural inheritance within which they are forged), as of the problems which arise when the understanding and practical control of the environment are limited or too rudimentary.

To recap then, we react to given situations according to how we perceive them, and interpretations are built out of the mental constructions of reality (hodological/cognitive maps or schemes) which develop in the course of our numerous experiences within our specific milieu. It is these which are challenged or removed when we are faced with the very strange or the 'uncanny'. According to Malinowski and Sartre, magic is dominant when control of the environment is weak. Magical beliefs and the (fearful) reactions which are based on such beliefs can on these terms be said to be the result of the states of uncertainty which are created by this challenge and by the negation of expectations. Feelings of fear can thus be said to derive from the conviction of loss of control and the sense of helplessness which become dominant in situations when (in Piagetian terms) the cognitive system can neither assimilate the environment into its own structure, nor adapt itself to the structure of the environment.[5] Further, because the environment is anything but clear-cut, and because an individual's contact with it is also mediated by a complex variety of meaning-making devices, the constructions and expectations created in the course of experience can often be erratic. Thus, objects and situations which pose a substantial threat can be assimilated into a system which codes them as harmless since they can be associated with familiar and safe elements. Similarly, a mental picture of reality can be restructured in such a way as to accommodate elements whose threat is unreal, but which have been described and appraised in a way which associates them with danger and distress. This, of course, is one of the ways in which irrational preconceptions and superstitious convictions can become part of a mental picture of reality. Whether such a picture will turn out to be temporary or permanent will again depend on the types of further interactions and

153

interpretations which take place. The amount of control an individual will feel in relation to specific objects and situations will thus not only depend on whether he or she can accommodate or assimilate them into the cognitive system, but also on the manner in which that system influences their appraisal – i.e. on the manner in which the complex variety of speculative instruments created in the course of previous experiences determines how such objects and situations are perceived and interpreted.

It has thus been observed that it is in the course of the growing child's (initially crude but increasingly complex) attempts to make sense of new experiences that fear appears to develop and assume specific contours. For the human infant, as with other animals, strangeness elicits alarm: sudden noise, quick changes in lighting, loss of support, jerky movements, and objects that rapidly advance or expand will cause an infant to show signs of distress. But what constitutes strangeness and the methods of coping with it will also change with the child's developing awareness and understanding of the environment. According to Seligman (1975), development is a process which involves movement from the new-born baby's almost complete lack of control over outcomes to the ability to make voluntary responses which can be recognized as influencing outcomes. If the child perceives its actions to be independent of what changes occur in the environment, or to have no influence on that environment at all, then a sense of helplessness will develop.[6] Seligman and his associates have also proposed an 'attributional analysis of helplessness' (Abramson et al. 1980) in order to explain why learning that outcomes are uncontrollable leads to the motivational, cognitive, and emotional 'deficits' which characterize helplessness. According to this analysis, the learning of helplessness depends on whether an individual attributes failures to universal barriers or else to the individual's own limitations, and also on the ways in which the cause of failure is perceived and interpreted. One of the most striking illustrations of this process is provided in Bruno Bettelheim's account of his personal experiences and observations as a prisoner at Dachau. Bettelheim noted that among the methods employed by the Gestapo to instil helplessness in their prisoners and victims was that of 'destroying all capacity for self-determination, all ability to predict the future and thus prepare for it' (Bettelheim 1961: 130–1). According to Bettelheim, 'under conditions of extreme deprivation, the influence of the environment can be total', but this depends, among other things, on 'whether the conviction is given that, no matter what one does, no positive response can be drawn from the environment through efforts of one's own' (ibid.: 147).

What is underlined by these accounts is that both the nature of the environment and the individual's cognitive appraisal of it have to be taken into consideration in any attempt to chart out the stages which mark the development of feelings of helplessness and fear. Before considering more specifically how all this bears on the discursive conventions surrounding contemporary horror fiction, as well as on the implications of such fictions in contemporary contexts, I propose to establish more firmly the ways in which fiction-making relates to the perceptual processes and cognitive appraisals underlying feelings of helplessness and fear. I propose to do this by looking more closely at some of the processes influencing the development and normal resolution of a type of fear which appears to presuppose a high order of imagination, and whose manifestations also appear to follow fairly clear time schedules during childhood. The discussion which follows takes its cue from Bruner *et al.*'s suggestion that the unique capacity for helplessness with which the human species seems to have evolved is of a kind which can be relieved by outside shaping and external devices, and that this capacity is usually 'accompanied by a propelling curiosity about the environment and by much self-reinforcing activity seemingly designed to achieve competence in that environment' (Bruner *et al.* 1966: 2–4).

COGNITION, PERCEPTION, AND THE FEAR OF DARKNESS

The fear of the dark has often been associated with the unease of separation and with the absence of the comfort and security provided by loved ones. In one of his discussions of infantile anxiety, Freud argued that children 'are afraid in the dark because in the dark they cannot see the person they love; and their fear is soothed if they can take hold of that person's hand in the dark' (Freud 1905, 1977 edn: 147). The fear of darkness is in fact most acute in children when they are alone and therefore without the direct reassurance of protection which is normally afforded by their trust in the people they know. But reassurance does not come exclusively from loved ones: a familiar environment which a child can see to contain no direct threats can also serve this purpose to varying degrees. Indeed, the 'visual cliff' experiments of Gibson and Walk (1960) suggest that infants will come to place more trust in their visual perceptions of situations and objects than in the reassurances offered by adults. In these experiments, infants were placed on the centre of a board laid across a sheet of heavy glass which covered patterned material lying directly beneath the glass on one side and, by dropping vertically, several feet below on the other. The infants tested were quite willing to cross over the 'solid' side of the table, but the majority refused to venture across the glass-covered 'deep' side, even when their mothers encouraged them to do so. The infants were also noted to place more trust in their visual perception of the situation than in tactile information: a number of them still refused to cross over to their mothers after touching and feeling the solid glass over the 'cliff'.

The importance of perceptual (and especially visual) cues in both the creation and the resolution of the fear of the dark is also suggested by the fact that a child's fears and anxieties in a dark environment are often only soothed when the child is *shown* that there is nothing to be afraid of. It is also of significance that the fear of darkness only manifests itself when the child's dependence on visual perception becomes marked, i.e. as the child becomes more independent in movement and in exploring and controlling the environment. Children do not normally fear the dark before around the second year of life, and such fears are usually at their most acute around the fifth year. The absence of sharp visual details and the curtailment of the ability to move can be said to give rise to a sense of disorientation in which familiar or recognizable surroundings become transformed into indeterminate darkness and strange shades. In other words, a sense of isolation is not the only or even the most disconcerting state which can be created in a dark environment. In a sense, the child cannot as yet trust surroundings to remain constant and unchanging when the sharp outlines which can be recognized when the lights are on can no longer be clearly perceived in darkness. One can interpret this type of uncertainty as an extension of Piaget's theories about the difficulties which children under the age of about 7 have with grasping the concept of conservation (i.e. that the mass of objects can remain unchanged even when there is a change in shape or appearance). The undefined nature of an environment shrouded in darkness, where substances appear to change their shape (as well as hiding recesses where potential threats may lurk), undermines the possibility of feeling control over outcomes. It is a sense of helpless vulnerability and a consequent state of anxiety which are most likely to prevail under these conditions. In this context, the slenderest perceptual clues are interpreted in terms of the various disturbing possibilities and images which have been encountered in other contexts.

Two points need to be stressed here. The first is that the sense of disorientation and vulnerability described above derives from the fact that the cognitive/hodological maps (or schemes) with which the child is trying to interpret the dark environment are not yet sophisticated enough to cope realistically and practically with the indeterminate and the unknown. The second point is that the methods in which the child reacts to this state of affairs – by plunging into what Sartre calls the magical world of emotions and ascribing incongruous meanings to what is perceived – raise important questions about the workings of the imaginative faculties which go into operation, make associations, and ascribe meanings in such situations. Significantly, most of the reports of childhood fears of this nature stress not so much the darkness itself but rather the terrifying imagery with which it becomes peopled. Further, the images associated with the ambiguous shades need not be intrinsically threatening – it might simply be the incongruity of their imagined presence which is found disturbing. Valentine, for instance, reported how a 5-year-old girl was terrified for several weeks because she 'saw' what she described as horrid things, 'Cabbages all round the room – and a girl going out of the window' (Valentine 1950: 226). This imaginative projection of disturbingly incongruous associations is worth pausing over.

A number of writers have argued that the capacity we have for taking things as significant – i.e. for seeing more in them than would meet the purely sensory eye – involves a process akin to that of fiction-making. Following Kant, Warnock insists that it is the 'fictions of the imagination' which allow us to perceive our familiar world, in the sense that it is through these 'fictions' that we construct (and thus perceive) the universal element in the world. Without the fictions of the imagination, she points out, 'we would be lost in an ocean of particular impressions' (Warnock 1976: 71). Fiction, as Gregory puts it, 'frees the nervous system from the tyranny of reflexes triggered by events, so that we respond not merely to what happens, but also to what might happen' (Gregory 1974: 439). It was also on the basis of considerations such as these that Sartre could assert that 'to experience any object as horrible, is to see it against the background of a world which reveals itself as *already* horrible (Sartre 1971: 89). The analogy of 'fictions' (rather than 'maps' or 'schemes') to refer to the mental constructs which give shape and unity to perception under-lines the fact that there is also an intentional and creative dimension to our methods of interpreting and making sense of even the most mundane of everyday events. This is a point which was also made powerfully by Sartre during his discussion (in *The Psychology of Imagination*) of what is involved when we interact with, interpret, and internalize an image. According to Sartre, 'the image, like the sign, is a consciousness' and 'a consciousness does not have an opaque and unconscious surface by which it can be seized and attached to another surface' (Sartre 1972: 27). What is happening when we react to an image is that one consciousness (our cognitive appraisal) has been motivated by another (a sign or an image):

> Between two consciousnesses there is no cause and effect rela-tionship. A consciousness is through and through a synthesis, completely withdrawn into itself: it is only at the very heart of this internal synthesis that it can join itself to another preceding or succeeding consciousness by an act of retention or protention. Moreover, if one consciousness is to act on another, it must be retained and recreated by the consciousness on which it is to act. There are no passivities, but internal assimilations of disinte-grations at the very heart of an intentional synthesis which is transparent to itself. One consciousness is not the cause of another: it motivates it.
>
> (ibid.)

One can thus say that cases like that of the girl who saw 'horrid things' in her dark bedroom involve an intentional synthesis of usually quite distinct consciousnesses, and that this synthesis is of a kind which accentuates the sense of disorientation created by the ambiguity of perceptual cues available in the dark environment. The incongruous shapes and figures which are 'seen' (i.e. which are imaginatively projected in the process of interpreting ambiguous data) also assume a magical significance which precludes control and which excludes the possibility of even recognizing the fact that what one is looking at is perceptually ambiguous. It is because this ambiguity is not recog-nized for what it is that the (projected) significance of the scene appears so incongruously disturbing.

These points can perhaps be made clearer through a brief consideration of our methods of making sense of illustrations which ambiguously represent three-dimensional objects on a two-dimensional surface. The ambiguity here derives from the fact that the illustration (or signifier) can fairly accurately be seen as referring to a variety of physical objects because many of the clues normally available to us in the three-dimensional sphere are missing, and hence cannot form part of the sensory data which normally form the basis for testing out the appropriateness or otherwise of hypothesized percepts. In the course of his discussion of how we interpret ambiguous images (like those in trick pictures), Wittgenstein noted that the fact that something that is ambiguous, and hence open to a different interpretation, can only be recognized when the realization is made that it can be seen as something quite different from what one had first taken it to represent. Wittgenstein also noted that interpretations are usually suggested by context, and that the fact that we can see the same illustration 'first as one thing, now as another' suggests that 'we interpret it and see it as we interpret it' (Wittgenstein 1958: 193–4). Some of the wider implications of these assertions have been underlined by Norman, who notes that in the famous trick picture in which a figure can be seen either as representing an old woman or as representing a young woman, for instance, there are also strict limits to the possibilities determining how the figure is seen. It can correctly be seen both as an old woman and as a young woman, but it cannot correctly be seen as a man (Norman 1978: 334). Concepts too, Norman argues, carry with them distinctions between correct and incorrect applications of them. What it is possible for us to see depends on how it is possible for us to conceptualize our experience, and

> the possible ways of seeing man's nature and his place in the universe are made available by the moral and intellectual traditions within one's culture. Thus there are limits to what can be said. And what is said can be more or less appropriate. The available traditions do not confine us once and for all; new ways of seeing can be developed and extended – but not arbitrarily.
>
> (ibid.)

Many of the examples used by *Gestalt* and cognitive psychologists to illustrate the workings of perception also stress the importance of background in determining what is seen. It is not just the features of an object, but also its context and the perceiver's past experience which are used to construct a percept. The extent to which our mental construction of reality is grounded in what Sartre termed 'the deterministic world of the usable' will be a deciding factor in the appraisal of what is involved in potentially frightful situations. Thus, the images with which children people a dark setting in the course of their attempts to 'classify' ambiguous or undefined surroundings are also directly related to the manners in which their interaction with a specific environment helped structure their conception of reality. Cultural differences, because they determine the range of possibilities of which an individual can become aware, have frequently been reported as influencing the ways in which objects and situations are perceived – i.e. the ways in which different 'maps', 'schemes', or 'fictions' are constructed in order to secure a meaning-giving structure within which the world can be experienced.[7] This assertion has specific implications which we shall need to consider more closely below, particularly as it relates to the complex cultural forces involved in the creation and uses of popular genres and the conventions underlying the phenomenon of horror fiction. But there is also a more general level to it which needs to be emphasized. An image can cause a disconcerted reaction because we see it as uncannily new or incongruous, or because of the dangerous associations which we ascribe to it. Such modes of seeing and ascribing have a cultural origin and develop as part of the process of creating and charting out meanings during our endeavours to establish and understand our position in relation to a specific environment.

In their endeavours to protect and frequently to control the young, adults will often warn against various imaginary or threateningly decked figures who will punish misbehaviour, or against, in the old cliché, sweet-proffering strangers whose friendly appearance is not to be trusted. The 'dance' of perceptual and cognitive development of necessity brings the child into contact with objects, figures, and situations which cannot (and often should not) be readily accommodated into a mental picture of secure reality. Nor are the 'data' on which the child has to work of an unambiguous nature. A great deal of parental teaching and many of the objects with which the growing child comes into contact often emphasize that appearances are not always to be trusted. Further, learning that substances remain the same irrespective of the shapes they assume (Piaget's concept of conservation) is not as natural or clear-cut as might appear to an adult who has already grasped the concept and come to take it for granted. The growing child comes in contact with objects which 'change' according to context (a plugged-in television set becomes a source of entertainment, and other electrictical implements become potentially lethal objects which parents warn about), or with shapes which change significance with changes in orientation (as in the alphabetical letters 'b', 'd', 'p', and 'q'). When there is doubt about the significance of perceived outlines, as much as when the trusted presence of a protecting adult is not readily available, it is not surprising that disquieting associations will also be projected on to visually ambivalent objects and conceived as forming a logical part of undefined surroundings (especially in the dark).

In all of this, the child can be said to be developing, using, and extending a complex series of cultural tools and symbols which gradually come to form the basis of meaning out of which a world view is formed. Those tools, it bears stressing, are not just adjuncts: our survival and ability to function as human beings depend on them. Understanding our position in a given context as one of helplessness, for instance, or recognizing our ability to activate avoidance or control, are both exercises in the deployment of interpretative and culturally based tools. As Bruner puts it, man's special status as a culture user means that his social–technical way of life 'goes to the bone', in that 'through evolution, [he] came increasingly to be linked to the amplifiers provided by culture and technology for making possible the expression of his powers' (Bruner 1972: 18). The use of such amplifiers involves what Geertz terms 'a traffic in significant symbols', i.e. anything 'that is disengaged from its mere actuality and used to impose meaning upon experience' (Geertz 1975: 45). Such symbolic forms include 'language, art, myth, theory, ritual, technology, law and the conglomerate of maxims, recipes, prejudices and plausible stories the smug call common sense' (ibid. 1983: 153). These tools are used by the individual

> sometimes deliberately and with care, most often spontaneously and with ease, but always with the same end in view: to put a construction upon the events through which he lives, to orient himself within 'the ongoing course of experienced things', to adopt a vivid phrase of John Dewey's.
>
> (ibid. 1975: 45)

One of the most crucial steps in cognitive development as described by Piaget, Bruner, and their followers is that involving the understanding and deployment of symbolic representation – a process which reaches maturity when the individual can conceive of reality as a special subset within the totality of things that available data would admit as hypotheses. In moments of uncertainty, the shapes taken by the fictions of the imagination can thus be argued to derive their impetus from the types of possibilities and significances with which we have come in contact in a particular culture, from the type of distinctions which we have come to make between what is 'real', what is possible, and what is 'unreal', and from the type of control which we have come to feel in relation to a specific environment.

PLAY, FICTION, AND THE DEFINITION OF REALITY

If the argument developed above is correct, then the achievement of adequate control of self and surroundings and the recognition of one's own potential and limitations are directly dependent on the extent to which an individual has been able to explore his or her interacting relation with a specific environment from a position of security. This consideration is presumably behind the emphasis which a large variety of psychologists (ranging from Freud, Klein, and Winnicott to Piaget, Bruner, and Goffman) have placed on the importance of play in emotional, cognitive, and social development. Thus, play has been argued to be essential for the exercise and mastery of feelings and desires, as well as of communicative skills and of the cultural amplifiers which make us fully human. When a child is actively engaged in play, he or she can be said to be coming to terms with various experiences and skills through what Garvey terms a 'non-literal attitude that allows play to be buffered from its consequences' (Garvey 1977: 13). Through play, a child can exercise and develop an understanding that what is done is not always what it appears to be: shapes and situations can be made to assume different significances in a child-controlled exploration of possibilities. As Bruner puts it, play 'is a means of minimising the consequences of one's action and of learning, therefore, in a less risky situation' (Bruner 1976: 38). In this sense, play makes it possible for the individual to try combinations of behaviour that would never be tried in situations involving functional pressure. Where more than one player is involved, the phenomenon of play can only occur when the participants are capable of what Bateson terms 'some degree of meta-communication, i.e. of exchanging signals which would carry the message "this is play"' (Bateson

162

1976: 120). Bateson notes the cognitive complexity implicit in such a message by expanding it thus: ' "These actions, in which we now engage, do not denote what would be denoted by those actions which these actions denote." The playful nip denotes the bite, but it does not denote what would be denoted by the bite' (ibid.: 121). The message 'this is play', as Bateson elaborates, thus 'sets a frame of the sort which is likely to precipitate paradox: it is an attempt to discriminate between, or to draw a line between, categories of different logical types' (ibid.: 128). Further, since play ceases to be play when an awareness of control over outcomes is absent, it can be seen as a means of developing a sense of competence and of forming an appraisal of the nature of fantasy as well as of the extent to which possibilities and limitations are determined by physical, personal, and social reality. All this points to a crucial cognitive function of play: it marks a vital step in the discovery of map–territory relations (Bateson's phrase). It is because play has been recognized to perform this function that social scientists have asserted its importance for the evolution of communication, as well as for the development and refinement of cognitive and symbolic tools ('maps', 'schemes', 'fictions') which will have their basis in the realistic world of the possible.

These processes can also be argued to underlie the developmental progress of the fascination of fear. The inability to comprehend ambiguous surroundings, and the lack of direct control, lead young children to 'incarnate' the unknown in a manner which emphasizes threatening aspects. In a sense, this can be seen as an exercise in self-preservation, since the terror thus generated causes the child to actively seek out, or at least attract by crying or screaming, the protection provided by parents and the comfort of the known. Growth in cognitive awareness makes this type of dependence on external protection and reassurance increasingly less absolute, so that the monsters embodying childhood fears come to lose much of their significance and disturbing features once the fears they originally embodied are understood to be unfounded and unnecessary. The processes involved in this development will include cognitive exploration. Fictional possibilities of a horrific nature can be considered from a position of control, so that the exercise becomes a type of game where 'risks' are taken in the knowledge that safety is not really threatened. This is often enough what happens in what Harding calls 'the technique by which in everyday social intercourse we invite each other to contemplate, and to evaluate, possible events and outcomes' – a technique which can be seen at its simplest in the 'suppose' or 'pretend' games in which children frequently engage during conversation (Harding 1967: 8).

Many horror stories, because they pose no real threat and function within clearly circumscribed parameters, have been argued to owe their popular appeal to the fact that they constitute linguistic and conceptual games of the type discussed above. As such they can be said to be exercises in the discovery and exploration of map–territory relations, in that they provide a safely distanced and stylized means of making sense of and coming to terms with phenomena and potentialities of experience which under normal (i.e. functional) conditions would be found too threatening and disturbing. Though it may not have been put in quite this way, this point has been made by a wide cross-section of commentators on the genre. Fraser, for instance, notes that 'for all their violences, violent entertainments normally involve a blanking out of the really unpleasant, and tend to promote a sense of security and invulnerability in the reader and viewer' (Fraser 1976: 66). Part I of this book has also explored the contours and functions of the reassuring roles performed by works of horror fiction. As already noted, one analogy which is frequently used to make this point is that of amusement park rides. Thus, the child sitting on the 'big dipper' at the fair can indulge in a thrilling exploration of what it would feel like to be on the brink of disaster, and to be momentarily deprived again of active control. But the exploration takes place in a context which gives a guarantee of security and is not really uncontrolled. There is only a tacitly negotiated pretence of lack of control. Both types of play (i.e. the fiction of the 'big dipper' and that involved in the institutionalized and genre-regulated contemplation of horrific possibilities) therefore involve and presuppose cognitive, emotional, and social processes which are more complex than is suggested by the assertion that they simply provide a socially sanctioned arena for the safe release of pent-up aggressiveness. When one underlines the playful nature of these activities, one is also making allowance for the fact that they involve explorations of map–territory relations. These, then, are social activities which hold out a promise that participants can place their vulnerability in trust while they flex their cognitive and emotional muscles, as it were, by exposing themselves to fears which were previously unmanageable. Such games have thus been argued to provide what Harding calls a 'melodramatised parallel' to individual anxieties, and to act as a salutary force by showing in a stylized way that imaginary perils can be survived or approached and understood in a rational manner (Harding 1967: 8–9). Bettelheim's (1976) modification of the catharsis theory into the suggestion that fiction provides the child with tools with which to manage chaotic feelings by giving them a local habitation and a name (discussed at the end of chapter 4 in this book) is in many ways an extension of this perspective.

These accounts, however, raise a number of issues and problems. For one thing, the notion assumes that the fictions will consistently follow a fairly uniform and clearly stylized pattern which will instantly carry the message 'this is play' to its audience. This, as was illustrated in part I of this book, is very often what does happen, and the assumptions and negotiated messages which the process involves raise interesting questions about the cultural settings which make it possible. However, this process is not as uniform or straightforward as that assertion might suggest. An author can use conventional and stylized patterns of story-telling in order to give the illusion that possibilities of experience are about to be explored in a familiarly reassuring manner. In such cases, the game the author intends for his audience is different from the one being proposed, so that the process becomes double-edged, in the sense that there is also a game being played on the audience's expectations. This is what happens when tales of terror break out of conventional patterns and challenge or disturb preconceptions – thus changing or breaking the rules after the game has started, as it were, and in the process modifying the author–text–reader interaction as well as the nature of the shared exploration of map–territory relations. The game analogy also takes it for granted that readers will react to the implicit 'this is play' message encoded in the conventional discursive patterns of (say) horror fiction in a fairly standard way – i.e. by tacitly agreeing to play along and exploring a series of possibilities and values from a discreet distance. When this type of agreement is made, of course, interesting questions are raised about the methods in which individuals make sense of experience. But it is also worth stressing that not all readers or viewers are likely to react in the same way to the fictionalized discussion of horrific potentialities and hypotheses. Harding suggests that the people who appear to derive most pleasure out of stories of terror and misfortune are those who are only partially or superficially satisfied that the world is really quite a safe and livable-in place (ibid.:

8–9). It is because of such secret and perhaps only half-conscious doubts, Harding points out, that many people derive satisfaction from having the possibilities of terror and destruction brought into the open. Thus, while children want to read about dangers escaped and disasters survived, older readers often prefer to contemplate the worst. The types of possibilities which are most frequently contemplated in the fictions of a particular culture, as well as the tone which is assumed in their relation, can therefore be read as important reflectors of that culture's appraisal of what constitutes reality, and of the types of competence which its members feel in relation to their environment.

In his often quoted essay on the 'uncanny', Freud argued that 'anyone who has finally rid himself of animistic beliefs' will be insensible to the type of uncanny feelings which arise when something actually happens in our lives which seems to confirm old discarded beliefs – or, in Harding's terms, half-conscious doubts. In Freud's view, 'the whole thing is purely an affair of "reality-testing", a question of the material reality of phenomena' (Freud 1919a, 1955 edn: 248). There are two problems with this account, and they are problems which have a direct bearing on the fact that different individuals will react differently to situations (in life or in fiction) like those discussed by Freud. For one thing, our perception of what constitutes 'the material reality of phenomena' can be erratic because of cultural and environmental influences, or because the tools which we happen to be using are not adequately refined. This partly accounts for the fact that interpretations and fictitious accounts which look utterly unrealistic to some people might actually be viewed as very possible and realistic by others (whose maps of reality are presumably different). Young children are thus disturbed by tales of monsters which to adults appear absurdly exaggerated precisely because of limitations in the tools which they are using to test out the reality or otherwise of such monsters. The exercise of 'reality testing' is also complicated by our habit of interpreting phenomena according to intentions and predispositions. As various social psychologists have noted, people's cognitive and evaluative processes are selective, in the sense that, as van der Pligt and Eiser put it, their 'attitudes and values lead them to see as salient those aspects of an issue in terms of which their own opinions seem most rational and justified' (van der Pligt and Eiser 1984: 173). Thus, with adults and children alike, the images and possibilities which are likely to be seen as most realistic are those which are most closely aligned with predisposed intentions, and which bear the greatest resemblance to customary perceptions of the world of reality and of the individual's relation to it. In the jargon of semiotics (and more specifically Barthes), these are the signs which have the most highly motivated or iconic levels of signification; in that of cognitive social psychology, these are the images which are most dimensionally salient.

Our need to impose significance on the empirical realities which surround us and the inhospitable nature of the states of uncertainty and helplessness have given rise to a number of dangerously self-contradictory attitudes and reinterpretations in our century's atmosphere of social, political, and economic insecurity. Where there is doubt about the (customarily assumed) security of habitual reality – when the real, in a sense, becomes unreal[8] – the illusion of control and significance, even when it is transparent, grotesquely despondent, or bloodlessly smug, is often clung to in preference to the threats of uncertainty. To labour a point, the types of fear which are likely to fester or manifest themselves in this kind of context will have origins and implications which can be ideologically enslaving and which can only be properly understood in relation to the viability or otherwise of the significances which our culture ascribes to itself and its surroundings. 'The uncanny fantasy of any generation', as Prawer puts its, 'has its roots firmly in the life of that generation' (Prawer 1980: 135). In this context one can begin to understand how often outmoded but 'legalized' science is frequently resorted to and made a popular (and magical) means of accounting for phenomena which defy easy classification or which are felt to be disarmingly disturbing. It is also within this context that one can begin to account for (on the one hand) modern society's ability to domesticate and normalize the unspeakable by claiming to 'understand' it when it has dressed it or its interpreters in suitably scientific-looking garb, and (on the other) for the various cults and fetishes which periodically grow around unrealizable fantasies. The intentions and interpretations influencing such attitudes betray nagging uncertainties, so that the deceptions which make them possible are frequently not fully internalized, and doubt and helplessly vacuous anxieties persist. It is presumably in such situations that satisfaction is derived from the contemplation of possibilities of terror and destruction. When the deceptions are internalized, on the other hand, they can be said to become the basis of a precarious ostrich-like existence.

The implications of these arguments are worth pausing over in terms of the bearing they have on the distinction made by Nietzsche between 'the actual causes of a thing's origin and its eventual uses, the manner of its incorporation into a system of purposes' (Nietzsche 1887, 1956 edn: 209). Nietzsche insisted that 'all processes in the organic world are processes of outstripping and overcoming, and that, in turn, all outstripping and overcoming means reinterpretation, rearrangement, in the course of which the earlier meaning and purpose are necessarily either obscured or lost' (ibid.). When reinterpretations are made without a clear awareness of the role and trend of the requirements of the specific system of purposes governing their direction and emphases, or when those purposes become obscured in habitual assumptions or myth, new modes of discourse and conceptions underlying motivation and behaviour will continue to remain invested with values and intentions which may have become redundant or even counter-productive. This does not mean that the understanding of self and surroundings can be anything but interpretative. It is, rather, to assert that the extent to which such understanding can be said to be viable or progressive depends largely on an awareness of the paradoxes of the hermeneutical circle which constitute 'the correlation between explanation and understanding, between understanding and explanation' (Ricoeur 1981: 221):

> If we follow the paradigm of the dialectic between explanation and understanding to its end, we must say that the meaningful patterns which a depth interpretation wants to grasp cannot be understood without a kind of personal commitment similar to that of the reader who grasps the depth semantics of the text and makes it his 'own'.
>
> (ibid.: 220)

In other words, 'the conditions of an authentic appropriation . . . are themselves paradigmatic', since such appropriation is inseparable from the explanatory procedures which mediate it, and since it is language which has the referential function of establishing the relation of human beings to the world. Understanding, as Ricoeur points out, 'has nothing to do with an *immediate* grasping of a foreign psychic life or with an *emotional* identification with a mental intention'. It is, rather, 'entirely *mediated* by the whole of explanatory procedures which precede and accompany it'. These procedures are the counterpart of personal appropriation, and as such they release 'the dynamic meaning' constituting the power of disclosing a world (ibid.).

Explanations and interpretations, therefore, can be said to become tautologically magical when the intentional processes underlying understanding are not acknowledged and qualified. When this happens, the motivated 'assimilations and disintegrations' of consciousness give rise to a self-enclosed world view in which the fantastic and the practically mundane are appraised with inadequately defined and loosely differentiating speculative instruments. To state this differently, thought becomes omnipotent in the sense that the mind's interactions with the symbolic forms at its disposal become circular and magically all-determining. There is clearly something wrong when this type of consciousness becomes what Berger *et al.* call a society's symbolic universe (Berger *et al.* 1974: 21), and forms the basis of overarching reality definitions which the individual needs to give meaning to life as a whole and which are essential to hold any society together and keep any particular situation going. Such a symbolic universe can make but limited reference to Sartre's 'deterministic world of the usable'. It is tautological, in that (to adopt Barthes's definition), it becomes a 'magical act ashamed of itself, which verbally makes the gesture of rationality, but immediately abandons the latter, and believes itself even with causality because it has uttered the word which introduces it' (Barthes 1973: 153).

A number of issues raised by this assertion as it applies to scientific interpretations and claims about the functions and consequences of fictional violence and horror have a direct bearing on many of the academic perspectives discussed in chapters 4 and 5 of this book.

STEREOTYPES AND THE MYSTIFICATION OF REALITY

These points can be illustrated through a brief consideration of a family of social stereotypes which at specific points in history were made to carry the burden of responsibility for unpalatable or confusing cultural realities, and which have also developed into customary images of fear. According to Thomas (1973), beliefs in witchcraft in a society technologically more backward than ours served not only as a means of accounting for the otherwise inexplicable misfortunes of daily life (a function also performed by other stereotypes like, in sixteenth-century England, fifth-column Frenchmen, Catholics, Jews, etc.), but also as a means of placating a growing unease created by moral and economic conflicts in a changing society. Accusations of witchcraft were usually intended to explain misfortune of a particular or personal nature, rather than calamities in general. At a period when social inequalities were becoming more marked, personal interests and cultural expectations came into conflict, in the sense that many individuals were faced with the task of reconciling the interests of personal property with the traditional demands of neighbourliness. Thomas argues that English-speaking communities before the sixteenth and seventeenth centuries had been based on a tradition of mutual help, so that the giving of food and drink, or the loan of equipment, had for a long time been considered neighbourly activities which were in the common interest. Beliefs in the power of witches grew at a period when this tradition came in conflict with the growth of personal property and appropriation, so that accusations of witchcraft were frequently directed against a neighbour by people who had failed to fulfil their accepted social obligations towards her. There was a pattern in such accusations which, as Thomas puts it, 'illustrates the essential conflict between neighbourliness and individualism which generated the tensions from which the accusations of witchcraft were most likely to arise' (Thomas 1973: 662). Thus, many witch cases arose after disputes over common land, gleaning, rights of way, or trespass, and a number of accusations of witchcraft were based on claims of retaliation against such local tyrants as the overseer of the poor who had put the children of the accused into compulsory service, or the village constable who had pressed their sons to be soldiers. Ironically, it was usually the 'witch' who was morally in the right, in that she was avenging a definite injury rather than acting out of mere vindictiveness. This, Thomas points out, was a pattern which corresponds with what many anthropologists have found elsewhere. The witch and her victim were usually two persons who ought to have been friendly towards each other, but were not. They existed in a state of hostility for which society provided no legitimate outlet, in that they could neither have recourse to open violence nor take each other to court. In this sense, witch beliefs reveal a great deal about the weak points in the social structure of the period and region in which they are prominent. Thus, accusations of witchcraft in Africa frequently spring from conflicts within the family, as in cases involving co-wives of a polygamous husband. In the England of the sixteenth and seventeenth centuries, on the other hand, the witch and her accuser were very seldom related. As Thomas puts it:

> The tensions which such accusations usually reflected arose from the position of the poor and dependent members of the community.

The charges of witchcraft were a means of expressing deep-felt animosities in acceptable guise. Before a witchcraft accusation could be plausibly made, the suspect had to be in a socially and economically inferior position to her supposed victim. Only then could she be presumed to be likely to have had recourse to magical methods of retaliation, for, had she been the stronger party, more direct methods of revenge would have been at her disposal.

(ibid.: 669)

The mental processes and evasions involved in the institution and justification of such accusations are worth considering more closely – not least because they appear to involve critical restructurings of world views (cognitive/hodological maps) as a result of clearly identifiable (though unacknowledged) purposes. Such restructurings can be seen to have wide-ranging consequences and implications, in that they will come to form the basis of further judgements once the 'map' they are forging is sufficiently established. The method of restructuring is also interesting for the purposes of the present argument in that it appears to proceed in a manner which involves complex linguistic games and deceptions which are rationalized through the juggling of attributes, analogies, perceptions, and meanings. Cognitive dissonance theory (Festinger 1957)[9] would predict that in situations where the individual finds him/herself holding two cognitions (i.e. ideas, attitudes, opinions, beliefs) which are inconsistent with each other, he or she will resolve the uncomfortable psychological conflict created by this dissonance by changing one or both cognitions in such a way as to render them more compatible, or else by adding more cognitions to help bridge the gap between them. Accusations of witchcraft as described by Thomas can be argued to have resulted partly from a state of cognitive dissonance which arose when individuals had to resolve the psychological conflict created by a set of mutually exclusive demands, desires, and expectations in a changing social situation. Such a conflict and its attendant uncertainties were resolved (or, more exactly, evaded) when the individual giving rise to the dissonance could be seen as not a neighbour towards whom one had duties, but as a conniver with demons and a threat to the common good. The very Christian virtues which the 'victim' felt uncomfortable about breaking ('Love thy neighbour as thyself') could thus be conveniently seen as justifying and even binding him or her to accuse the 'witch' and thus protect honest Christians against the evil one. The exchanging of tales about the wicked and horrible deeds committed by witches not only helped in the reinforcement of such justifications: such stories also continued to act as conservative guardians of the values and ideological purposes underlying accusations of witchcraft long after their attendant beliefs and conflicts had ceased to be of direct social or personal relevance. As Sulloway puts it:

> The ideological forces which govern the creation of myth during major revolutions do not just dissipate once their task has been accomplished; rather they continue to inhere within the structure of myth they have created. As revolution becomes dogma, myth increasingly assumes the role of its conservative guardian in order to continue to mediate between stability and change long after the revolutionary change has passed away.
>
> (Sulloway 1979: 502)

As I argued in part I of this book, many of the stock characters and fears contemplated in horror fiction can be seen to have origins and associations similar to those encoded (and frequently buried) in stereotypes like that of the witch. Stereotypes of psychopaths, juvenile delinquents, uncontrollable monsters, and invading demons – as well as larger unifying myths like those of 'beasts within' and 'clockwork mechanisms' allegedly underlying motivation and behaviour – reflect but some of the recurring analogical games resorted to in the course of contemporary society's attempts to evade the implications of unpleasant social and existential realities. Rather than providing tools for progressive and constructive interpretations, these stereotypes and the contexts within which they function and have meaning, in many cases become means of evading the real implications of the uncertainties and discomforts which appear to be endemic to the constantly changing social, political, and economic conditions of our technologically oriented cultures. And, since many of them are based on outdated concepts, they can also be argued to compound confusion and perpetuate redundant ways of seeing. The fact that there are significant links between the concerns or weaknesses of a particular society and the types of terrors which become the focus of its fascinated observation has of course frequently been noted by critics of the horror genre. Moretti, for instance, makes a forceful case for the contention that 'the literature of terror is born precisely out of the terror of a split society and out of the desire to heal it' (Moretti 1982: 68). Thus, Frankenstein's monster (the utterly unknown) is described as serving 'to displace the antagonisms and horrors evidenced within society to outside society itself', while *Dracula* (with its thinly veiled themes of repressed sexuality and class conflicts) is argued to represent 'a refined attempt by the nineteenth-century mind not to recognise itself' (ibid.: 81). In these terms Moretti proposes a refined Marxist reading of the literature of terror, asserting that its function is that of taking up within itself determinate fears in order to transform them into other (unreal) fears, with the purpose of saving readers from having to face up to what might really frighten them:

> It is a 'negative' function: it distorts reality. It is a work of 'mystification'. But it is also a work of 'production'. The more these great symbols of mass culture depart from reality the more, of necessity, they must expand and enrich the structures of false consciousness: which is nothing other than the dominant culture. They are not confined to distortion and falsification: they form, affirm, convince. And this process is automatic and self-propelling. Mary Shelley and Bram Stoker do not have the slightest intention to 'mystify' reality: they interpret it in a spontaneously mendacious manner.
>
> (ibid.: 83)

The implications of map/schemes analogies as developed in accounts of cognitive functioning can also be profitably applied to the patterns in which myths develop and give rise to the genre conventions which come to enframe and perpetuate them (and hence the values they embody). Thus, myths too preserve and organize information about the world of experience. In this sense, they also store and suggest perceptual patterns and methods of ascribing meaning which derive from earlier as well as ongoing interpretations and assumptions. The genre conventions within which popular myths are stored and expressed can on these terms be viewed as (popular) maps of cultural realities. Such maps can develop into self-enclosed analogical constructs which become interpretative strait-jackets evoking exclusively magical effects. The analogical tools which they store can also, however, form the basis of innovatively realistic interpretations of experience – as happens in cases when gifted writers use genre conventions in order to extend and/or challenge the preconceptions on which such conventions are based. Whether a particular genre will assume the first or the second of these cultural and cognitive functions depends mainly on how flexibly and imaginatively it is handled and reacted to by writers, readers, and professional commentators. Part I of this book, it will be recalled, also discussed some of the methods in which genre writers can either become totally dominated by the genre conventions which they happen to be following, or else use such conventions as a ground for the extension of ideas – i.e. as ways of making what is widely recognizable the basis for the introduction of new ways of seeing and thinking about experience and reality, or even about those ways of seeing themselves (as happens in works which deliberately draw attention to the conventions, mechanics, and clichés of the genre in order to, say, underline their inadequacies, or else draw out the real horrors of the situations to which they refer). Much of the more popular and successful type of contemporary horror fiction does not do this: it endorses assumptions and reinforces preconceptions, transforming areas of communal unease into provinces of sanitized and safely padded thrills – self-enclosed and self-referring, leading nowhere except to evasions of its own real meanings.

At the risk of sounding repetitive, it is worth stressing again that stereotypes and literary/cultural archetypes (like 'fantasy') do not just develop out of thin air: they form part of complex meaning-making processes which are inspired by identifiable social and psychological purposes. They also form part of the myths which societies construct in order to help make sense of the world of experience, as well as derive reassurance about perceived aspects of that experience which appear to pose a threat to control, comprehension, happiness, and/or survival. In this sense they form an important component of the meaning-making tools (or cultural amplifiers, in Bruner's phrase) of contemporary society. This chapter has explored some of the processes underlying the methods in which tools of this type are developed and deployed, and drawn attention to some of the uses of analogies (maps and games) which have in their turn been found appropriate and helpful for the understanding of the processes which underlie the creation and development of genre conventions like those of horror fiction.

It has been the contention of this chapter that childhood and adult fears are underscored by a sense of helplessness in the face of the very strange. Adult fears are similar to those of children in the sense that both involve the interpretation of disturbing ambiguities in terms of the fictions of the imagination inspired by the multiple rhythms of interaction with an environment. In each case, a complex process of dramatization, or of making sense through analogy and (when conditions allow) playful exploration, can be said to be in operation. The types of fear which arise when (in Sartre's phrase) 'the world of the utilisable vanishes abruptly and the world of magic appears in its place' (Sartre 1971: 90–1) inevitably raise questions about the cultural and social structures, as well as the symbolic tools, which help to form and give expression to children's and adults' conceptions of reality. Our understanding of what can be referred to as real, and of what possibilities can be applied to the appraisal of a particular situation, is dependent on the systems of purposes and frames of reference which operate within our particular cultural context. It is these systems and frames which give rise to possibilities for knowledge and thus largely determine (or enframe) the interpretations of reality which are available to us. In this sense, popular and academic redescriptions of perceived reality constitute important components of social discourse, and hence of social reality, in that they give expression to the structuring of experience in coherent terms and images in order to make sense of such experience by ascribing motives to action or causes to events.

An important implication of this argument is that we can only establish the viability or otherwise of the significance which we ascribe to specific situations by identifying and analysing the models of reality out of which such ascriptions are compounded. It is this exercise which has formed the focus of this book.

ENDWORD:
Consuming impotence

A video-rental outlet in south London (though it could be in any part of the western world) prominently displays a series of posters outside its shop window. The themes and images on show are instantly familiar to the late twentieth-century popular consciousness. They include well-known faces from the world of movies, emblematic poses and icons, and aggressive-sounding titles and captions printed in variously coloured and shaped lettering. Through a complex but firmly established series of associations, these signs arouse curiosity by playing on feelings of uncertainty, anxiety, and fear. But they also function within parameters which disarm and sanitize the very anxieties which they encourage and keep in discursive circulation. Even at their most ghastly and nauseous, they and the context in which they are presented can usually be recognized as proffering magical solutions and soothing (if ostrich-like) cures for the horrifying and disturbing states which they invite us to consider. In this sense, they are also agents of reassurance. Their paradoxically mixed functions as dredgers of anxiety and winchers of magically stilted confidence in large measure account for their continued popularity – in the sense that (as many writers in this field have noted) they provide an amusement-park type of excitement for anyone who wishes to indulge in it. At the same time, however, this mixture of functions also underlines a certain tendentiousness about the signs of horror fiction – a tendentiousness which is linked to the roles they perform as guardians of established values within the consumerist culture of which they have become increasingly prominent and popular components.

In the top right-hand corner of the video-rental shop window, a poster displays a huge, torn, and grotesque-looking claw, apparently reaching out towards whoever happens to be facing it. Just behind the claw, a deformed, putrefying, and vaguely human-looking skull smashes out of an exploding television screen. The poster suggests immediacy and the urgency of frozen animation: the skull appears to have just burst out of the set, and there are flashes of discharged electrical power surrounding it. The pin-sharp eyes, harshly arched eyebrow, and generally malevolent expression suggest the threat of pent-up aggressive violence – long frustrated and now revealed at the moment of triumphant release. The figure's mouth is open, its snarl displaying inordinately large, sharp, but also sick-looking and jagged teeth. There is also a second claw clutching the side of the smashed TV set from the inside, in a manner which suggests that the festering body attached to the head is levering itself to climb out of a prison which is now incapable of containing the shattering force of its supernatural energy. There is an electricity lead snaking out of the set; it is attached to a plug which is, like the creature's skull, full of highlighted electrical discharges. It flies out towards the front bottom corner of the poster, and past the graphically lettered and gaudily coloured title: 'THE VIDEO DEAD'. A prominent caption is printed in white at the top right-hand corner and against a dark background which is also interspersed with jagged lines of further electrical discharges. The caption proffers a gloating invitation: 'LOOK WHAT'S BURIED INSIDE YOUR TELEVISION.'

In another corner of the shop window, a second poster displays Arnold Schwarzenegger looking defiantly past and over the point of focus of the camera which has presumably captured him in this pose. He is standing sideways and wearing a sling vest, so that his bulging, flexed, and shining arm muscles appear to jut out of the picture towards the viewer. Equally prominent is a large sub-machine-gun which Schwarzenegger holds in both hands with what looks like a firm and expert grasp. The gun points skywards, but it is also slightly tilted towards the camera, suggesting that its owner is poised for action, waiting for the slightest move before pointing and opening a blast of fire. Flames and columns of smoke provide the backdrop. Another prominent feature on Schwarzenegger's arm is a large wrist-watch whose metallic slickness both matches and helps to highlight the shining ripples of his bulging biceps. Unlike the monster of the telly (with its tufts of sick-looking hair and untidily decaying flesh), Schwarzenegger is well groomed: his hair is firmly greased back and his jaw is almost defiantly clean-shaven. There is, in fact, a harshly cosmopolitan air about this tough and hardened handler of violence and heavy metal who roams the burning streets in a sling vest. He is, the picture's details suggest, a respectable citizen – one of us. If his pose threatens danger, it is a danger which is also meant to reassure honest and right-thinking citizens. It is the refuse of society, or even unpalatable creatures like that of the TV set on the other poster, who should feel threatened by Schwarzenegger's look, muscle, and metal.

Both posters depend for their effect on our ability to decode them in the light of our familiarity with a series of popular films and images. This of course underlines the extent to which our modes of perceiving (and hence of interpreting and reacting to the realities and dangers of the world around us) have been influenced by these latter-day versions of popular myths and by speculative instruments which have a long and complex history. Thus, the associations suggested by the first poster partly derive from the fact that, for all the supposedly futuristic-looking flashes of flying electricity, the pose captured and depicted here is a staple and recurring cliché of the horror-film industry. The monster climbing out of the TV set looks like, and (for the effect it is meant to create) depends on, our recollections of scenes in which vampires and/or zombies climb out of their coffins/graves and reach out to grab and devour the nearest available victim. The television set out of which the monster is climbing is, in fact, lying horizontally, its 'feet' facing the front – a position which is highly unusual for a TV set, but which forcefully suggests (in this context, anyway) a coffin. The poster thus attempts to update the implications of a hackneyed set of images by aligning them with popular images of technological wizardry. Concerns and disturbing ideas whose meanings and force derive from superstitious and magical beliefs developed during earlier centuries' (often crude) attempts to make sense of incomprehensible phenomena are thus proposed to the viewer as relevant and as forming part of a scientifically perceived universe. The dressing up depends for its effect on a slick (though relatively unimaginative) use and combination of images.

Schwarzenegger's pose in the second poster forms part of a family of images with an equally long progeny, but whose foremost and most familiar contemporary exponent is Sylvester Stallone's Rambo. Like Rambo, Schwarzenegger is here clearly meant to be seen as a tough guy of the likeable variety, the type who will fight for his rights, defend those of others, and beat or blast the hell out of anybody who stands in the way of these pursuits. The poster's captions compound this impression. The name 'SCHWARZENEGGER' is printed in large red capitals over the head of its pictured owner; and under his elbow,

178

in equally bold red lettering, stand the words 'RAW DEAL'. Below this, in lower-case but prominent white lettering, is the phrase: '*Nobody* gives him a Raw Deal.' The notions underlying these mythological constructs are in many ways a rather grotesque offspring of liberal individualism – they set up the tough resourcefulness of the lone individual as the ultimate hope of a corrupt society. At the same time, there are also magical and quasi-superstitious meanings placed here on the individual's ability to be tough, to survive almost impossible odds through an astute and muscle-bound use of brute force. And among the complex web of ideas underlying the pose, as well as the threats and cures which it simultaneously suggests, is the notion that human beings are essentially savage beasts whose modes of functioning are mechanically determined and controlled. On the basis of this assumption, a host of contemporary popular images repeatedly project the message that those who shall inherit the earth are the fittest – i.e. those who have taken the trouble to pump up their muscles and learn the techniques of combat warfare, who can automatically switch on to the 'combat mode' in times of trouble, and who are thus tough and strong enough to spit in the face of traders of raw deals. Rambo, though he is anything but the first-born of the line of popular heroes embodying these values, is probably the most representative of the 1980s version. His screen cousins are many-faceted and they range from the ostensibly self-mocking to the self-righteously dead earnest. They include the likeably naïve but tough Crocodile Dundee (of the Paul Hogan series), who applies the survival techniques he has learnt in the Australian outback to the supposedly more sophisticated jungles of New York social and inner-city life, and in the process manages to work his way to the top of the American Dream. In what is presumably meant to be taken as harmlessly 'escapist' (but reassuring) fun, his solutions to inner-city problems are simple: make sure you can draw out a larger knife than that held by any city bum who may attack you; don't allow yourself to get caught up in the niceties of (so-called) civilization, it is safer and saner to barge through them. The *Death Wish* movie series in many ways projected a more hard-faced version of the same notions. In this highly successful sequence, the tough protagonist (played by Charles Bronson) was cheered as he assumed the role and responsibilities of self-appointed and self-styled guardian of justice, and exercised his rights by shooting down the scum of the city streets. The Bronson character too was forcefully shown to have learned the hard way that the world can only be made

179

habitable by those who are able to face up to the 'fact' that we are all beasts, that reacting to other beasts' aggressiveness in wimpishly 'civilized' fashions is self-destructive, and that we need to harness and channel our own bestiality in ways which will enable us to dispose of any less considerate beasts who might be disrupting the social order and our position within it. Given the growth in the popularity of such orientations, it is perhaps not surprising that the horrific monsters depicted in films like *Aliens* or the 1980s remake of *The Thing* tend to be destroyed through a combination of nerve and heavy ammunition – a trend which is well caught in the sequence towards the end of *Aliens* when, tense in a descending lift and bracing herself for the final confrontation with the monsters, Sigourny Weaver adjusts the heavy artillery with which she is laden and assumes a pose which suggests daring determination and force by virtue of the fact that it mimics Sylvester Stallone's now mythic pose as defiant Rambo in combat gear.

In the course of his semiotic analysis of popular and influential images coming from the America of the 1980s, Blonsky argues that such images reflect a critical shift from the socially oriented popular iconography of the 1960s and 1970s (with their 'fantasy of changing the world and confronting society') to a situation where the popular fantasies reflected and reinforced in dominant images betray 'the urge to accept society and live within its values' (Blonsky 1985: xxxiii). Pleasure, Blonsky argues, has become 'the great naturalizer', with the result that sex and politics, for instance, are now often equated with 'romance and knowledgeable eating and drinking'. The projection of militarism, heavy artillery, and disciplined aggressiveness as sexy commodities is part of this cultural construction of meaning:

> I pass a poster in the subway, an ad for a pleasure product. . . . It shows a man in uniform on a ship coming towards me. Again on the street seeing that poster, I several times mistook the man for a military, not a merchant marine officer. The mistake was intended; the intent was to add the value of pleasure to current militarism. Only in the Reagan Age in America the Bland could a uniform, after Vietnam, be popular again.
>
> (ibid.: xxviii–xxix)

The Rambo family of images forms part of a complex cultural reality. A lot of its appeal presumably derives from its suggestion that there are (or should be) simple and effective (tough, hard-punching, even personalized) solutions to the problems of society. Such a notion, of course, can only be perceived as reassuring if one approaches it from a perspective which is also willing to label the problems and their sources as simple (and thus amenable to magical blasting). The suspension of disbelief which makes the images credible, in other words, requires specific conceptual frameworks, and the orientations which make such perspectives and evasions possible can be argued to grow out of interpretative habits which have a broad base in a wide cross-section of the signs of contemporary popular culture. Thus, obstacles to happiness and success are often neatly and reductively identified in the mythology of (say) advertising as externalized and magically defeatable 'monsters' of ugliness, social inadequacy, insufficiently consumerist orientations. The roots of anxiety have thus ostensibly (though misleadingly) become fairly easy to label and locate. And, while they flatter themselves that they have moved beyond superstitious and enslaving orientations, the more 'advanced' (i.e. industrialized) cultures of the modern world continue to read themselves in terms of signs and images that simultaneously titillate and dissolve anxiety in magical fashions, and which are frequently based on outdated and regressive assumptions about human nature, behaviour, and existence.

It is not an accident that it is at this period that there should have been a notable growth in the number of 'professionals' who have made the writing of horror stories their full-time (and often very lucrative) occupation. In his contribution to a collection of essays discussing and giving 'inside' (mostly adulatory) information about the phenomenal contemporary success of Stephen King, Robert Bloch (author of *Psycho*) considers why it is that writers like himself choose to 'frighten rather than enlighten, why dwell upon and within a domain of darkness, dread and death'. Insisting that he is 'neither a philosopher nor a psychiatrist', Bloch offers what he describes as 'the easy explanation':

> On the basis of personal belief and observation, I'd say that those of us who direct our storytelling into darker channels do so because we are perhaps a bit more mindful than most regarding our childhood confusions of identity, our conflicts with unpleasant realities and our traumatic encounters with imaginative terrors. Although there are significant exceptions, it would appear that the majority of writers who deal with the supernatural have repudiated the tenets

of organised religion. In so doing they may have lost the fear of hellfire but they've also sacrificed any hope of heaven. What remains is an all-too-vivid fear of pain and death and a final, total, eternal oblivion.

(in Underwood and Miller 1987: 24)

The paradox of Bloch's position is in many ways symptomatic of its age. He sees himself as forming part of a group of writers who 'deal with the supernatural' but consider themselves to belong to a secular-ized society and culture. The fact that 'the majority of writers' in this industry 'have repudiated the tenets of organized religion' underlines the curiously disembedded (and disembodied) nature of their posi-tion. The horror industry has domesticated the supernatural and turned it into a commodity with considerable market value – particu-larly when it is traded in contexts which have endorsed its divorce from the institutionalized structures of religion which traditionally supervised its interpretations and meaning. At the same time, how-ever, those structures and their tenets and rituals continue to provide many of the horror-monger's central images and ideas, as well as the background for his shock effects. As I argued in the first part of this book, the assumptions and conceptual frameworks underlying the conventions of horror fiction often derive from half-baked processes of secularization. It is precisely because these conventions are uncer-tainly (and often vacuously) positioned between superstition and (poorly digested) science that the only mode within which they can adequately function is the magical. There are parallels to be drawn here with the manner in which, in many of the industrialized coun-tries of the western world in the 1980s, popular culture appears to have been dominated by frequently frantic calls for a return to traditionally safe and conservative values – often in the face of changing realities which emphatically demand the construction of newer and more sharply tuned interpretative instruments. There is, in other words, a desire to retreat from the uncertainties created by the dislocations endemic to change, but not at the expense of the comforts and titillations which have been made accessible by the technological advances underlying that change.

The application of simple and simplistic labels and solutions to the modern world's problems is not likely to resolve those problems; and dwelling on stereotyped and caricatured representations of the sources of concern is likely to compound the disturbing confusions and uncertainties – particularly when, as happens in much popular horror fiction, the reflections and ascriptions of values are conducted in terms of images based on superseded concepts and beliefs. Writers like Bloch can at times produce works which draw out and illustrate the terrors growing out of and feeding on such states of uncertainty. But, given the fact that they also frequently depend on the compounding and reinforcement of outdated assumptions for their effects, they are also manifestly incapable of proposing or providing anything near a solution to the uncomfortable states which they describe. It is also appropriate perhaps that such states should also have been fitted so neatly into the consumerist cultures of the late twentieth century, and there transformed into an increasingly lucrative source of economic growth and financial success. It is, in short, this curious investment of and in uncertainty which propels and maintains the continuing growth of the western world's horror-fiction industry – an industry which has developed into one of the most oddly successful means of production and consumption of the modern age.

Most of this book has been concerned with identifying what the continued popularity of the horror genre suggests about the methods in which the contemporary (popular as well as educated) consciousness imposes meaning upon experience. The arguments developed here have been based on a premise which in fact underscores some of the most challenging contemporary thinking in various fields – i.e. that our methods of making sense are analogically structured, and that human perception and behaviour are shaped by what have been variously described as internal fictions, mental models, schemes, or maps of reality formed and refined in the course of experience. As part II of this book has striven to show, this perspective raises a number of issues which can be used as basis for developing research methods and ways of reading cultural phenomena like horror fiction that will avoid the inadequacies of more simplistic and reductionist approaches. As a reminder of the fact that meanings are constructed against the background of, and using the tools provided by, complex social formations, this perspective can form the basis of a more viable understanding of the cultural, social, and political structures and discursive conventions within the parametes of which phenomena like horror fiction assume specific meanings and project variously loaded messages and values. The preceding chapters have also contended that the methods in which such meanings and messages are read, evaluated, and reacted to by their interpreters are also importantly mediated by the same structures and conventions which give meaning to the genres themselves. It follows from this that, if we are dissatisfied by the trend of contemporary depictions of horrific situations, or confused/worried by the fact that we find such depictions fascinating (or that others claim to find them entertaining), then we should be looking more critically at the structures and conventions which make them (and our reactions) possible. As this book has repeatedly pointed out, though they usually come dressed in flashily modern guises and trendy poses, many of these structures and conventions are built out of assumptions whose driving force and foundations have little contact with the present-day world of practical reality.

The examples of contemporary horror fictions and the fields of popular and academic discourse discussed in this book suggest that our age is one in which myths are made (often sceptically, generally uncertainly) to perform the functions of magic as Malinowski conceived it – i.e. of patching over (rather than resolving) those unbridgeable gaps and hiatuses in our knowledge or in our powers of practical control (Malinowski 1937: 638). As a result, a variety of symbols and modes of perceiving remain enmeshed in our attempts to appraise and evaluate our true bearings long after they have lost any direct relevance. The types of fear which are likely to prevail in this context will have origins and implications which cannot be properly understood or resolved if our awareness of competence or control in relation to our environment is no more than an exercise in self-deception, or if our lives are structured around a resigned sense of helplessness and ruled by the politics of bitter vacuousness.

NOTES

CHAPTER 1 HORROR FICTION AND SOCIAL UNEASE – AN OVERVIEW

1 Summers reprints the first chapter of *Varney the Vampire* in full, on the grounds that its author 'has certainly studied the Vampire legends with some care' and 'for all his lurid coloratura he has made definite researches into authentic and rare material' (Summers 1929, 1980 edn: 105). Summers ascribes the authorship of the 1847 'very lengthy but well written and certainly exciting romance' (ibid.: 103) to Thomas Preskett Prest – 'one of the most prolific as he was one of the most admired authors of this school' (ibid.: 103–4) – to whom he also ascribes other penny dreadfuls of the period like *The Skeleton Clutch; or, The Goblet of Gore, Sawney Bean, the Man-eater of Midlothian*, and *The Black Monk or, The Secret of the Grey Turret*. For a more critical review and an accessible summary of *Varney the Vampire*, see Twitchell (1981).

2 It is worth noting in this connection that, in his history of western attitudes to death, Ariès ascribes to the eighteenth century the development of what he terms 'a curious form of macabre eroticism': love and desire aroused by the dead body and the beautiful victim (Ariès 1981: 375). According to Ariès, earlier contemplations of death reflected very different values and concerns. Unlike fifteenth- and sixteenth-century representations of decomposition and a (theological) emphasis on the corruption and corruptibility of the flesh, eighteenth-century artists unabashedly contemplated the dead body in and for itself, so that 'in the world of the imagination, death and violence have merged with desire' (ibid.). Ariès notes that this phenomenon was most apparent in a growing number of stories about love with the dead and 'a literature that in the nineteenth century would soon become popular' (ibid.: 377):

> Let us not look too hard for the reality that lies beneath these fanciful tales. Even if there is some truth to them, and there must have been, the real is only a passing effect of the imaginary. What is essential here takes place in the imagination. The most important events, those heaviest with consequences, do not belong to real life but to the world of fantasies. Like the writings of the doctors, these fantasies assume that the cadaver has a kind of existence of its own that arouses desire and excites the senses.
>
> (ibid.: 381)

Within this general picture, it is not surprising to find that discussions of vampires and vampirism first became marked in the eighteenth century, and that the *Oxford English Dictionary* gives the first citation for the word 'vampire' at 1734.

3 Pirie is presumably referring to Hamilton Deane's adaptation of *Dracula*, which was first staged in June 1924 and which was eventually exported to New York (with a slightly modified play-script) in October 1927, when Bela Lugosi and Edward Van Sloan first played the roles of Dracula and Van Helsing respectively. It was this stage version which also served as the basis of Tod Browning's film adaptation of the story in 1931 (for Universal Pictures) when Lugosi and Van Sloan also appeared in the screen parts which were to make them household names for two decades. According to Silver and Ursini, Hamilton Deane's stage adaptation of Stoker's tale superseded an earlier version by Henry Irving (dated 1897) which lasted for over four hours and consisted of more than forty scenes (Silver and Ursini 1975: 50).

4 Cf. Inglis (1981), Jackson (1981), and Tolkein (1975).

5 According to Clarens, Cohen's *I Was a Teenage Werewolf* cost 'a paltry $150,000' and 'grossed an astonishing $2,300,000 in a short time' (Clarens 1968: 171). It was the first of a spate of films with titles like *Teenage Monster*, *Teenage Zombies*, and *Teenage Caveman*, in which 'traditional terrors were modified to accommodate the theme of puberty betrayed' (Daniels 1977: 207). Cohen himself (who was 29 years old at the time) produced two further and equally successful 'teenage' horror films in the same year (1957) – *I Was a Teenage Frankenstein* and *Blood of Dracula*. Clarens notes that Cohen decided to translate the well-known formulas of the horror movie into terms and contexts which adolescents could more readily identify as their own after 'studying the results of a poll that earmarked the age group of a high percentage (70 per cent, to be exact) of the movie-going public as lying between twelve and twenty-five years'. The implications of these trends have not been missed by more recent horror movie-makers as is evidenced, for instance, by such 1987–8 teenage-oriented adaptations of the werewolf motif as *Teen Wolf*, *Teen Wolf Too*, and the TV series *Werewolf*.

6 The contrast between civilization and man's evolutionary origins had also been at the centre of Arnold's earlier and much more accomplished *Creature of the Black Lagoon* (1954). The Creature here was a man-fish – described by one of the scientists in the film as 'an evolutionary dead end' – who has unaccountably survived the eons since his race was spawned. The film had two sequels, the last of which (*The Creature Walks Among Us*, directed by John Sherwood in 1956) portrayed the gill-man being operated upon by 'civilized' men, dressed up in American clothes, and reduced to a caged, powerless freak. Prawer comments in relation to this film that 'the horror/science-fiction framework enables the film to broach without offence momentous themes and sensitive issues of the late fifties: deculturization, torture, genocide, exploitation' (Prawer 1980: 55).

7 The study reported by DeFleur and Dennis was conducted by Brigitte Goldstein for her MA thesis on 'The television's portrayal of the mentally ill' at the University of New Mexico in 1980.

8 Not all the films about visitors from outer space made in the 1950s presented such creatures as malevolent and destructive. One of the most famous exceptions, *The Day the Earth Stood Still* (1951), told of an

evangelistic alien who comes to earth to warn of the cosmic implications of a nuclear conflict between humans.

9 See Stan Cohen's *Folk Devils and Moral Panics* (1972) for a highly influential analysis of the social construction of the images of youth.

CHAPTER 2 HEROICS AND HELPLESSNESS – THE CASE OF JAMES HERBERT

1 *Sunday Times Magazine*, 11 September 1983: 86.

2 In the interests of (pedantic) accuracy, it should perhaps be pointed out that Herbert frequently describes his heroines as having small rounded breasts and as tending towards the boyish in appearance.

3 On the American pulp-magazines of the first part of this century, see Daniels (1977: 144–5, 157–60, 171–8).

4 For a challenging appraisal of Wertham's *Seduction of the Innocent* and of the campaign against the horror comics of the 1950s more generally, see Barker (1984a).

5 A detailed study of the Hank Janson novels was conducted by R. J. King in his unpublished Ph.D. thesis 'Hank Janson and James Bond – an analysis of aspects of the social and cultural significance of popular fiction' (King 1970). King meticulously examines and gives synopses of all (bar a few issues he could not trace) of the tediously large number of Hank Janson novels published at quarterly intervals between 1950 and 1970, and traces a series of changes in attitude and tone, particularly in relation to the eponymous hero of the novels (who progresses from a Chicago newspaper crime reporter in the early novels to an international spy-network operator in the later ones). King also traces a number of changes in the handling of sex and violence themes, and underlines the contrast between an onanistic–sadistic attitude to women in the early novels (where there are regular references to 'frothy' underwear, and where all potential sexual encounters end in bloody confrontation), and a more 'liberated' approach in the later instalments. According to King, the novels published in the shadow of the popularity of James Bond in the 1960s project women in a more 'personalized' image of glamour which, he claims, is also reflected in the development of pin-up modelling during this period.

6 See J. Strachey (ed.) *The Standard Edition of the Complete Psychological Works of Sigmund Freud*, Vol. 17: 240–1.

7 See, for instance, *The Fog* (Herbert 1975: 250).

CHAPTER 3 LANGUAGE, MODES OF SEEING, AND MAGIC – THE COVENANT OF STEPHEN KING

1 Reports of interviews with King (usually coinciding with the publication of one or other of his books) are scattered through a large cross-section of the popular press. Besides the interviews with Hugh Herbert (in the *Guardian* of 14 May 1983) and Andrew Duncan (in the *Telegraph Sunday*

Magazine of 8 May 1983), which are quoted in this chapter (and which coincided with the British publication of his twelfth book, *Christine*), I have also used other published reports of King's ruminations on the horror genre. These include King's introductory essays to his own collection of short stories *Night Shift* (1978) and to the Signet Classic one-volume edition of *Frankenstein, Dracula,* and *Dr Jekyll and Mr Hyde* (1978); his guest appearance on the BBC Radio 4 chat show *Midweek* on 11 May 1983; and reports in the *Guardian* of 30 August 1977, the (London) *Evening News* of 2 April 1979, *MS London* of 9 April 1979, and *19* of March 1980.

2 See King (1982a: 9–11) and the interview with Duncan (1983: 36).

3 The quotation is taken from chapter 6 of Le Fanu's *Carmilla* (1872).

4 King's comparison of the ghost with the werewolf occurs in the course of his admiring discussion of Straub's *Ghost Story* in *Danse macabre* (King 1982a: 284 ff.). The similarities and mutual influences between King's and Straub's work are noteworthy, not least because they have co-authored a bestseller combining magical adventures and horror motifs (*The Talisman* 1984). In *Danse macabre*, King quotes Straub's acknowledgement of the influence of *'Salem's Lot* in the genesis of *Ghost Story*. Like King, Straub is very much aware of his genre antecedents, and *Ghost Story* is full of allusions to earlier works and passages which at times read like straight borrowings from classics like *The Turn of the Screw*. According to Straub (as quoted by King), *Ghost Story* 'started as a result of [his] having just read all the American supernatural fiction [he] could find . . . because [he] wanted to find out what [his] tradition was' (King 1982a: 286). It is partly because of this concern for tradition that the work of Straub and King is held in such high esteem by other horror writers. According to Daniel Farson, for instance, 'if horror fiction is gaining respect, it is largely due to the success in America of Stephen King and Peter Straub' (Farson 1981: 30); and Marc Alexander (author of *Ghoul, Ogre, Bloodthirst,* and *Plague Pit*) declares *Ghost Story* to mark a new trend in the horror genre which will cause it 'to be regarded with the same respect it had in the days of Edgar Allan Poe' (as cited in Farson 1981: 33).

5 A wide-ranging study of noted as well as less frequently acknowledged doubles in literary history is provided by Miller (1985), who sees doubling as expressing not only the apparatus of the unconscious but also the essence of modern imagination and authorship, an extension, in effect, of Eliot's 'dissociation', Empson's 'ambiguity', and Derrida's 'deconstruction'. Otto Rank's psychoanalytic study of the double (which bases most of its evidence on literary and anthropological examples) is available in an English version (Rank 1971) translated and edited by Harry Tucker.

6 A similar point (but with a different application) is made by Hudson, who argues that

> every generation of students is susceptible to its teachers' presupposi-
> tions, and . . . these presuppositions are potent just to the extent that
> they are unspoken. It is assumptions, prejudices and implicit metaphors

that are the true burden of what passes between teacher and taught. Facts, skills, details are in comparison ephemeral, in the sciences especially, but in the arts as well. They are also identifiable – and rejectable. What the teacher spells out, the pupil can question. What he assumes, especially from a position of unchallenged legitimacy, his pupils will tend to swallow unawares.

(Hudson 1972: 43)

CHAPTER 4 CATHARSIS AND THE MYTH OF THE BEAST

1 Similar statements frequently appear in the popular press. Writing in the *Radio Times* (London: BBC Publications, 1984, vol. 242, no. 3146: 14), Alan Frank, for instance, proclaimed that

It might be logically argued that horror movies provide a 20th-century safety valve for the release of those baser human traits that in more violent times found expression in watching grisly public spectacles such as the hangings that took place at the original Tyburn.

A sustained elaboration of this type of argument was our point of focus in chapter 3, which considered the logic and implications of contemporary invitations to mad horrors as exemplified in the work of Stephen King.

2 The neurophysiological experiments of Delgado and Smith *et al.* are summarized (among other places) in Hilgard *et al.* (1979: 320) and in Goldstein (1975: 6 ff.). The experiments were originally reported in the following publications:

Delgado, J. M. R. (1967) 'Aggression and defense under cerebral radio control', in C. D. Clemente and D. B. Lindsley (eds) *Aggression and Defense: Neural Mechanisms and Social Patterns*, Los Angeles: University of California Press, 171–93.

Delgado, J. M. R. (1969) *Physical Control of the Mind*, New York: Harpers.

Delgado, J. M. R., Roberts, W. W., and Miller, N. E. (1954) 'Learning motivated by electrical stimulation of the brain', *American Journal of Physiology* 179: 587–93.

Smith, D., King, M., and Hoebel, B. G. (1970) 'Lateral hypothalamic control of killing: evidence for a chalinoceptive mechanism', *Science* 167: 900–1.

The ability to control aggression in humans through the physical stimulation of the brain is reported (among other places) in:

Heath, R. G. (1963) 'Electrical self-stimulation of the brain in man', *American Journal of Psychiatry* 120: 571–7.

3 Cf. Fromm (1975: 23–4 and *passim*).

4 The interweaving of biological speculation with social and moral considerations in the nineteenth century is interestingly analysed by Burrow, who views the processes of interpretation in operation here as

the attempts of an initially rationalist, utilitarian approach to the study of social relations and institutions to comprehend non-rational modes of thought and conduct and the existence and viability of institutions which seem, though cherished, to serve no purpose that is readily describable in utilitarian terms.

(Burrow 1966: 2)

Williams similarly asserts that 'theories of evolution and natural selection in biology had a social component before there was any question of re-applying them to social and political theory' (Williams 1980: 86). This was a point which was noted as early as 1865 by Friedrich Engels, who declared himself 'struck . . . with the remarkable likeness [between Darwin's] account of plant and animal life and the Malthusian theory' (cited in Bannister 1979: 14). Engels expounded on the implications of this likeness in a note on 'The struggle for life' (written in 1875 and subsequently published in the *Dialectics of Nature*):

The whole Darwinian theory of the struggle for existence is simply the transference from society to organic nature of Hobbes' theory of the *bellum omnium contra omnes*, and of the bourgeois theory of competition, as well as the Malthusian theory of population. When once this feat has been accomplished (the unconditional justification for which, especially as regards the Malthusian theory, is still very questionable), it is very easy to transfer these theories back again from natural history to the history of society, and altogether too naïve to maintain that thereby these assertions have been proved as eternal laws of society.

(Engels 1954: 404)

It is worth stressing that it was precisely on what were asserted to be 'natural laws' that the social theories and explanations of behaviour propounded by many Social Darwinists (as well as many of their intellectual and ideological heirs) were proclaimed and believed to be based. William Graham Sumner, for instance, noted how Huxley had 'drawn our attention to the fact that nature's discipline does not consist of a word and a blow . . . but a blow without a word' (cited in Bannister 1979: 103). 'The law of the survival of the fittest was not made by man,' asserted Sumner; so that 'we can only, by interfering with it, produce the survival of the unfittest' (ibid.: 105).

5 The dramatic dimension of Freud's formulations was also noted by Jung, who speaks of Freud 'mak[ing] the unconscious – at least metaphorically – take the stage as the acting subject' (*Jung, Collected Works*, vol. 9, part 1: para. 2). Jung himself, it bears noting, applied the implications of dramatic catharsis to his own theory of archetypes, underlining a quasi-theatrical (as distinct from consciously rational) process of psychic functioning:

As the archetypes, like all numinous contents, are relatively autonomous, they cannot be integrated simply by rational means, but require a dialectical procedure, a real coming to terms with them, often conducted by the patient in dialogue form, so that, without knowing it, he puts into effect the alchemical definition of the *meditatio*: 'an inner colloquy with one's good angel'. Usually the process runs a dramatic course, with ups and downs. It expresses itself in, or is accompanied by, dream symbols that are related to the 'représentations collectives', which in the form of mythological motifs have portrayed psychic processes of transformation since the earliest times.

(ibid.: para. 85)

6 For evidence and arguments rebutting Freud's account of Breuer's reasons for discontinuing his treatment and study of hysteria, see Ellenberger (1970: 483–4) and Sulloway (1979: 78–80, 83–5, 490).

7 This mode of conceptualizing mental structures and processes in terms and images derived from drama can also be seen to characterize more recent attempts to apply the Freudian perspective to discussions of horror fictions. Twitchell, for instance, sets out to explain why adolescents find horror fascinating by realigning the protagonists of the (Freudian) psyche and attributing new dramatic functions to them:

> Essentially, horror can be thought of as the price exacted by the superego to let the ego learn about the id. For the most part we are not really interested in horror, in having our neck hairs raised; rather we are interested in something for which we must experience horror, namely knowledge of forbidden levels of sexuality.

(Twitchell 1983: 44–5)

Writing from a Lacanian perspective, Lenne similarly argues for the virtues of horror movies by postulating various parallels and 'identifications' between the build-up of dramatic tension on the screen and the drama of conflicting emotions taking place 'inside' the spectator:

> Le déroulement de l'intrigue prend en effet l'aspect d'une montée progressive de la tension jusqu'à la crise finale, dont l'effet s'apparente à la libération cathartique. Mais il s'en faut que l'attitude du spectateur se conforme aveuglément à cette operation . . . tout en se conformant à l'identification proposée ou imposée par le film, il ne peut empêcher que ses tendances et ses pulsions inconscientes prennent forme sur l'écran dans la partie adverse. Tout ce qu'il ne peut ou n'ose faire 'dans la vie' (sur le plan *libido/* sur le plan *destrudo*) il le fait par l'entremise du monstre.

(Lenne 1970: 35–6)

Similar trends can be traced in Britton *et al.* (1979), Huss and Ross (1972), and Twitchell (1985).

CHAPTER 5 CLOCKWORK COPY-CATS AND THE STUDY OF HORRIFIC INFLUENCES

1 Maureen O'Connor (in the *Guardian* of 13 December 1983: 13) and Michael Tracy (in *The Times* of 25 February 1984: 8) give interesting accounts of the conflict between the researchers, politicians, and propagandists involved in the controversial report of the Parliamentary Group Video Enquiry (published on 22 November 1983). In an article

which appeared in *New Society* on 10 November 1983 (and which created a controversy in its own right), Martin Barker underlined the similarities in tone and content between the journalistic campaign mounted against 'video nasties' in Britain in 1983 – which culminated in the Video Recordings Act of 1984 – and the campaign which was mounted against American horror comics in the early 1950s – which in Britain led to the Children and Young Persons (Harmful Publications) Act of 1955. Barker insists that effects studies have been too tied up with policy-making to be coherently developed, conceptually, and repeatedly points to the histrionic and usually vague nature of the claims made in popular accounts of the dangers of such material for children (Barker 1983, 1984a,b). Barker's research has led him to the conclusion that the campaign of the 1950s in Britain was mainly spearheaded by the Communist Party looking for a morale-boosting victory against an 'influence' of American origin. Claims about effects in that campaign, Barker notes, were much larger and more specific in the early stages than they were towards the end (when they concentrated on morally imprecise issues) (ibid.: 1984a). Thus, early in the campaign, Peter Mauger could argue (in an article entitled 'Children's reading', published in 1951 in *Arena*, the cultural journal of the British Communist Party) that the young American soldiers fighting in Korea had been hardened for the cruelties of war by being brought up on horror comics. Specific claims of this nature, according to Barker, were dropped when the impossibility of proving them and their openness to criticism made them a liability for the campaign.

In this relation, Mary Harron (writing in the *Times Educational Supplement* of 21 October 1983) also noted how 'Fleet Street's obsession with video reached a crescendo in July and August, providing useful fillers at a time when hard news is in short supply.' In Harron's view, the series of shock-horror news stories about crimes allegedly committed 'under the influence of videos' reflected the extent to which the video had become 'a fashionable defence' which grabs the headlines, though it is only one influence among many.

2 As formulated in chapter 6 of Thorndike's *Animal Intelligence*, the 'law of effect' states that:

> Of several responses made to the same situation, those which are accompanied or closely followed by satisfaction to the animal will, other things being equal, be more firmly connected with the situation, so that, when it recurs, they are more likely to recur; those which are accompanied or closely followed by discomfort to the animal will, other things being equal, have their connections with the situation weakened, so that, when it recurs, they will be less likely to occur. The greater the satisfaction or discomfort, the greater the strengthening or weakening of the bond.
>
> (Thorndike 1911)

In *Science and Human Behavior*, Skinner insists in this relation that 'the Law of Effect is not a theory' but 'simply a rule for strengthening behavior', since, 'when we reinforce a response and observe a change in its frequency, we can easily report what has happened in objective terms' (Skinner 1953: 81). In Skinner's view, it is 'in explaining *why* it has happened [that] we are likely to resort to theory'. If the argument developed in this chapter is correct, Skinner's discomfort with explicit theoretical explanation – because it 'is probably of little help in a functional analysis' (ibid.: 84) – is a measure of his (and behaviourism's) failure to appreciate the nature and importance of the speculative instruments informing his observations and 'objective reports'.

3 Cf. Poole, who, following Kuhn's definition of the 'paradigm' (in *The Structure of Scientific Revolutions*, 1970), identifies the paradigm of objectivity in the sciences as 'materialist-behaviourist-positivist', and quotes the list of precursors of behaviourism identified in the *Encyclopaedia Britannica* (Poole 1972: 50ff.). These include: materialist and mechanist philosophy, the English empiricists and associationists of the eighteenth and nineteenth centuries, and the dominance of the mechanical world view in the physical science of the eighteenth and nineteenth centuries, which also penetrated into biology. The influence on Watson of 'animal psychology, objectivistic biology, Russian reflexology and American pragmatism' is also cited in the *Encyclopaedia Britannica* as a basis for the assertion that behaviourism is 'first and foremost an extension of the methods of animal psychology to the study of man'.

The manner in which the positivist conceptual framework was expressed (and eventually superseded) in different academic disciplines is critically reviewed in Quentin Skinner's editorial introduction to *The Return of Grand Theory in the Human Sciences* (Skinner 1985). In this connection, see also Capra (1982: 37–62, 166–93) and Hudson (1975: 148–50). Hudson interestingly underlines the discrepancies between materialism and positivism as the joint bases of behaviourism, and he points to the historical link 'between materialism, as a philosophy and as a way of life, and puritanism'.

4 See Gunter (1985), Brown and Tedeschi (1976), and Kane *et al.* (1976).
5 In an article entitled 'Same time next year', Baron and Reiss analyse some of the evidence behind claims to the effect that, say, news reports of suicides lead to imitative behaviour, and that this link can be proved by statistically recorded rises in suicide rates after the broadcasting of such reports. According to these writers, the logic of much of this type of field research 'does not meet the special burdens of proof associated with quasi-experimental studies that use aggregate data to make inferences about individual behavior' (Baron and Reiss 1985: 347). 'The issues explored by aggregate studies of imitative behavior', Baron and Reiss insist, 'are momentous, but so too are the dangers of misconstruing the results of those studies' (ibid.: 362). It is thus possible to present detailed statistical evidence supporting completely different interpretations from those asserted by researchers who work from 'assumptions about the evocative properties of mass media violence'. Baron and Reiss in fact offer detailed evidence supporting 'an equally parsimonious and comprehensive explanation of observed peaks in mortality after media

events', in order to drive home the point that 'imitation effects attributed to mass media events (prize fights and television news stories about suicides) are statistical artifacts of the mortality data, the timing of media events, and the methods employed in past research'.

6 As examples of studies which focus on differing reactions as a consequence of differing interpretations and understanding, see Gunter (1985), Atkin (1983), and Reeves (1978). Studies of the more positive cognitive implications of the media include Singer and Singer (1983), Bryant and Anderson (1983), Christenson and Roberts (1983), Gunter (1984), and Greenfield (1984).

CHAPTER 6 CONSCIOUSNESS, FICTION, AND THE TERRORS OF UNCERTAINTY

1 Major shaping influences on applications of game/rules and theatre/roles analogies to the study of social behaviour were G. H. Mead and Erving Goffman respectively. See, for example, Mead's *Mind, Self, and Society* (Chicago: University of Chicago Press, 1934) and *The Philosophy of the Act* (Chicago: University of Chicago Press, 1938); and Goffman's *The Presentation of Self in Everyday Life* (New York: Doubleday Anchor, 1959) and *Behavior in Public Places* (New York: Free Press of Glencoe, 1963). Goffman's ideas have been ingeniously applied to an analysis of the impact of electronic media on social behaviour by Meyrowitz (1985); and some of the applications of the roles analogy to the genre conventions of popular literature are interestingly discussed in Cawelti (1976). Bennett and Woolacott (1987) have also systematically applied the games analogy to an analysis of the cultural and ideological transactions underlying a complex series of texts which have James Bond as their point of focus.

2 For more detailed discussions of the ontogenesis of fear, see Bowlby (1973) and Tuan (1979). Citing S. Schachter and G. Mandler as his sources, Bamber also stresses that recent work in the area of emotional theory follows a 'two factor approach' which takes account of both physiological arousal and cognitive appraisal. On these grounds, Bamber distinguishes 'between stimuli which automatically arouse the autonomic nervous system (ANS) because the organism has been preprogrammed in a given way, and stimuli which are signals for a cognitive–emotional interpretation and evaluation to come into operation' (Bamber 1979: 54). For a discussion of some of the more general and educational implications of the contention that emotions are basically forms of cognition, see Peters (1972).

3 See, for example, Valentine (1950: 211).

4 Thomas offers an interesting application and critique of Malinowski's thesis (Thomas 1973: 774–800), and finds fault with it on the grounds that the correspondence between magic and social needs was never more than approximate, so that 'the absence of a technical remedy was not in itself sufficient to generate a magical one' (ibid.: 785–6). Thomas, however, also offers convincing evidence from English popular beliefs during the sixteenth and seventeenth centuries to substantiate the claim

that magic was seldom invoked when a technical solution was available. 'Society's magical resources', Thomas points out, 'were the result of its cultural inheritance, as much as of its current problems' (ibid.: 786).

5 Cf. Bamber, who argues that 'whenever highly organised activities are interrupted in the sense that their completion is physically delayed, then the ANS (autonomic nervous system) is aroused in a manner similar to arousal resulting from stimuli which are preprogrammed releasers' (Bamber 1979: 54–5).

6 Seligman's speculations were based on a series of experiments in which dogs were first restrained in a Pavlovian hammock and given a series of electric shocks which they could neither avoid nor control. Unlike other dogs which had not been subjected to this type of inescapable shock, the dogs in these experiments were later found to be virtually incapable of learning how to avoid discomfort when the shocks were escapable. When they were placed in a Skinner type of shuttle box (or two-sided chamber), in which they could escape shock by jumping a barrier from one side to the other, these dogs revealed a disturbing tendency to accept punishment with fatal resignation. According to Seligman, they had learned helplessness. After observing this pattern of behaviour, Seligman made the following generalization:

> When an organism has experienced trauma it cannot control, its motivation to respond in the face of later trauma wanes. Moreover, even if it does respond, and the response succeeds in producing relief, it has trouble learning, perceiving and believing that the response worked. Finally, its emotional balance is disturbed: depression and anxiety, measured in various ways, predominate.
>
> (Saligman 1975: 22–3)

There are many points on which this method of generalizing can be (and has been) criticized, not least with reference to the loose and indiscriminate use made here of such complex concepts as those described by terms like 'organism', 'trauma', 'perceiving', and 'believing'. But the implications of Seligman's argument, particularly as this has been refined in his later writings (which took more serious account of individual differences and questions as to when and where helplessness is likely to generalize when humans are involved), are challenging and of direct relevance to the argument developed in the present chapter.

7 It has been noted, for instance, that people who spend all their lives living in small clearances in dense forests do not appear to experience distant objects, so that, when they are taken out of their forest and shown distant objects, they see these objects not as distant but as small (Gregory 1977: 162).

8 Cf. Brooke-Rose (1981: 3–11).

9 Aronson provides a readable and well-illustrated introduction to Festinger's cognitive dissonance theory, as well as to some of its offshoots (Aronson 1984: 113–79). A summary of some famous critiques of this theory, and Festinger's own rebuttal of these critiques and defence of his theory can be found in Cohen (1985: 126–44).

REFERENCES

Abramson, L. Y., Garber, J., and Seligman, M. E. P. (1980) 'Learned helplessness in humans: an attributional analysis', in J. Garber and M. E. P. Seligman (eds) *Human Helplessness: Theory and Applications*, New York and London: Academic Press.

Ardrey, R. (1961) *African Genesis: a Personal Investigation into the Animal Origins and Nature of Man*, London and Glasgow: Collins/Fontana.

Ariès, P. (1981) *The Hour of Our Death*, Harmondsworth: Allen Lane.

Aronson, E. (1984) *The social animal*, 4th edn, New York: W. H. Freeman.

Atkin, C. (1983) 'Effects of realistic TV violence vs. fictional violence on aggression', *Journalism Quarterly* 60: 615–21.

Bamber, J. H. (1979) *The Fears of Adolescents*, New York and London: Academic Press.

Bandura, A. (1965) 'Influence of models' reinforcement contingencies on the acquisition of imitative responses', *Journal of Personality and Social Psychology* 1: 589–95.

—— (1977) *Social Learning Theory*, Englewood Cliffs, New Jersey: Prentice-Hall.

Bandura, A. and Walters, R. H. (1959) *Adolescent Aggression: a Study of the Influence of Child-training Practices and Family Interrelationships*, New York: Ronald Press.

Bannister, R. C. (1979) *Social Darwinism: Science and Myth in Anglo-American Social Thought*, Philadelphia: Temple University Press.

Barker, M. (1983) 'How nasty are the nasties?', *New Society* 66: 231–3.

—— (1984a) *A Haunt of Fears: the Strange History of the British Horror Comic Campaign*, London: Pluto Press.

—— (ed.) (1984b) *The Video Nasties: Freedom and Censorship in the Media*, London: Pluto Press.

Barlow, G. and Hill, A. (1985) *Video Violence and Children*, London: Hodder & Stoughton.

Baron, J. N. and Reiss, P. C. (1985) 'Same time next year: aggregate analyses of the mass media and violent behaviour', *American Sociological Review* 50: 347–63.

Barthes, R. (1973) *Mythologies*, London: Paladin.

Bateson, G. (1976) 'A theory of play and fantasy', in J. S. Bruner, A. Jolly, and K. Sylva (eds) *Play – Its Role in Development and Evolution*, Harmondsworth: Penguin. (Originally published in 1955 in *Psychiatric Research Reports* 2: 39–51.)

Belschner, W. (1975) 'Learning and aggression', in H. Selg (ed.) *The Making of Human Aggression: a Psychological Approach*, London: Quartet Books.

Belson, W. (1978) *Television Violence and the Adolescent Boy*, London: Saxon House.

Bennet, T. and Woolacott, J. (1987) *Bond and Beyond: the Political Career of a Popular Hero*, London: Macmillan Education.

Berger, P. L. (1970) *A Rumour of Angels: Modern Society and the Rediscovery of the Supernatural*, Harmondsworth: Penguin.

Berger, P. L., Berger, B., and Kellner, H. (1974) *The Homeless Mind*. Harmondsworth: Penguin.

Berkowitz, L. (1964) 'The effects of observing violence', *Scientific American* 210(2). Reprinted in Aronson, E. (ed.) (1977) *Readings about the Social Animal*, 2nd edn, San Francisco: W. H. Freeman, pp. 177–89.

Berkowitz, L. and Green, R. G. (1966) 'Film violence and the cue properties of available targets', *Journal of Personality and Social Psychology* 3: 525–30.

Bettelheim, B. (1961) *The Informed Heart: the Human Condition in Modern Mass Society*, London: Thames & Hudson.

— (1976) *The Uses of Enchantment: the Meanings and Importance of Fairy Tales*, London: Thames & Hudson.

Bjorkqvist, K. and Lagerspetz, K. (1985) 'Children's experience of three types of cartoon at two age levels', *International Journal of Psychology* 20: 77–93.

Black, M. (1962) *Models and Metaphors: Studies in Language and Philosophy*, New York: Cornell University Press.

Blonsky, M.(ed.) (1985) *On Signs*, Oxford: Blackwell.

Booth, W. C. (1961) *The Rhetoric of Fiction*, Chicago: University of Chicago Press.

Bowlby, J. (1973) *Separation: Anxiety and Anger*, London: Hogarth.

Britton, A., Lippe, R., Williams, T., and Wood, R. (1979) *The American Nightmare: Essays on the Horror Film*, Toronto: Festival of Festivals.

Brody, S. (1977) *Screen Violence and Film Censorship – a Review of Research*, London: HMSO.

Brooke-Rose, C. (1981) *A Rhetoric of the Unreal: Studies in Narrative and Structure, especially of the Fantastic*, Cambridge: Cambridge University Press.

Brown, J. A. C. (1963) *Techniques of Persuasion: from Propaganda to Brainwashing*, Harmondsworth: Penguin.

Brown, R. C. and Tedeschi, J. T. (1976) 'Determinants of perceived aggression', *Journal of Social Psychology* 100: 77–87.

Bruner, J. S. (1972) 'Immaturity – its uses, nature and management, *Times Educational Supplement*, 27 October: 18, 63.

— (1976) 'Nature and uses of immaturity', in J. S. Bruner, A. Jolly, and K. Sylva (eds) *Play – Its Role in Development and Evolution*, Harmondsworth: Penguin.

— (1979) *On Knowing: Essays for the Left Hand*, expanded edn, Cambridge (Massachusetts) and London: Harvard University Press.

Bruner, J. S., Olver, R., and Greenfield, P. M. (1966) *Studies in Cognitive Growth*, New York: Wiley.

Bryant, J. and Anderson, D. R. (eds) (1983) *Children's Understanding of Television: Research on Attention and Comprehension*, New York: Academic Press.

Burrow, J. W. (1966) *Evolution and Society: a Study in Victorian Social Theory*, Cambridge: Cambridge University Press.

Butler, M. (1981) *Romantics, Rebels and Reactionaries: English Literature and Its Background 1760–1830*, Oxford: Oxford University Press.

Cannadine, D. (1981) 'War, death, grief and mourning in modern Britain', in J. Whaley (ed.) *Mirrors of Mortality: Studies in the Social History of Death*, London: Europa Publications.

Capra, F. (1982) *The Turning Point: Science, Society, and the Rising Culture*, London: Wildwood House.

Cavendish, R. (1975) *The Powers of Evil in Western Religion, Magic, and Folk Belief*. London: Routledge & Kegan Paul.

Cawelti, J. (1976) *Adventure, Mystery and Romance*, Chicago: University of Chicago Press.

Charters, W. W. (1935) *Motion Pictures and Youth*, New York: Macmillan.

Christenson, P. G. and Roberts, D. F. (1983) 'The role of television in the formation of children's social attitudes', in M. J. A. Howe (ed.) *Learning from Television*, London: Academic Press.

Clarens, C. (1968) *Horror Movies: an Illustrated Survey*, London: Secker & Warburg.

Cohen, D. (1985) *Psychologists on Psychology*. London: Ark Paperbacks. (First published in 1977 by Routledge & Kegan Paul.)

Cohen, S. (1972) *Folk Devils and Moral Panics: the Creation of the Mods and Rockers*, London: MacGibbon & Kee.

Collingwood, R. G. (1938) *The Principles of Art*, Oxford: Clarendon Press.

Daniels, L. (1977) *Fear: a History of Horror in the Mass Media*, London: Paladin.

DeFleur, M. L. and Dennis, E. E. (1985) *Understanding Mass Communication*, 2nd edn, Boston: Houghton Mifflin.

Dollard, J., Miller, N. E., Doob, L. W., Mowrer, O. H., and Sears, R. R. (1939) *Frustration and Aggression*, New Haven and London: Yale University Press.

Doob, A. W. and Macdonald, G. E. (1979) 'Television viewing and fear of victimization: is the relationship causal?', *Journal of Personality and Social Psychology* 37: 170–9.

Duncan, A. (1983) 'Meeting the demon King', *Telegraph Sunday Magazine*, no. 343, 8 May: 35–8.

Ellenberger, H. F. (1970) *The Discovery of the Unconscious: the History and Evolution of Dynamic Psychiatry*, Harmondsworth: Allen Lane.

Engels, F. (1954) *Dialectics of Nature*, Moscow: Foreign Languages Publishing House.

Eysenck, H. J. and Nias, D. K. B. (1980) *Sex, Violence and the Media*, London: Paladin.

Farson, D. (1981) 'Success for the menace masters', *Telegraph Sunday Magazine*, no. 274, 27 December: 30–3.

Feshbach, S. (1961) 'The stimulating versus cathartic effects of a vicarious aggressive activity', *Journal of Abnormal and Social Psychology* 63: 381–5.

Festinger, L. (1957) *A Theory of Cognitive Dissonance*, Stanford: Stanford University Press.

Fiske, J. and Hartley, J. (1978) *Reading Television*, London: Methuen.

Foucault, M. (1979) *The History of Sexuality: Vol. 1 – An Introduction*, Harmondsworth: Penguin.

Fraser, J. (1976) *Violence in the Arts*, illustrated edn, Cambridge: Cambridge University Press.

Freud, S. (1905, 1977 edn) *Three Essays on the Theory of Sexuality*, in A. Richards (ed.) *The Pelican Freud Library, Vol. 7: On Sexuality*, Harmondsworth: Penguin.

    (1919a, 1955 edn.) 'The "uncanny"' ', in J. Strachey (ed.) *The Standard Edition of the Complete Psychological Works of Sigmund Freud*, vol. 17, London: Hogarth Press and Institute of Psycho-Analysis, pp. 218–52.

    (1919b, 1955 edn.) '"A child is being beaten": a contribution to the study of the origin of sexual perversions', in J. Strachey (ed.) *The Standard Edition of the Complete Psychological Works of Sigmund Freud*, vol. 17, London: Hogarth Press and Institute of Psycho-Analysis, pp. 117–204.

    (1930, 1963 edn) *Civilization and Its Discontents*, London: Hogarth.

    (1933, 1973 edn) *New Introductory Lectures on Psychoanalysis*, in J. Strachey and A. Richards (eds) *The Pelican Freud Library*, vol. 2, Harmondsworth: Penguin.

Freud, S. and Breuer, J. (1895, 1955 edn) *Studies on Hysteria*, in J. Strachey (ed.) *The Standard Edition of the Complete Psychological Works of Sigmund Freud*, vol. 2, London: Hogarth Press and Institute of Psycho-Analysis.

Froeberg, J., Karlsson, C., Levi, L., and Lidberg, L. (1971) 'Physiological and biochemical stress reactions induced by psychosocial stimuli', in L. Levi (ed.) *Society, Stress and Disease*, vol. 1, Oxford: Oxford University Press.

Fromm, E. (1975) *The Anatomy of Human Destructiveness*, New York: Fawcett Crest.

Garvey, C. (1977) *Play*, Glasgow: Fontana/Open Books.

Geertz, C. (1975) *The Interpretation of Cultures*, London: Hutchinson.

    (1983) *Local Knowledge: Further Essays in Interpretive Anthropology*, New York: Basic Books.

Gerbner, G. (1980) 'Children and power on television: the other side of the picture', in G. Gerbner, C. J. Ross, and E. Zigler (eds) *Child Abuse: an Agenda for Action*, New York: Oxford University Press.

Gerbner, G. and Gross, L. (1976a) 'Living with television: the violence profile', *Journal of Communication* 26: 173–99.

    (1976b). 'The scary world of TV's heavy viewer', *Psychology Today* 89, 41–5.

Gerbner, G., Gross, L., Eleey, M., Jackson-Beeck, M., Jeffries-Fox, S., and Signorielli, N. (1977) 'The violence profile no. 8', *Journal of Communication* 27: 171–80.

Gerbner, G., Gross, L., Jackson-Beeck, M., Jeffries-Fox, S., and Signorielli, N. (1978) Cultural indicators: violence profile no. 9', *Journal of Communication* 28: 176–207.

Gerbner, G., Gross, L., Signorielli, N., Morgan, M., and Jackson-Beeck, M. (1979) 'The demonstration of power: violence profile no. 10', *Journal of Communication* 29: 177–96.

Gerbner, G., Gross, L., Morgan, M., and Signorielli, N. (1980) 'The "mainstreaming" of America: violence profile no. 11', *Journal of Communication* 30: 10–29.

Gibson, E. J., and Walk, R. D. (1960) 'The "visual cliff"',' *Scientific American* 202: 64–71.

Goldstein, J. H. (1975) *Aggression and Crimes of Violence*, New York: Oxford University Press.

Greenfield, P. M. (1984) *Mind and Media: the Effects of Television, Computers and Video Games*, Glasgow: Fontana.

Gregory, R. L. (1974) 'Psychology: towards a science of fiction', *New Society*, 23 May: 439–41.

—— (1977) *Eye and Brain: the Psychology of Seeing*, 3rd edn, London: Weidenfeld & Nicolson.

Gunter, B. (1984) 'Television as a facilitator of good behaviour amongst children', *Journal of Moral Education* 13: 152–9.

—— (1985) *Dimensions of Television Violence*, Aldershot: Gower.

Gunter, B. and Wober, M. (1983) 'Television viewing and public trust', *British Journal of Social Psychology* 22: 174–6.

Habermas, J. (1970) *Toward a Rational Society*, Boston: Beacon Press.

Hall, G. S. (1904) *Adolescence: Its Psychology and Its Relation to Physiology, Anthropology, Sociology, Sex, Crime, Religion and Education*, 2 vols, New York: Appleton.

—— (1914) 'A synthetic genetic study of fear', *American Journal of Psychology* 25: 149–200, 321–92.

Hall, S. (1980) 'Encoding/decoding', in S. Hall, D. Hobson, A. Lowe, and P. Willis (eds) *Culture, Media, Language*, London: Hutchinson.

Harding, D. W. (1962) 'Psychological processes in the reading of fiction', *British Journal of Aesthetics* 2: 133–47.

—— (1967) 'Considered experience: the invitation of the novel', *English in Education* 1: 7–15.

—— (1971) 'The bond with the author', *Use of English* 22: 307–25.

Harré, R. (1981) 'Rituals, rhetoric and social cognitions', in J. P. Forgas (ed.) *Social Cognition: Perspectives on Everyday Understanding*, New York and London: Academic Press.

Harré, R., Clarke, D., and De Carlo, N. (1985) *Motives and Mechanisms: an Introduction to the Psychology of Action*, London: Methuen.

Herbert, H. (1983) 'A frightening morality', *Guardian*, 14 May: 6.

Herbert, J. (1974) *The Rats*, London: New English Library.

—— (1975) *The Fog*, London: New English Library.

—— (1976) *The Survivor*, London: New English Library.

—— (1977) *Fluke*, London: New English Library.

—— (1980) *The Dark*, London: New English Library.

—— (1981) *The Jonah*, London: New English Library.

—— (1983) *Shrine*, London: New English Library.

Hilgard, E. R., Atkinson, R. L., and Atkinson, R. C. (1979) *Introduction to Psychology*, 7th edn, New York: Harcourt Brace Jovanovich.

Hirsch, P. M. (1980) 'The "scary world" of the nonviewer and other anomalies: a reanalysis of Gerbner *et al.*'s findings on cultivation analysis', part 1', *Communication Research* 7: 403–56.

200

Hoggart, R. (1958) *The Uses of Literacy: Aspects of Working-class Life with Special Reference to Publications and Entertainments*, Harmondsworth: Penguin.

Howitt, D. and Cumberbatch, G. (1974) 'Audience perceptions of violent television content', *Communication Research* 1: 204–23.

(1975) *Mass Media Violence and Society*, London: Elek Science.

Hudson, L. (1972) *The Cult of the Fact*, London: Jonathan Cape.

(1975) *Human Beings: an Introduction to the Psychology of Human Experience*, London: Jonathan Cape.

Hughes, M. (1980) 'The fruits of cultivation analysis: a reexamination of some effects of television watching', *Public Opinion Quarterly* 44: 287–302.

Huss, R. and Ross, T. J. (eds) (1972) *Focus on the Horror Film*, Englewood Cliffs, New Jersey: Prentice-Hall.

Huxley, T. H. (1894) *Evolution and Ethics and Other Essays*, London: Macmillan.

Inglis, F. (1975) *Ideology and the Imagination*, Cambridge: Cambridge University Press.

(1981) *The Promise of Happiness: Value and Meaning in Children's Fiction*, Cambridge: Cambridge University Press.

Jackson, R. (1981) *Fantasy: the Literature of Subversion*, London: Methuen.

Jahoda, M. (1977) *Freud and the Dilemmas of Psychology*, London: Hogarth.

James, W. (1890) *Principles of Psychology*, 2 vols, New York: Holt.

Johnson, R. W. (1982) 'The myth of the 20th century', *New Society*, 9 Dec.: 432–3.

Jones, E. (1931) *On the Nightmare*, London: Hogarth.

Jung, C. G. (1956, 1972 edn) *Four Archetypes* (reprinted from H. Read, M. Fordham, and G. Adler (eds) *The Collected Works of C. J. Jung*), London: Routledge & Kegan Paul.

Kane, T., Joseph, J. M. and Tedeschi, J. T. (1976) 'Personal perception of the Berkowitz paradigm for the study of aggression', *Journal of Personality and Social Psychology* 33: 663–73.

King, R. J. (1970) 'Hank Janson and James Bond: an analysis of aspects of the social and cultural significance of popular fiction', unpublished Ph.D. dissertation, University of Birmingham Faculty of Arts.

King, S. (1976) *'Salem's Lot*, London: New English Library.

(1977) *The Shining*, London: New English Library.

(1978) *Night Shift*, London: New English Library.

(1980) *The Dead Zone*, London: Futura.

(1982a) *Danse macabre*, London: Futura.

(1982b) *Cujo*, London: Futura.

(1983) *Christine*, London: New English Library.

Krook, D. (1959) *Three Traditions of Moral Thought*, Cambridge: Cambridge University Press.

Kuhn, T. (1970) *The Structure of Scientic Revolutions*, 2nd edn, Chicago: University of Chicago Press.

Leavis, F. R. (1948) 'Mass civilization and minority culture', in *Education and the University*, 2nd edn, Cambridge: Cambridge University Press.

Leavis, Q. D. (1932, 1979 edn) *Fiction and the Reading Public*. Harmondsworth: Penguin.

Lefkowitz, M. M., Eron, L. D., Walder, L. O., and Huesmann, L. R. (1977) *Growing Up to be Violent: a Longitudinal Study of the Development of Aggression*, New York and Oxford: Pergamon Press.

Lenne, G. (1970) *Le Cinéma 'fantastique' et ses mythologies*, Paris: Editions du Cerf.

Lorenz, K. (1966) *On Aggression*, London: Methuen.

MacIntyre, A. C. (1958) *The Unconscious: a Conceptual Analysis*, London: Routledge & Kegan Paul.

Malinowski, B. (1926) 'Magic, science and religion', in J. Needham (ed.) *Science, Religion and Reality*, London: Sheldon Press.
— (1937) 'Culture', in E. R. Seligman and A. Johnson (eds) *Selections from the Encyclopaedia of Social Sciences*, New York: Macmillan.

Marx, K. (1890, 1976 edn) *Capital*, vol. 1, Harmondsworth: Penguin.

Meyrowitz, J. (1985) *No Sense of Place: the Impact of Electronic Media on Social Behavior*. New York: Oxford University Press.

Midgley, M. (1980) *Beast and Man: the Roots of Human Nature*, London: Methuen.

Miller, K. (1985) *Doubles: Studies in Literary History*, Oxford: Oxford University Press.

Moretti, F. (1982) 'The dialectic of fear', *New Left Review* 136 (Nov.–Dec.): 67–85.

National Institute of Mental Health (NIMH) (1982) *Television and Behavior: Ten Years of Scientific Progress and Implications for the Eighties. Vol. 1: Summary Report*, Rockville, Maryland: US Department of Health and Human Services.

Nietzsche, F. (1887, 1956 edn) *The Genealogy of Morals*, New York: Doubleday Anchor Books.

Norman, R. (1978) 'On seeing things differently', in R. Beehler and A. R. Drengson (eds) *The Philosophy of Society*, London: Methuen.

Orwell, G. (1970) *Collected Essays, Journalism and Letters*, vol. 3, London: Penguin.

Osborn, D. K. and Endsley, R. C. (1971) 'Emotional reactions of young children to TV violence', *Child Development* 42: 321–31.

Pearson, G. (1984) 'Falling standards: a short, sharp history of moral decline', in M. Barker (ed.) *The Video Nasties*, London: Pluto.

Peters, R. S. (1972) 'The education of the emotions', in R. F. Dearden, P. H. Hirst, and R. S. Peters (eds) *Education and the Development of Reason*, London: Routledge & Kegan Paul.

Pickard, P. M. (1961) *I Could a Tale Unfold: Violence, Horror and Sensationalism in Stories for Children*, London: Tavistock.

Pirie, D. (1973) *A Heritage of Horror: the English Gothic Cinema, 1946–1972*, London: Gordon Fraser.

Poole, R. (1972) *Towards Deep Subjectivity*, London: Allen Lane.

Prawer, S. S. (1980) *Caligari's Children: the Film as Tale of Terror*, Oxford: Oxford University Press.

Praz, M. (1933) *The Romantic Agony*, Oxford: Oxford University Press.

REFERENCES

Prickett, S. (1979) *Victorian Fantasy*. London: Harvester Press.
Punter, D. (1980) *The Literature of Terror: a History of Gothic Fictions from 1765 to the Present Day*, London: Longman.
Rank, O. (1971) *The Double: a Psychoanalytic Study*, trans. and ed. H. Tucker, Chapel Hill: University of North Carolina Press.
Reeves, B. (1978) 'Perceived TV reality as a predictor of children's social behaviour', *Journalism Quarterly* 55: 682–9, 695.
Ricoeur, P. (1978) *The Rule of Metaphor: Multi-disciplinary Studies of the Creation of Meaning in Language*, London: Routledge & Kegan Paul.
    (1981) *Hermeneutics and the Human Sciences: Essays on Language, Action and Interpretation*, Cambridge: Cambridge University Press.
Rodman, G. (1984) *Mass Media Issues: Analysis and Debate*, 2nd edn, New York: Brooklyn College of the City University.
Rowland, W. D. (1983) *The Politics of TV Violence: Policy Uses of Communication Research*, Beverly Hills: Sage.
Sartre, J. P. (1971) *Sketch for a Theory of the Emotions*, London: Methuen. (Original French edition: 1939.)
    (1972) *The Psychology of Imagination*, London: Methuen. (Original French edition: 1940.)
Schott, F. (1975) 'What is aggression?', in H. Selg (ed.) *The Making of Human Aggression*, London: Quartet Books.
Segal, H. (1973) *Introduction to the Work of Melanie Klein*, London: Hogarth.
Selg, H. (ed.) (1975) *The Making of Human Aggression: a Psychological Approach*, London: Quartet Books.
Seligman, M. E. P. (1975) *Helplessness: On Depression, Development and Death*, San Francisco: Freeman.
Silver, A. and Ursini, J. (1975) *The Vampire Film*, London: Tantivy Press.
Silverstone, R. (1981) *The Message of Television*, London: Routledge & Kegan Paul.
Singer, D. G. and Singer, J. L. (1983) 'Learning how to be intelligent consumers of television', in M. J. A. Howe (ed.) *Learning from Television: Psychological and Educational Research*, London: Academic Press.
Singer, J. L. and Singer, D. G. (1981) *Television, Imagination and Aggression: a Study of Preschoolers*, Hillsdale, New Jersey: Erlbaum.
Skinner, B. F. (1953) *Science and Human Behavior*, New York and London: Macmillan.
    (1973) *Beyond Freedom and Dignity*, Harmondsworth: Penguin.
Skinner, Q. (ed.) (1985) *The Return of Grand Theory in the Human Sciences*, Cambridge: Cambridge University Press.
Speisman, J. C., Lazarus, R. S., Mordkoff, A. M., and Davison, L. (1964) 'Experimental reduction of stress based on ego-defense theory', *Journal of Abnormal and Social Psychology* 68: 367–80.
Spengler, O. (1932) *The Decline of the West*, London: Allen & Unwin.
Stevenson, R. L. (1885, 1978 edn) *The Strange Case of Dr Jekyll and Mr Hyde*, New York: New American Library.
Storr, A. (1962) 'The psychology of aggression', *New Society* 1(2) (11 October): 13–16.
Straub, P. (1979) *Ghost Story*, London: Futura.

Sulloway, F. J. (1979) *Freud, Biologist of the Mind: Beyond the Psychoanalytic Legend*, London: Burnett Books/André Deutsch.

Summers, M. (1929, 1980 edn) *The Vampire in Europe*, Wellingborough, Northamptonshire: Aquarian Press.

Tannenbaum, P. H. (1980) 'Entertainment as vicarious emotional experience', in P. H. Tannenbaum (ed.) *The Entertainment Functions of Television*, Hillsdale, New Jersey: Erlbaum.

Thomas, K. (1973) *Religion and the Decline of Magic: Studies in Popular Beliefs in Sixteenth- and Seventeenth-century England*, Harmondsworth: Penguin.

Thorndike, E. L. (1911) *Animal Intelligence*, New York: Macmillan.

Todorov, T. (1973) *The Fantastic: a Structural Approach to a Literary Genre*, Cleveland and London: Press of Case Western Reserve University.

Tolkien, J. R. R. (1975) 'On fairy stories', in *Tree and Leaf, Smith of Wooton Major, etc.*, London: Allen & Unwin. (Originally published in 1947.)

Tracey, M. and Morrison, D. (1979) *Whitehouse*, London: Macmillan.

Tuan, Y. F. (1979) *Landscapes of Fear*, Oxford: Blackwell.

Tudor, A. (1974) *Image and Influence: Studies in the Sociology of Film*, London: Allen & Unwin.

Tumber, H. (1982) *Television and the Riots: a Report for the Broadcasting Research Unit of the British Film Institute*, London: British Film Institute.

Twitchell, J. B. (1981) *The Living Dead: a Study of the Vampire in Romantic Literature*, Durham, NC: Duke University Press.

—— (1983) 'Frankenstein and the anatomy of horror', *Georgia Review* 37: 41–78.

—— (1985) *Dreadful Pleasures: an Anatomy of Modern Horror*, New York: Oxford University Press.

Underwood, T. and Miller, C. (eds) (1987) *Kingdom of Fear: the World of Stephen King*, London: Hodder & Stoughton.

Valentine, C. W. (1950) *The Psychology of Early Childhood: a Study of Mental Development in the First Years of Life*, 4th ed, London: Methuen.

van der Pligt, J. and Eiser, J. R. (1984) 'Dimensional salience, judgment, and attitudes', in J. R. Eiser (ed.) *Attitudinal Judgment*, New York: Springer-Verlag.

Warnock, M. (1976) *Imagination*, London: Faber.

Watson, J. B. (1913) 'Psychology as the behaviourist views it', *Psychological Review* 20: 157–77.

Williams, B. (ed.) (1981) *Obscenity and Film Censorship: an Abridgement of the Williams Report*, Cambridge: Cambridge University Press.

Williams, R. (1974) *Television: Technology and Cultural Form*, Glasgow: Fontana/Collins.

—— (1980) *Problems in Materialism and Culture*, London: Verso and New Left Books.

Winn, M. (1977) *The Plug-in Drug*, New York: Viking.

Winnicott, D. W. (1958) *Collected Papers: Through Paediatrics to Psychoanalysis*, London: Tavistock.

Wittgenstein, L. (1958) *Philosophical Investigations*, 2nd edn, Oxford: Blackwell.

Wober, M. and Gunter, B. (1982) 'Television and personal threat: fact or artifact? A British survey', *British Journal of Social Psychology* 21: 239–47.

Wollheim, R. and Hopkins, J. (eds) (1982) *Philosophical Essays on Freud*, Cambridge: Cambridge University Press.

Zillman, D. (1980) 'Anatomy of suspense', in P. H. Tannenbaum (ed.) *The Entertainment Functions of Television*, Hillsdale, New Jersey: Erlbaum.

Zinberg, N. E. and Fellman, G. A. (1967) 'Violence: biological need and social control', *Social Forces* 45: 533–41.

INDEX

207